D1432463

London
2009

WHAT'S NEW | WHAT'S ON | WHAT'S BEST

www.timeout.com/london

Contents

London by Area

Essentials

Published by Time Out Guides Ltd
Universal House
251 Tottenham Court Road
London W1T 7AB
Tel: + 44 (0)20 7813 3000
Fax: + 44 (0)20 7813 6001
Email: guides@timeout.com
www.timeout.com

Managing Director Peter Fiennes
Financial Director Gareth Garner
Editorial Director Ruth Jarvis
Deputy Series Editor Dominic Earle
Editorial Manager Holly Pick
Assistant Management Accountant Ija Krasnikova

Time Out Guides is a wholly owned subsidiary of Time Out Group Ltd.

© Time Out Group Ltd
Chairman Tony Elliott
Financial Director Richard Waterlow
Group General Manager/Director Nichola Coulthard
Time Out Magazine Ltd MD Richard Waterlow
Time Out Communications Ltd MD David Pepper
Time Out International Ltd MD Cathy Runciman
Production Director Mark Lamond
Group IT Director Simon Chappell
Head of Marketing Catherine Demajo

Time Out and the Time Out logo are trademarks of Time Out Group Ltd.

This edition first published in Great Britain in 2008 by Ebury Publishing
A Random House Group Company
Company information can be found on www.randomhouse.co.uk
10 9 8 7 6 5 4 3 2 1

Distributed in US by Publishers Group West
Distributed in Canada by Publishers Group Canada

For further distribution details, see www.timeout.com

ISBN: 978-1-84670-101-6

A CIP catalogue record for this book is available from the British Library

Printed and bound by Firmengruppe APPL, aprinta druck, Wemding, Germany

The Random House Group Limited supports The Forest Stewardship Council (FSC), the leading international forest certification organisation. All our titles that are printed on Greenpeace approved FSC certified paper carry the FSC logo. Our paper procurement policy can be found at www.rbooks.co.uk/environment.

Time Out carbon-offsets all its flights with Trees for Cities (www.treesforcities.org)

London Shortlist

The **Time Out London Shortlist 2009** is one of a series of annual guides that draws on Time Out's background as a magazine publisher to keep you current with what's going on in town. As well as London's key sights and the best of its eating, drinking and leisure options, it picks out the most exciting venues to have opened in the last year and gives a full calendar of events from September 2008 to December 2009. It also includes features on the important news, trends and openings, all compiled by locally based editors and writers. Whether you're visiting for the first time in your life or the first time this year, you'll find the *Time Out London Shortlist* contains all you need to know, in a portable and easy-to-use format.

The guide divides central London into five areas, each containing listings for Sights & Museums, Eating & Drinking, Shopping, Nightlife and Arts & Leisure, and maps pinpointing their locations. At the front of the book are chapters rounding up these scenes city-wide, and giving a shortlist of our overall picks. We include itineraries for days out, plus essentials such as transport information and hotels.

Our listings give phone numbers as dialled within London. To dial them from elsewhere in the UK, preface them with 020; from abroad, use your country's exit code followed by 44 (the country code for the UK), 20 and the number given.

We have noted price categories by using one to four pound signs (**£-££££**), representing budget, moderate, expensive and luxury.

Major credit cards are accepted unless otherwise stated. We also indicate when a venue is NEW, and give **Event highlights**.

All our listings have been double-checked, but places do sometimes close or change their hours or prices, so it's a good idea to call a venue before visiting. While every effort has been made to ensure accuracy, the publishers cannot accept responsibility for any errors that this guide may contain.

Venues are marked on the maps using symbols numbered according to their order within the chapter and colour-coded as follows:

❶ Sights & Museums
❶ Eating & Drinking
❶ Shopping
❶ Nightlife
❶ Arts & Leisure

Map key	
Major sight or landmark	■
Railway station	■
Underground station	⊖
Park	▢
Hospital	▢
Casualty unit	✚
Church	✚
Synagogue	✿
Congestion Zone	◐
District	MAYFAIR
Theatre	●

Time Out London Shortlist 2009

EDITORIAL
Editor Simon Coppock
Copy editors Lesley McCave, Patrick Welch
Additional editorial Carol Baker, Jonathan Derbyshire
Proofreader Marion Moisy
Indexer Rob Norman

DESIGN
Art Director Scott Moore
Art Editor Pinelope Kourmouzoglou
Senior Designer Henry Elphick
Graphic Designers Gemma Doyle, Kei Ishimaru
Digital Imaging Simon Foster
Advertising Designer Jodi Sher
Picture Editor Jael Marschner
Deputy Picture Editor Katie Morris
Picture Researcher Gemma Walters
Picture Desk Assistant Marzena Zoladz

ADVERTISING
Commercial Director Mark Phillips
Advertising Manager Alison Wallen
Advertising Sales Ben Holt, Alex Matthews, Jason Trotman
Advertising Assistant Kate Staddon
Display Production Manager Sally Webb
Copy Controller Chris Pastfield

MARKETING
Marketing Manager Yvonne Poon
Senior Publishing Brand Manager Luthfa Begum
Sales & Marketing Director, North America Lisa Levinson
Marketing Designers Anthony Huggins, Nicola Wilson

PRODUCTION
Production Manager Brendan McKeown
Production Controller Caroline Bradford
Production Co-ordinator Julie Pallot

CONTRIBUTORS
This guide was researched and written by Simone Baird, Tim Benzie, Jonathan Derbyshire, Natasha Edwards, Anna Faherty, Anna Norman, Andrew Staffell, Patrick Welch and the writers of *Time Out Guide to London* and *Time Out London* magazine.

PHOTOGRAPHY
Photography by pages 8, 21, 34, 58, 70, 73 (left), 83, 107, 118, 125, 128, 159, 160, 163, 187, 188, 198, 206 Britta Jaschinski; page 11, 25, 113, 203, 209 Heike Bohnstengel; page 13 National Maritime Museum; page 14, 26, 27, 31, 51, 52, 53, 56, 96, 116, 148, 167, 178, 191 Jonathan Perugia; page 19 Kate Peters; page 35 Getty Images; page 36 Debbie Bragg; page 39 Tony Shepherd/The Dance Umbrella; page 44 Doug Southall, Pepper Pictures; page 45 (left) London Word Festival; page 45 (right) Alan Shortis; pages 48, 74 Peter Watts; pages 50, 108, 168, 169, 170 Rob Greig; page 54 Barry J. Holmes; page 59 Michael Cockerham; page 63 Tate Photography; pages 66 Simon Leigh; pages 69, 81, 88, 110, 139, 145, 146 Ming Tang Evans; page 73, 140 Alys Tomlinson; page 76 James O Jenkins; pages 87, 94, 121 Michael Franke; page 91 Courtesy of Saatchi Gallery, London *Zhang Xiaogang, 2007*; page 92, 184 Susie Rea; page 100, 181 Olivia Rutherford; page 134, 142, 143 Andrew Blackenbury; page 156 Tricia de Courcy Ling; page 164 Hayley Harrison; page173 Nerida Howard; page175 Oliver Knight; page 183 diamondrodgers.com.

The following images were provided by the featured establishments/artists: pages 43, 122, 133, 153, 194, 204.

Cover Olimpio Fantuz / 4Corners Images

MAPS
JS Graphics (john@jsgraphics.co.uk).

About Time Out

Founded in 1968, Time Out has expanded from humble London beginnings into the leading resource for those wanting to know what's happening in the world's greatest cities. As well as our influential what's-on weeklies in London, New York and Chicago, we publish more than a dozen other listings magazines in cities as varied as Beijing and Mumbai. The magazines established Time Out's trademark style: sharp writing, informed reviewing and bang up-to-date inside knowledge of every scene.

Time Out made the natural leap into travel guides in the 1980s with the City Guide series, which now extends to over 50 destinations around the world. Written and researched by expert local writers and generously illustrated with original photography, the full-size guides cover a larger area than our Shortlist guides and include many more venue reviews, along with additional background features and a full set of maps.

Throughout this rapid growth, the company has remained proudly independent, still owned by Tony Elliott four decades after he started Time Out London as a single fold-out sheet of A5 paper. This independence extends to the editorial content of all our publications, this Shortlist included. No establishment has been featured because it has advertised, and no payment has influenced any of our reviews. And, for our critics, there's definitely no such thing as a free lunch: all restaurants and bars are visited and reviewed anonymously, and Time Out always picks up the bill.

For more about the company, see www.timeout.com.

Don't Miss
2009

Wellcome Collection

WHAT'S BEST
Sights & Museums

When a city has as many historic attractions as London (we've got more World Heritage Sites than any other city), it should be no surprise that the sightseeing news is about renewal. The White Tower, oldest part of the Tower of London (p162), will be renovated to the tune of £2m over the next two years, with the ongoing work being used as an opportunity to show visitors the ancient fabric of the building. Just up river, the Monument (p159) reopens in December 2008 after extensive improvements, and the extraordinary (too often overlooked) Westminster Cathedral (p78) is due to get much needed repair work as we go to press. There have also been successful reopenings all year, notably the superb new London Transport

Museum (p127), now an absolute must-see, and the return of a grand old Victorian station as St Pancras International (p144).

The South Bank remains the key destination for tourists and has seen the arrival of several new attractions (including new mayor Boris Johnson at City Hall, p59). The Movieum (p65) opened in County Hall, right by the London Eye (p65). Near Borough Market (p71), there are the gory London Bridge Experience (p62) and the reopened Fashion & Textile Museum (p59). It also looks like the idiosyncratic, obsessional Topolski mural (p67) will soon reopen in the arches behind the Southbank Centre.

Other new, small-scale museums have already begun to work their way into Londoners' affections:

Best new
- Household Cavalry Museum (p80)
- Movieum (p65)
- London Bridge Experience (p62)

Most welcome returns
- London Transport Museum (p127)
- St Pancras International (p144)
- Topolski's Studio & Memory of the Century (p67)
- Whitechapel Art Gallery (p179)

Best free
- British Museum (p141)
- Natural History Museum (p86)
- Tate Britain (p78)
- Victoria & Albert Museum (p86)

Best secret
- Old Operating Theatre, Museum & Herb Garret (p65)
- Petrie Museum (p143)
- Wellcome Collection (p144)

Best views
- London Eye (p65)
- Parliament Hill on Hampstead Heath (p171)
- St Paul's Cathedral (p161)
- Westminster Cathedral (p78)

Best outdoor
- Swimming in the Hampstead Heath pools (p171)
- Thames Clipper back from the O2 Arena (p188)
- Watching the herons in Regent's Park (p99)

Best late events
- British Museum (p141)
- Tate Britain (p78)
- Victoria & Albert Museum (p86)

we enjoyed spying on the horses and stablehands through the glass screen at the Household Cavalry Museum (p80) and can't get enough of last year's Wellcome Collection (p144). Watch out too for the expanded Jewish Museum (www.jewish museum.org.uk), due to reopen in Camden in 2009, as well as the purpose-built Centre of the Cell (www.centreofthecell.org) and restored Keats House (www.city oflondon.gov.uk/keats).

Brilliant though these all are, first-time and return visitors alike will spend most of their time at the headline attractions. That means the 'Babylon' blockbuster show at the British Museum (p141) should be a big success, and millions will enjoy the glittering gemstones of the new Vault at the Natural History Museum (p86), the new Launchpad at the Science Museum (p86), the Planetarium at the Royal Observatory (p186) and the new treetop walkway at Kew Gardens

SEE YOUR WORLD
DIFFERENTLY
visit the science museum

Get your hands on some interactive stuff. Feast your eyes on a 3D IMAX movie.
You've never seen science this refreshing.

⊖ South Kensington • www.sciencemuseum.org.uk

FREE MUSEUM ENTRY

(p185). Even before £2m-worth of children's zoo opens in 2009 at London Zoo (p171), the kids can enjoy a new hummingbird exhibit.

Contemporary art remains a key cultural mover in London. Sponsorship of the Saatchi Gallery (see box p91) should ensure it's free when it does finally open. Also gratis are the exemplary Turbine Hall installations at Tate Modern (p66) – Dominique Gonzalez-Foerster has been announced as the latest artist to take on the challenge – and the intriguing Fourth Plinth in Trafalgar Square (see box p76). Shows at Project Space 176 (p175), in a former Methodist chapel, have demonstrated the range and intelligence not-for-profit spaces can deliver, and the reopening in spring 2009 of a massively expanded Whitechapel Art Gallery (p179) will bring one of our long-term favourite galleries back into full operation.

Doing the geography

This book is divided by area. The **South Bank** primarily covers riverside Bankside, home of Tate Modern and the revamped Southbank Centre. Over the river, **Westminster & St James's** covers the centre of UK politics, while the impressive Victorian museums of **South Kensington**, the Knightsbridge department stores, and the boutiques and restaurants of still-fashionable **Chelsea** lie to the west.

The **West End** includes most of what is now central London. We start north of unlovely Oxford Street, in the elegant, slightly raffish shopping district of **Marylebone**. South, between Marylebone and St James's, is **Mayfair**, as expensive as its reputation but less daunting, with fine mews and pubs. Eastward is **Soho**, notorious centre of filth and fun, then **Covent Garden**,

London Transport Museum p8

so popular with tourists that locals often forget about the charms of its boutique shopping. North of Soho is **Fitzrovia**, its elegant streets speckled with inviting shops and restaurants, while the squares and Georgian terraces of literary **Bloomsbury**, home of academia and the British Museum, are east across Tottenham Court Road.

The **City** comprises the once-walled Square Mile of the original city, compelling for its long history and now adjoined by London's focal area for bars and clubs, Shoreditch; **Holborn** and **Clerkenwell** have great food and nightlife.

Around these central districts **neighbourhood London** has clusters of fine restaurants, bars and clubs, servicing what are mainly residential zones, as well as some of London's must-see attractions: Greenwich, Kew and Hampton Court Palace.

Making the most of it

Some tips for getting the best out of London in 2009. Don't be scared of the transport system: invest in an Oyster travel smartcard (p213) and travel cashless through the city by bus and tube. Buses are best for getting a handle on the topography. Some good sightseeing routes are RV1 (riverside), 7, 8 and 12, along with the Routemaster Heritage Routes (p77); the no.11 is one of our favourites, pp48-50. Don't be afraid to wander at will: crime in central London is low, and walking can be the best way to appreciate its many character changes. No one thinks any the less of someone consulting a map – so long as they dive out of the stream of pedestrian traffic. And most people will be happy to help with directions: Londoners' reputation for standoffishness is largely undeserved.

To avoid the worst of the crowds try to steer clear of the big draws at weekends and on late-opening nights, when the population turns out in force. Aim to hit exhibitions in the middle of their run – or prepare yourself for crowds. Last entry can be up to an hour before closing time (we specify where last entry is more than an hour before the doors shut), so don't turn up just before a place closes. Some sights close at Christmas and Easter – ring ahead to confirm openings.

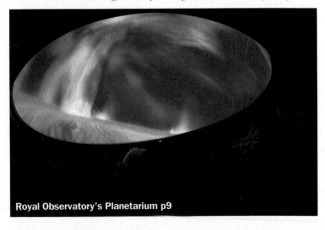

Royal Observatory's Planetarium p9

Sake no hana

WHAT'S BEST
Eating & Drinking

London has now established itself as one of the world's top dining destinations, catering for the demands of an ever more gastronomically savvy public. Despite all the talk of credit crunches and impending recession, there's no obvious reduction in Londoners' willingness to swap hard-earned wages for a square meal, nor any abatement in the rapidity at which new venues spring up – and close down.

This is the age of the celebrity chef, in which figures like Gordon Ramsay dominate not only our TV screens but also the newspaper reviews – partly because they have the money to generate powerful PR campaigns, but equally because their experience and talent often

make for successful restaurants. Ramsay's empire expands apace. Notably, he's entered the gastropub market, having already acquired and revamped three properties: first the Narrow in Limehouse, then Chiswick's Devonshire, and most recently the Warrington in Maida Vale (p172). With a new gastropub opening practically every week, we hardly needed another three, but Ramsay's take on the genre is slick and professional, producing good, solid, reliable food and well-oiled service. The problem is getting hold of a table without making a booking a month in advance. Nor is the great man infallible: we were underwhelmed by his revamp of Foxtrot Oscar, a brasserie on Royal

Hospital Road, and, despite its Michelin star, his modern European restaurant La Noisette, closed in spring 2008. However, Maze (p106) is still one of our favourites, so we're excited about the opening of Maze Grill right next door.

Other chefs with a similarly expansionist creed as Ramsay are Gary Rhodes, who has put his name to three restaurants (his best is Rhodes W1, p101), and Tom Aikens, the ex-Pied à Terre, Joël Robuchon-trained chef whose fine-dining restaurant was followed in 2006 by the more informal Tom's Kitchen, and then in early 2008 by Tom's Place (p92), a posh pastiche of an old-school chippie, which is making a big fuss of its strict policy of sourcing only sustainable fish. (This isn't the only recent opening with an ecological agenda: another is Water House, p181, the second venture from the people behind the lauded, super-green Acorn House, p144.)

Successful non-chef restaurateurs have continued to strengthen their arsenal. Oliver Peyton opened a Peyton & Byrne café, following his brilliant bakery shop, in the Wellcome Collection (p144) and Alan Yau – the mastermind behind Hakkasan (p138), Busaba Eathai (p145), Yauatcha (p120) and the original modern noodle-bar Wagamama (p146) – sold his former restaurants to open Sake no hana (p82), a Japanese fine-dining restaurant of exceptional calibre, as well as lay the groundwork for a new chain (see box p126). At about the same time, Hakkasan and Busaba were voted the first and second best restaurants in the capital by *Time Out* magazine's food critics.

The revival of home-grown cooking gets stronger and stronger, largely inspired by the pioneering work done over the last decade at

SHORTLIST

Best new eats
- Dehesa (p117)
- Hibiscus (p106)
- Kiasu (p190)
- L'Autre Pied (p101)
- Sake no hana (p82)
- Wild Honey (p108)

Best of British
- Great Queen Street (p129)
- Hereford Road (p190)
- Hix Oyster & Chop House (p155)
- Magdalen (p69)
- St John (p156)

Best global scoff
- Amaya (p89)
- Hakkasan (p138)
- Nahm (p95)
- Providores & Tapa Room (p101)
- Zuma (p89)

Best for vegetarians
- Food for Thought (p128)
- Ottolenghi (p172)

Best drop-in nosh
- Busaba Eathai (p145)
- Hummus Bros (p118)
- S&M Café (p172)
- Song Que (p180)

Best gastropubs
- Anchor & Hope (p68)
- Botanist (p92)
- Cow (p190)
- Eagle (p155)
- Pig's Ear (p92)

Best traditional boozers
- Lamb (p145)
- Nag's Head (p95)
- Princess Louise (p130)
- Ye Old Mitre (p152)

Best wines & cocktails
- East Room (p164)
- Loungelover (p180)
- Vinoteca (p157)
- Westbourne House (p190)

wagamama

delicious noodles
rice dishes
freshly squeezed juices
wine ǀ **sake**
japanese beers

bloomsbury ǀ borough / london bridge ǀ brent cross
camden ǀ canary wharf ǀ covent garden ǀ croydon
earls court ǀ fleet street ǀ haymarket ǀ islington
kensington ǀ knightsbridge ǀ leicester square
mansion house ǀ moorgate / citypoint
old broad street / bank ǀ putney ǀ royal festival hall
soho ǀ tower hill ǀ victoria ǀ wigmore ǀ wimbledon

positive eating + positive living

wagamama.com

BEWARE

BY RICHARD WILSON, COMMISSIONED BY
THE WAPPING PROJECT FOR VEUVE CLICQUOT (2007)
PHOTOGRAPH THOMAS ZANON-LARCHER

WAPPING FOOD AT THE WAPPING PROJECT
WAPPING HYDRAULIC POWER STATION
WAPPING WALL LONDON E1W 3SG 00 44 207 680 2080

WWW.THEWAPPINGPROJECT.COM

Kiasu

Fergus Henderson's St John (p156), and the capital's gastropubs can be thanked for bringing the word about honest, robust British scoff to the plates of the masses. With so many around it takes a lot to stand out from the crowd, but any gastropub we recommend in the following pages is top-notch. You can also enjoy carefully cooked modern British food in slightly more proper surroundings: try the fine new restaurants Hereford Road (p190) and Northbank (p165).

London's new openings aren't, of course, all about British food. In fact, more than anything else, it's diversity that makes London one of the world's leading culinary centres. Over the past year we've seen excellent entrants to the competitive modern European bracket, particularly Wild Honey (p108) and L'Autre Pied (p101), with young pretender Marcus Eaves at the helm. We've enjoyed good new restaurants doing great versions of French (La Petite Maison, p106; Côte, p117), Spanish (Dehesa, p117) and Singaporean (Kiasu, p190) food. Indeed, the cuisines of Asia continue to be especially well represented here, with notable newcomers including

Indian 'street-food' restaurant Urban Turban (p190), in the mould of the already successful Imli (p119) and Masala Zone chain (p129).

It's often said that London is a prohibitively expensive city, with complaints about the price of eating out invariably joining gripes about the cost of a hotel room. There's truth in both complaints. But the city does benefit from an excellent, and growing, range of good-value, high-quality canteen restaurants. Old favourites include Wagamama, Carluccio's Caffè (p179), Busaba and Strada; newer kids on the block include Hummus Bros (p118), Masala Zone, Ping Pong (p69), Leon (p89), Itsu (p92) and Wahaca (p130). Wherever you are in central London, you're unlikely ever to be far from a branch of one of these chains.

Arguably, London still lacks the calibre and range of cocktail and wine bars that distinguish other major cities such as New York or Sydney. On the other hand, those places don't have illustrious traditional pubs such as the splendidly refurbished Princess Louise (p130). And the ante is being upped for London's cocktail bars by places such as

Notting Hill's Westbourne House (p190) and the East Room (p164), a recent Shoreditch addition to the group of brilliant bars that also includes Milk & Honey (p119) and Player (p120). At East Room wines are dispensed from machines measure-by-measure, in itself an interesting new trend.

Neighbourhood watch

The **South Bank** has a cluster of great options around foodie-magnet Borough Market, and increasingly interesting venues near the revivified Southbank Centre. **Covent Garden**, however, remains terrible for dining; still, Wahaca and Masala Zone offer better food and fairer prices than the overpriced chains. The options in nearby **Soho** are much better, with more canteens (Busaba Eathai, Hummus Bros) joined by classy upmarket restaurants such as the excellent Arbutus and Dehesa. **Mayfair** is principally the domain of high-end hotel-housed fine dining, backed by top-name chefs; Maze and Chisou are less austere than many, even if they aren't much cheaper. **Marylebone**, however, is another food-lover's heartland. Excellent dining options here include outposts of the Royal China dim sum mini-chain, L'Autre Pied and superb global fusion at Providores & Tapa Room. The predictably expensive vicinity of **South Kensington & Chelsea** is home to a few undeniable gems, including Zuma and Assaggi.

The City, unsurprisingly, isn't much of a destination for evening eats, but a handful of good restaurants help soak up those bonuses – try Sauterelle and 1 Lombard Street, both French. It also has some fine traditional pubs: Ye Old Mitre and the Black Friar are favourites. Neighbouring **Clerkenwell** is home of the

famous St John and many other first-rate venues, among them Smiths of Smithfield, Vinoteca, Moro and Le Comptoir Gascon duo. It also has a number of superb pubs – including gastropub pioneer the Eagle. **Shoreditch**, to the north-east, must have London's greatest concentration of bars: members' bar East Room, chilled-out Bar Kick and overblown Loungelover stand out. Nearby, **Brick Lane**'s 50-plus curry houses might be legendary, but with very few exceptions they're mediocre. Serious curry pilgrims need to head out to Tooting for cheap, regional options; to Wembley's Ealing Road for Gujarati- and Mumbai-style food, or to Southall, a Punjabi home from home.

Dos & don'ts

Don't expect to be able to get a table at a buzz restaurant any day of the week without booking at least a week ahead. If you do find yourself caught without a reservation, try a gastropub, where at least you can wait indoors; somewhere cheap, where throughput is likely to be quick; or the growing number of restaurants (among them Arbutus, J Sheekey, Maze and Moro) where you can eat casually sat up at the counter.

Many restaurants add a 10 to 15 per cent service charge to the bill; check whether they have before leaving extra, and be wary of the common and despicable practice whereby a restaurant adds a service charge, then still gives the customer the option of adding a further tip at the credit-card payment stage.

Smoking is now illegal in enclosed public places. However, many restaurants, bars and pubs have designated sheltered and/or heated outdoor smoking areas.

Rough Trade East p24

WHAT'S BEST
Shopping

The opening of Europe's largest shopping mall 'in an urban area' – Westfield London (see box p180) – scheduled for Christmas 2008 might seem at odds with the continued rise of eco-aware consumerism and home-grown artisans, but then London has always been contrary when it comes to splashing the cash.

The city is as well known for its exuberant street markets and secondhand bookdealers as it is for cutting-edge fashion boutiques, superluxe department stores and none-more-traditional shopping arcades. London's increasingly visible ethnic diversity helps to keep the shopping scene bold and exciting, and the luxury end of the market especially seems pretty

much immune to the effects of credit crunches and economic downturns: whether talking about high-end designer gear or luxury luggage, analysts suggest this retail sector is likely to remain decidedly buoyant.

Less encouraging is the closure of small, independent shops, which find themselves caught in a pincer movement between rising rents and deep online discounting. Nonetheless, many idiosyncratic shops remain fixtures, either because of the sheer quality of their products (James Smith, p146) or by clever updating (Burlington Arcade, p109; Old Curiosity Shop, p152).

The emblematic department stores – step forward Selfridges

(p104), Liberty (p123) and the recently revamped Fortnum & Mason (p82) – are also showing a willingness to adapt to the times that can only enhance their traditional virtues.

Fashion forward

The buzz at 2008's London Fashion Week centred on House of Holland, Vivienne Westwood's new Red Label and Christopher Kane, but most young Londoners will still spend their shopping time scooping up the extra-bargain fashion at Uniqlo (p113) and Primark (p112). Those who are slightly older tend to favour COS (p121) and Reiss (p140), which rolled out a flock of new accessories shops in 2008. In fact, these mid-range stores are enjoying something of a resurgence, as shoppers become disillusioned with the 'throwaway' trend for supercheap sweatshopped clothes. Capsule collections and appealing 'heritage' lines are hooking even the most discerning shoppers into the mid-range places, but for top-quality designerwear on the cheap, check the Consume section of *Time Out* magazine each week for details of sample sales.

For unique pieces, you're still best off veering away from the high street and jumping in on the capital's continuing love affair with the boutique. If your budget has a bit of give in it, there are plenty of places where you can pick up established but unhyped designers: A Butcher of Distinction (p181), Alice & Astrid (p190), Bread & Honey (p166), KJ's Laundry (p103), Koh Samui (p131), Matches on Ledbury Road (p192) and Sefton (p173) are just a start.

If money isn't an issue at all, London has flagships for all the major international designers, as well as nicely curated selections

SHORTLIST

Best new
- Georgina Goodman (p111)
- Luella (p111)
- Ortigia (p93)
- Oxfam Boutique (p192)

Cutting-edge concepts
- Dover Street Market (p109)
- Shop at Bluebird (p93)
- Three Threads (p166)

Best boutiques
- A Butcher of Distinction (p181)
- Bread & Honey (p166)
- KJ's Laundry (p103)
- Koh Samui (p131)

Best sensory experience
- Borough Market (p71)
- Columbia Road Market (p181)
- Miller Harris (p112)

Best shoes
- Foot Patrol (p121)
- Kurt Geiger (p111)
- Tracey Neuls (p104)

Best of British
- A Gold (p181)
- Fortnum & Mason (p82)
- James Smith & Sons (p146)

Best retro clothing
- Alfie's Antiques Market (p103)
- Beyond Retro (p181)
- Rellik (p192)

Most eccentric
- Old Curiosity Shop (p152)
- Playlounge (p123)

Best books and music
- Foyles (p121)
- Rough Trade East (p182)
- Skoob (p147)

Most charming streets
- Camden Passage (p173)
- Exmouth Market (p157)
- Lamb's Conduit Street (p146)

in the likes of Harvey Nichols (p90). Hip Dover Street Market (p109) remains a favourite destination for the fashion pack.

Vintage stores are still hugely popular, meeting the twin appetites for cabaret-style dressing up and truly one-off outfits. The latest addition to the pack is the eco-aware Oxfam shop (p192), which opened in early 2008; other good bets include Beyond Retro (p181) and Rellik (p192). The markets – Camden (p172), Portobello Road (p192) and Alfie's Antiques (p103) – are another reliable source, whether you're searching for vintage Dior or for an original Harrington.

Cultural artefacts

More independent bookshops are lost every year (Metropolitan Books and Quinto in 2008), but plenty remain for the bibliophile. For atmosphere, Daunt (p103) – with its beautiful Edwardian conservatory – and the several antiquarian booksellers along pedestrianised, picturesque Cecil Court take some beating, while the revitalised Foyles (p121) is still on top form for new books. Don't neglect the museum shops for specialist tomes and knick-knacks: the Southbank Centre (p73), Tate Modern (p66) and London Transport Museum (p127) shops are all great.

Record and CD shops have also taken a beating in recent times, with Berwick Street seeing several closures and the wonderful Fopp chain biting the dust, but indie temple Rough Trade East (p182) has settled firmly into its 5,000sq ft of the Old Truman Brewery.

To market, to market

The most central of London's markets is Berwick Street (p121), which can be a lot of fun, but stalls of fruit and veg aren't really enough to make it a shopping destination. Borough Market (p71), on the other hand, is superb for foodies – committed eaters do well also to check out Broadway Market in Hackney and Cabbages & Frocks in Marylebone (both held on Saturday), as well as the host of farmers' markets currently spread across the capital. Lush flower market Columbia Road (p181) is a lovely Sunday morning outing, with stallholders shouting out the Latin plant names in Cockney accents; try to get there before 11am. Old Spitalfields Market (p182) and the nearby Sunday (Up)Market are great for fashion, crafts and vintage clobber.

London's most famous markets are also both going strong: despite the huge fire that swept through Camden Lock in early 2008 and the ongoing disturbances of major redevelopment, Camden's collection of markets are still a major tourist attraction, and – if you can stomach the crowds – Portobello Road Market is a good place for antiques and bric-a-brac. (Alfie's, not far off in Marylebone, is more laid-back.)

On the streets

With more than 40,000 shops and 80 markets, shopping in London can be exhausting. So limit the territory you cover in each outing, sticking to one or two earmarked areas at a time.

Regent Street is home to the flagships of many mid-range, high street clothing chains. For a taste of retail past, **St James's Street** is full of anachronistic specialists, including London's oldest hatter and the royal shoemaker, while Mayfair's royal arcades are best represented by the revamped Burlington Arcade. Stuffy **Savile Row** has been given a shake-up in recent years by a handful of tailoring upstarts – even an Abercrombie & Fitch.

Mayfair – especially Conduit Street and Bond Streets Old and New – remains the domain of catwalk names (including British big guns Mulberry, Burberry and Vivienne Westwood, and newcomers Georgina Goodman and Luella Bartley). To the north, it's best to hurry across heaving **Oxford Street** and duck instead into pedestrianised Gees Court and St Christopher's Place – pretty, interconnecting alleyways lined with cafés and shops that lead to the bottom of Marylebone. Curving **Marylebone High Street** is a village-London cliché these days, but it still has excellent fashion, perfumeries, gourmet food shops and design stores.

A couple of London's most celebrated streets have recently been lifted out of decades in the chain-dominated doldrums. **Carnaby Street** fell prey to tacky souvenir shops, but has been salvaged by an influx of quality youth clothing brands and by Kingly Court. (Behind Carnaby, cobbled Newburgh Street has a further cache of one-off jewellery and clothes shops.) Also synonymous with the Swinging London of Mary Quant, the **King's Road** morphed into shopping-mall mediocrity but has recently been revived by a crop of hip stores following the lead of the Shop at Bluebird.

Nor should **Covent Garden** be written off as a tourist trap. Apple is eyeing up a site near the piazza, while to the north-west, cobbled Floral Street and the offshoots from Seven Dials remain fertile browsing ground. Don't miss sweet little Neal's Yard, with its wholefood cafés and organic herbalist. A little further north

from here, Lamb's Conduit Street is a quiet retreat that's crammed with appealing indie shops.

Unless you're looking to work the platinum AmEx card among the global designer salons along Sloane Street or marvel at the art nouveau food halls of Harrods, there's little reason to swing by **Knightsbridge**. Drop in on pretty Ortigia, though, and the cute shops of Elizabeth Street to the south.

For luxe designer labels without the crush, **Notting Hill** (especially where Westbourne Grove meets Ledbury Road) overflows with posh, feminine boutiques. On the other side of town, **Brick Lane** (especially around the Old Truman Brewery) and its offshoot Cheshire Street have a dynamic collection of offbeat clothing and homeware shops. The boutiques of **Islington** are also usually worth having a nose around, especially those on Camden Passage.

DON'T MISS: 2009

Ortigia p23

Amersham Arms

Nightlife

If it's been a while since you were on the disco trail in London, you'll find that the geography has been comprehensively redrawn. Early in 2008, the closure within months of each other of four famous and long-running clubs – Canvas, the Cross, the Key and Turnmills – was a hell of a shock for the city's clubbers, no matter that was long expected (each closed because of district or building redevelopment).

Nightclubs renewed

There are new venues on the horizon, however. The biggest will be Fabric's 2,500-capacity space beside the O2 (p188) – the four rooms of the original Fabric (p157) hold 'only' around 1,800. Due to open in early 2009, the venue is

to host a lot of gigs but also one-off club nights. In King's Cross, Pacha are to open a multifloor 'house' of club rooms, bars and outdoor terraces at around the same time – they've already refurbed their current location (p79).

For more underground changes, 'east London' creeps ever further east: Shoreditch feels positively central now, with Dalston and Limehouse regularly appearing on the nightlife map. There are even signs of a counter-move further into the City (see box p167) – not an area known for its clubs, it offers an attractive combination of easier licensing conditions (there are few residents to object to late-night noise) and ready access to bankers with large disposable incomes.

SHORTLIST

Best new venues
- Amersham Arms (p187)
- Corsica Studios (p71)
- East Village (p166)
- Island (p132)
- Proud (p174)
- Victory (p132)

Best indie mash-ups
- Durr at the End (p132)
- Smash n Grab at Punk (p124)

Best for bands
- Bardens Boudoir (p182)
- Luminaire (p174)
- Shepherd's Bush
  Empire (p192)

Best for cutting-edge jazz
- Vortex Jazz Club (p184)

Best leftfield dance action
- End (p132)
- Fabric (p157)

Best small clubs
- Notting Hill Arts Club (p192)
- Plastic People (p168)

The best out clubs
- Popstarz at SIN (p125)
- Dancing through to tomorrow
  in 'Vauxhall Village' (p188)

Best for crazy dress-up
- Bethnal Green Working
  Men's Club (p182)
- Volupté (p152)
- Lady Luck at On
  the Rocks (p184)

Best cabaret and drag
- Bistrotheque (p183)
- Royal Vauxhall Tavern in
  'Vauxhall Village' (p188)
- Soho Revue Bar (p125)

Best comedy
- Clark's at Lowdown
  at the Albany (p104)
- Comedy Camp at
  Barcode (p124)
- Comedy Store (p124)

The music is all about bassbins, baby. Pity the sound engineer at nights such as Bastard Booty Bass and Dirty Canvas, at which cult DJs like Hannah Holland and Blaise Bellville tear speaker stacks to shreds with baile funk, grime and old jungle riddims. Dancehall, electro and pop interventions keep things from getting surly, in what is a surprisingly girl-friendly scene.

Tea dances & dress-up

The effort many clubbers make with their outfits – whether at an indie club, electro rave or retro swing dance – leaves today's clubland with more in common with 1984 than 1994.

Boombox had its last dress-up for New Year's Eve 2007/08, but the fashion pack have no shortage of parties to pose at. Performance artist Scottee and drag superstar Jodie Harsh are the darlings of this scene, hosting over-the-top For3ign at Bar Music Hall (p166). It's not

Kitsch Cabaret

Madame Jojo's

THE HEART OF SOHO'S DARKNESS

www.madamejojos.com

all gorgeous-gorgeous designer threads, either – think creativity and DIY style, ironic fancy dress that nods to superheroes or film icons, or strapping some old thing on an outfit and calling it art. For inspiration, visit cult websites like dirtydirtydancing.com. Remember, darlings: too much is *never* enough.

It also seems that every secretary is a now burlesque performer on the side. Having gone mainstream, straight burlesque shocks no one (unless it's done really badly), so performers are going weird. Freaks of all shapes and sizes are stepping up, and circus tricks often contain elements of horror so gross they make Jim Rose look quaint.

At the other end of the scale, tea dances are back and sweeter than ever. Forget post-ironic club kids slapping on some lippy and a string of pearls, we mean tea dances put on by pensioners in the ballrooms they frequented after the War – you'll be waltzed off the floor.

Live music, dead venues

We said a sad sayonara to the Spitz, a Spitalfields Market venue adored by folktronica types, which lost its battle with developers in 2007, and the Astoria (p123) is to be demolished to make way for new transport links, albeit with no date set. We were pleased, though, to say a chipper hello to new Dalston venue, Cafe Oto (p183), which joins the characterful, low-rent Bardens Boudoir (p182) and superbly programmed jazz venue the Vortex Jazz Club (p184).

Musically, in spite of all those samey-same indie guitar bands that will keep doing their thing until the day of reckoning, we saw an increasingly inventive approach from the young 'uns in the last year. Twiddling electro sounds all the way up to exciting were the truly marvellous Fuck Buttons,

Micachu & the Shapes began their London takeover with vacuum cleaner-starring neo-skiffle, Foals hit the Top Five with their edgy take on math rock and the ferocious dubstep of Benga, Burial and Kode9 continued to remind us not all is sunshine and tweetie birds. Too challenging? Get all fired up for action and then go babble through the likes of the Enemy at the reopened Proud (p174). Or our On The Up shows (www.timeout.com/london/ontheup) are monthly (and free) at the Carling Academy Islington – and our tips for stellar success bear up well thus far.

The smaller, trashier venues are the best fun, of course. Forget Camden and head to the Old Blue Last (p168) and Hoxton Square Bar & Kitchen (p183) to join punters as young and riotous as the bands. We still love the Luminaire (p174) and have really appreciated the hip new bands and Japanese psychedelia at Corsica Studios (p71).

Is there even a divide between guitars and dance music? Not so as you'd notice. Club nights offering a heady mix of both are everywhere, exemplified by the opening of the Amersham Arms (p187). The Barfly (p173) maintains its mosh-'em-up, mash-'em-up club nights, while Durr at the End (p132) – the West End club that defies the area's reputation for high-dollar suburban meat markets – still sees the indie stroke electro heads and fashion kids worship at the altar of Light Speed Champion and the Chap.

Gay disco

For out and out hedonism, the 'Vauxhall Village' (p188) is still where to go, whether on a Friday night or Sunday lunchtime – Horse Meat Disco, for example, gets a perfect cross-section of freaks and uniques out every other Sunday afternoon. There's also suddenly half a dozen 'gay salons' at which literary types talk books and 1980s records (Polari at Green Carnation, p124) or nod sagely at other arty lesbian types (Tart, 28 Shacklewell Lane, Dalston). Good news for the West End arrived in the form of mixed indie party Popstarz, which deserted King's Cross for SIN (p125).

Just for laughs

For surefire stand-up, the big hitter is always the Comedy Store (p124), but we've had serious fun with the appreciative audiences at Comedy Camp (Barcode, p124) and Clark's at Lowdown at the Albany (p104), home to the new wave of offbeat, erudite comedians. For the latest comedy trend – comic storytelling – check out Sarah Bennetto's Storytellers Club and Anthology at Inn on the Green.

While London's nightlife is lively all year, anyone who's after comedy in late July or August is likely to be disappointed. Despite some nights bucking the trend, most performers go to the Edinburgh Festival and so most venues are dark. Come in June or October instead: comedians will either be trying out a fresh show or touring their Edinburgh triumph.

Making the most of it

Whatever you're doing, always check how things are running before you set off: countless festivals, street closures and bits of engineering tinkerage throw spanners in the works through the year, particularly at Christmas, Easter, New Year's Eve, during public holidays and through August. Transport details are regularly updated at www.tfl. gov.uk. And you'll kick yourself if you came all this way to see an event, only to arrive the one weekend it isn't on – check www.timeout.com/london to coordinate your visit or, if you're

already here, buy the weekly mag for its comprehensive listings.

Still, in London there's something going on, no matter the day, no matter the hour. So if you miss out due to a useless mate forgetting to get tickets or a last-minute change of plan, it isn't the end of the world. Even long-in-the-tooth Londoners fall across brand new happenings just by taking the wrong street, and the best way to get a taste of 'real London' – instead of the city every postcard-collecting tourist sees – is to go with the flow. Someone tells you about a great party? Check it out. You read about a new band on the tube? Get a ticket. Sure, you've got some 'essentials' mapped out in your head, but if you miss them this time, come back another year.

Once you're here, be sure to get to grips with our transport system. Don't worry, it's not as daunting as you might think. The tube is self-evident, but stops running come midnight (New Year's Eve is the sole exception). Black cabs are pricey and hard to find at night, but safe. There are also licensed minicabs; some bigger nightclubs run their own service. But avoid illegal minicabs, touted outside every club. Far better to check out the excellent Night Bus system before you leave your hotel (the Journey Planner at www.tfl.gov.uk can be handy). A few minutes working out which bus gets you back can save hours of blurry-visioned confusion later. For more on transport, see pp211-215.

In addition to our mag and website, www.dontstayin.com is excellent for on-the-ground clubbing news, and record shops are invaluable for flyers and advice about what's going on. We love the friendly folk at Rough Trade East (p182), but indie fans should also check www.irlondon.co.uk.

Place p35

WHAT'S BEST
Arts & Leisure

Until the Olympics finally arrive in 2012, every year's arts story is likely to be the same: spiralling costs on the Olympic facilities are being met by savage cuts in funding to arts institutions. Yet, amid all the politicking, London's arts scene is buoyant. The reborn Southbank Centre (p73) claims a rise to 18 million visitors since its reopening in 2007 (its programme has certainly been eye-catching since Jude Kelly took over as artistic director), and new funding has been found for the pioneering Battersea Arts Centre (p189).

As we go to press, there is even news of a new venue opening – or rather an old venue, County Hall, being taken over. The Greater London Theatre (www.greater

londontheatre.co.uk) is, in fact, three theatres based around the grand debating chamber that once belonged to the Greater London Council. There are also several new multi-arts venues: King's Place (see box p177) combines office space, classical music and sculpture galleries, the refurbished Shunt (p72) continues to plough its unusual furrow through performance art, cabaret and live music, and both Corsica Studios (p71) and Unit 7 (p184) are gig-cum-club-cum-artist communities.

However, the city's sports venues are rapidly improving too. The new South Stand has made Twickenham (p186) into the largest rugby stadium in the

WINNER
27 MAJOR AWARDS!

'THE MOST HAPPY,
SUNNY, FUNNY
SHOW IN TOWN'
SUNDAY EXPRESS

'A HIT! JUST GO!'
MAGIC

hairspray

'THE MUSICAL WITH EVERYTHING
A TRIUMPH!'
OBSERVER

world, planning has been sought for the redevelopment of the Oval cricket ground, and work began on the Olympic Stadium in spring 2008. More surprisingly, dreams of global sports franchises are still alive: the NFL announced it will play regular season games at Wembley (p175) until 2010.

Classical music & opera

After a long period of turbulence, Edward Gardner's first year as music director of the English National Opera (ENO) seems to have created a new sense of enthusiasm at the Coliseum (p132). 'From my point of view,' he says, 'my job is to get musical standards at every level as high as possible.' Things remain pretty traditional at the Royal Opera House (p134), but it was here that Harrison Birtwhistle premiered his magnificent and challenging *Minotaur* in April 2008. Meanwhile, the Southbank Centre has been developing a very decent music programme: keep an eye out for the Stockhausen Festival in late 2008 and the Vienna Philharmonic Orchestra's neat pairing of Haydn and Bruckner's last symphonies in February 2009.

Nonetheless, much of the city's classical music action happens in superb venues on a much more intimate scale. John Gilhooly, the director of one of them – the exemplary Wigmore Hall (p105) – is keeping things lively with the appointment of Brad Mehldau to run a jazz series; Cadogan Hall (p93) and LSO St Luke's (p169) are also terrific venues, and a number of London's ancient churches host fine concerts: the magnificently refurbished St Martin-in-the-Fields (p77) continues to host concerts – popular candlelit Vivaldi and Mozart recitals, as well as some more unusual fare at lunchtimes.

SHORTLIST

Best new venues
- Greater London Theatre (p31)
- King's Place (see box p177)

Best revamp
- St Martin-in-the-Fields (p77)

Best auditoriums
- Cadogan Hall (p93)
- Coliseum (p132)
- Lilian Baylis Theatre at Sadler's Wells (p175)

Best cinemas
- BFI Southbank (p72)
- Curzon Soho (p125)
- Odeon Leicester Square (p126)

Biggest theatrical events
- Sam Mendes's Bridge Project (see box p68)
- Jude Law in *Hamlet* at Wyndham's (p135)

Best off-West End theatres
- BAC (Battersea Arts Centre) (p189)
- Donmar Warehouse (p132)

Most innovative work
- London Sinfonietta at King's Place (see box p177)
- Punchdrunk (p34)
- Royal Court Theatre (p95)
- Spring Loaded (p41)

Best bargains
- Prince Charles (p126)
- Promenade tickets at the Globe (p66)
- Standing tickets at the Coliseum (p132)
- Standing tickets at the Proms (p88)
- £10 Monday at the Royal Court Theatre (p95)

Best of the West End
- Avenue Q (p134)
- God of Carnage (p132)
- Into the Hoods (p134)
- Jersey Boys (p126)

Southbank Centre p31

Film

The BFI (British Film Institute)
Southbank (p72), a key part of
the South Bank renewal, continues
to impress with the most ambitious
programming of any London
cinema. However, the controversial
appointment in 2008 of Greg Dyke
as chairman of the BFI (he spent
most of his career prior to the
appointment as a television
executive) has raised fears the
programme may pitch from
popular to blandly populist.
The jury is out until Dyke's first
London Film Festival (p37). This is
Britain's largest public film event,
screening over 300 movies from 60
countries; Dyke promised in *The
Times* to make it, erm, 'glitzier'.

The Leicester Square cinemas
still dominate the starry premières,
although the Vue multiplex at the
O2 Arena (p188) has been making
a concerted bid for a larger share.

Notwithstanding the dismally
wet summer of 2007, outdoor
screenings are established on the
the London events calendar: check
www.timeout.com for the best of
them – the Somerset House (p149)
programme is always worth a look.

Theatre & dance

The distinctions between dance
and theatre have been creatively
blurred with increasing frequency.
One example is *Into the Hoods* at
the Novello (p134), an exhilarating
street-dance take on Sondheim that
made it all the way to Theatreland
from Edinburgh. The usual West
End song-and-dance formula for
success – and a million more people
turned out for shows this year than
last – is rather more mundane:
according to the Society of London
Theatres, it's all down to the
popularity of star castings from
TV talent contests. We say try the
likes of *Hairspray* (p135) or *Jersey
Boys* (p126) for easy entertainment
with casts reassuringly free of
reality-show winners. Interestingly,
Jude Kelly is putting on *Lost and
Found Orchestra,* the latest from
the people behind the West End hit
Stomp!, at the Southbank Centre for
the Christmas season 2008/09.

The trend for wonderfully
immersive, offbeat dance-drama
continues – Punchdrunk (www.
punchdrunk.org.uk) made a roaring,
extended success of their Edgar
Allen Poe adaptation *The Masque
of the Red Death* (and its ferocious
after-parties) in the Battersea Arts
Centre. Check their website to find
out about a follow-up.

There is also plenty of more
formal dance in London. Spring
Dance, programmed by Sadler's
Wells, brought the New York
City Ballet, the Stuttgart Ballet
(performing *Romeo & Juliet*) and
Carlos Acosta and Sylvie Guillem
(reprising their smash *Push!*) to the

vast stage of the London Coliseum for a month in March 2008. Indeed, Allen Robertson, *Time Out*'s outgoing dance critic, considers dance to be London's most vital artform, citing the city's unique combination of different dance traditions and cultures, and the availability of venues to suit all scales of performance, from the Royal Opera House through Sadler's Wells (p175) to the intimate Place (p147).

London has also been able to attract the best international dance companies due to the commitment of Dance Umbrella (www.dance umbrella.co.uk), whose annual autumn festival – entering its fourth decade in 2009 – draws large audiences for often rather challenging work. Revived after a seven-year hiatus in 2007, the Spring Loaded festival (www. theplace.org.uk) provides another unbeatable showcase for the most adventurous choreographers.

Times are also pretty good for straight theatre in the West End.

Yasmina Reza, behind the monster hit *Art*, seems to have done it again with *God of Carnage* at the Gielgud (p132), while the always inventive Donmar Warehouse (p132) has decamped temporarily for a season at the major West End theatre Wyndham's (p135). The season culminates with Kenneth Branagh directing Jude Law as Hamlet in summer 2009. South of the river, the highlight of the year will be at the Old Vic (p72), where Simon Russell Beale performs in *The Winter's Tale* and *The Cherry Orchard* as part of Sam Mendes's Anglo-American Bridge Project collaborations (see box p68).

What's on

We've included long-running musicals we think are likely to survive into 2009. However, a new crop will inevitably open through the year, along with seasons at individual venues. *Time Out* magazine and www.timeout. com have the most informed and up-to-date listings.

Twickenham p31

WHAT'S ON
Calendar

Underage Festival p46

The following is our selection of annual events, as well as the best one-offs announced by the time this guide went to press. To stay totally current with what's happening, buy the weekly *Time Out* magazine and check www.time out.com/london; always confirm dates before making travel plans.

Dates of public holidays are picked out in **bold**.

September 2008

7 **Regent Street Festival**
www.regentstreetonline.com

7 **Brick Lane Festival**
www.bricklanefestival.com

11 Sept-4 Jan 2009
Francis Bacon
Tate Britain, p78
www.tate.org.uk/britain

13 **Great River Race**
Thames, Richmond to Greenwich
www.greatriverrace.co.uk

13-14 **Mayor's Thames Festival**
Westminster & Tower Bridges
www.thamesfestival.org

20-21 **Open House London**
Various locations
www.openhouselondon.org
Free access to over 600 buildings.

24 Sept-5 Oct **Raindance**
Various central London venues
www.raindance.co.uk
Britain's largest indie film festival.

27 **Great Gorilla Run**
Mincing Lane, the City
www.gorillas.org/greatgorillarun
Fund-raising 7km run, in gorilla suits.

26 Sept-1 Feb 2009 **Rothko**
Tate Modern, p66
www.tate.org.uk/modern

30 Sept-8 Nov **Dance Umbrella**
Various locations
www.danceumbrella.co.uk
The city's headline dance festival.

Until Dec **Music of
Olivier Messiaen**
Southbank Centre, p73

www.messiaenfestival.com
Year-long exploration of the work of the French composer (until Dec).

October 2008

Ongoing Dance Umbrella (see Sept); Francis Bacon (see Sept); Music of Olivier Messiaen (see Sept); Raindance Festival (see Sept); Rothko (see Sept)

5 **Pearly Kings & Queens Harvest Festival**
St Martin-in-the-Fields, p77
www.pearlysociety.co.uk
A 3pm service for the professional Cockneys, in traditional outfits.

16-19 **Frieze Art Fair**
Regent's Park, p99
www.friezeartfair.com

mid Oct-early Nov
London Film Festival
BFI Southbank, p72
www.lff.org.uk

26 **American football**
Wembley Stadium, p175
The New Orleans Saints versus the San Diego Chargers in a regular NFL game.

28 **Diwali**
Trafalgar Square, p78
www.london.gov.uk
The Festival of Light is celebrated by Hindu, Jain and Sikh communities.

late Oct-late Apr 2009 **Shell Wildlife Photographer of the Year**
Natural History Museum, p86

November 2008

Ongoing Dance Umbrella (see Sept); Francis Bacon (see Sept); Music of Olivier Messiaen (see Sept); Rothko (see Sept); London Film Festival (see Oct); Shell Wildlife Photographer of the Year (see Oct)

2 **London to Brighton Veteran Car Run**
From Serpentine Road, Hyde Park
www.lbvcr.com

5 **Bonfire Night**

8 **Lord Mayor's Show**
Various streets in the City
www.lordmayorsshow.org

Fashion and high art

Touching down in London in July 2009, Chanel's Mobile Art Show takes the travelling exhibition to a new dimension. Here, as Chanel becomes the latest luxury fashion empire to compete on the contemporary art catwalk, it's no longer a question of transporting the art from one institution to another but of shipping the entire gallery, a slinky white capsule by architect diva Zaha Hadid.

Inside the capsule is work by some 20 artists, inspired by Chanel's famous quilted handbag – a fashion marketing plug that most treat with a light touch: a Nobuyoshi Araki film mixes images of lushly sexual flowers and girls in Chanel chain bondage, Wim Delvoye shows stuffed tattooed pigs and pigskin handbags, while young Argentine artist Leandro Erlich created a compelling video installation of a drizzly Parisian street. The MP3 soundtrack, narrated in gravelly chain-smoker drawl by veteran film actress Jeanne Moreau, transforms it all into something curator Fabrice Bousteau justly describes as more like a 'landscape or a film set'.

But make no mistake: Hadid's 'container' will draw at least as much attention as the art. It amply demonstrates her mix of technical ingenuity (in devising the lightweight, demountable structure) and fascination with new forms of flowing, organic space. Rather like a sculpture – or a handbag – itself.
■ www.chanel-mobileart.com

DO SOMETHING
OUT OF THE ORDINARY

Escape to a green oasis of calm and tranquility, just minutes away from central London

Outstanding and unique treasure houses, offering a glimpse of life in the 17th and 18th centuries.

Ham House and Garden, Richmond

Osterley Park and House, Isleworth

For opening times call Ham House and Garden on 020 8940 1950 or Osterley Park and House on 020 8232 5050 or visit www.nationaltrust.org.uk

 THE NATIONAL TRUST

Dance Umbrella p36

A grand inauguration procession for the City's new Lord Mayor.

8-29 Investec Challenge
Twickenham Stadium, p186
www.rfu.com
England's rugby union players take on the might of the Southern Hemisphere.

9 Remembrance Sunday Ceremony
Cenotaph, Whitehall

14-23 London Jazz Festival
Various locations
www.serious.org.uk

mid-late Nov
State Opening of Parliament
House of Lords, Westminster, p74
www.parliament.uk
Limited public access, but you can watch the Queen arrive by coach.

Nov-Dec **Christmas Tree & Lights**
Covent Garden, Regent Street & Trafalgar Square
www.london.gov.uk/www.covent gardenmarket.co.uk/www.regent streetonline.com

December 2008

Ongoing Francis Bacon (see Sept); Music of Olivier Messiaen (see Sept); Rothko (see Sept); Shell Wildlife Photographer of

the Year (see Oct); Christmas Tree & Lights (see Nov).

early Dec **VIP Day**
Oxford, Regent & Bond Streets
Three major shopping areas are pedestrianised, with entertainments laid on.

12-14 Bankside Frost Fair
Tate Modern & the Globe, p66
visitsouthwark.com/frostfair

mid Dec **Spitalfields Festival**
Various locations
www.spitalfieldsfestival.org.uk
Classical music, walks and talks.

20-23 Slow Food Market
Southbank Centre, p73
www.southbank.co.uk

25 Christmas Day

26 Boxing Day

31 New Year's Eve Celebrations
Trafalgar Square, p78
The crowded, booze-free focal point of London's celebrations. Fireworks from the riverbank are much more fun.

January 2009

Ongoing Francis Bacon (see Sept); Rothko (see Sept); Shell Wildlife Photographer of the Year (see Oct)

The Famous
WEMBLEY MARKET

SUNDAYS   9am – 4pm

This is the largest Sunday Market
In the UK with over 600 stalls.
WEMBLEY STADIUM CAR PARK
LONDON HA9 0WS
Wembley Park Tube

For info
wembleymarket.co.uk

01895 632221
Not open on Stadium event days

1 New Year's Day

early Jan **London International Mime Festival**
Various locations
www.mimefest.co.uk

14-18 **London Art Fair**
Business Design Centre, Islington
www.londonartfair.co.uk

February 2009

Ongoing Shell Wildlife Photographer of the Year (see Oct)

5 Great Spitalfields Pancake Race
Dray Walk, Brick Lane
7375 0441/www.alternativearts.co.uk
Charity race, flipping pancakes from frying pans as they go.

7 Chinese New Year Festival
Chinatown, Leicester Square & Trafalgar Square
www.chinatownchinese.co.uk

mid Feb **Children's Literature Festival**
Southbank Centre, p73
www.southbankcentre.co.uk

late Feb-early Mar **Word Festival**
Various East End locations
www.londonwordfestival.com
See box p45.

March 2009

Ongoing Shell Wildlife Photographer of the Year (see Oct); Word Festival (see Feb)

mid Mar **Human Rights Watch International Film Festival**
Various locations
www.hrw.org/iff

16 (tbc) **St Patrick's Day Festival**
Various locations
www.london.gov.uk

late Mar-early Apr **London Lesbian & Gay Film Festival**
BFI Southbank, p72
www.llgff.org.uk

29 Oxford & Cambridge Boat Race
On the Thames, Putney to Mortlake
www.theboatrace.org

April 2009

Ongoing Shell Wildlife Photographer of the Year (see Oct); Lesbian & Gay Film Festival (see Mar)

10 Good Friday

13 Easter Monday

mid Apr (tbc) **La Linea**
Various locations
www.imaginamultimedia.com/comono
Latin American music festival.

mid Apr **Camden Crawl**
Various locations in Camden
www.thecamdencrawl.com
Fine showcase of new musical talent, traditionally almost entirely of the indie guitar variety.

mid Apr **East End Film Festival**
Various locations
www.eastendfilmfestival.com

mid Apr-mid May **Spring Loaded**
Place, p147
7121 1100/www.theplace.org.uk
Dance festival showcasing some 30 choreographers over three weeks.

20-22 **London Book Fair**
Southbank Centre & Earl's Court
www.londonbookfair.co.uk

26 **London Marathon**
Greenwich Park to the Mall
www.london-marathon.co.uk

May 2009

Ongoing Spring Loaded (see Apr).

4 Early May Bank Holiday

mid May-early June **Cockpit Arts**
Cockpit Yard, Bloomsbury, & Deptford Centre, Deptford
7419 1959/8692 4463/www.cockpitarts.com
Series of open weekends at designer-makers' studios.

19-23 (tbc) **Chelsea Flower Show**
Royal Hospital grounds, Chelsea
www.rhs.org.uk

25 Spring Bank Holiday

June 2009

Ongoing Cockpit Arts (see May)

4-5 (tbc) Beating Retreat
Horse Guards Parade, Whitehall
*www.army.mod.uk/ceremonialand
heritage/index.htm*
An evening of Cavalry drumming.

**June Hampton Court
Palace Festival**
www.hamptoncourtfestival.com
Big-name concert series, with mostly
classical pops and hoary rockers
appearing over three weeks.

June-July Jazz Plus
Victoria Embankment Gardens,
Westminster
7375 0441/www.alternativearts.co.uk
Free lunchtime concerts by contemporary jazz musicians.

June-Aug Opera Holland Park
www.operahollandpark.com

June-Aug Coin Street Festival
Bernie Spain Gardens, South Bank
www.coinstreet.org

13 Trooping the Colour
Horse Guards Parade, St James's
www.trooping-the-colour.co.uk
The Queen's official birthday parade.

**13-14
Open Garden Squares Weekend**
Various locations
www.opensquares.org

Private squares opened to the public.

mid June Architecture Week
Various locations
www.architectureweek.co.uk

mid June Meltdown
Southbank Centre, p73
www.southbank.co.uk
A fortnight of contemporary music and
culture, curated each year by different
musicians – Massive Attack in 2008.

**22 June-5 July Wimbledon Lawn
Tennis Championships**
www.wimbledon.org

late June LIFT
Southbank Centre, p73
A week of international theatre.

late June-early July
City of London Festival
Various locations around the City
www.colf.org
A themed festival of mostly free music
and art events.

July 2009

Ongoing Coin Street Festival
(see June); Jazz Plus (see June);
Opera Holland Park (see June);
the Wimbledon Lawn Tennis
Championships (see June); City
of London Festival (see June)

Hendrick's Chap Olympics p44

early July **Pride London**
Oxford Street to Victoria
Embankment
www.pridelondon.org
A huge annual gay and lesbian parade
that is the culmination of a week of
cultural events.

July **Chanel's Mobile Art Show**
www.chanel-mobileart.com
See box p37.

July **Hendrick's Chap Olympics**
Bedford Square, Bloomsbury
The Hop, Skip and G&T, Pipe Smokers'
Relay and other events are fiercely con-
tested every Thursday in July.

July **Greenwich & Docklands
International Festival**
www.festival.org

July-Aug **Dance Al Fresco**
Regent's Park, p99
www.dancealfresco.org

mid July **Somerset House
Summer Series**
Somerset House, p149
www.somerset-house.org.uk/music
A series of outdoor concerts.

mid July-mid Sept
Marble Hill House Concerts

mid July-mid Sept
**BBC Sir Henry Wood Promenade
Concerts (The Proms)**

Royal Albert Hall, p88
www.bbc.co.uk/proms

16-20 **Second Npower
Ashes Test**
Lord's, p171
The English and Australian cricket
teams battle it out for the little urn.

late July **Rise**
Finsbury Park
Anti-racist music festival.

late July
Rushes Soho Shorts Festival
Various locations in Soho
www.sohoshorts.com
Free short film and video screenings.

late July **World London Festival**
Southbank Centre, p73
www.southbank.co.uk
Two weeks of global sounds.

August 2009

Ongoing Opera Holland Park (see
June); Coin Street Festival (see
June); Marble Hill House Concerts
(see July); Dance Al Fresco (see
July); BBC Sir Henry Wood
Promenade Concerts (see July)

early Aug **Innocent Summer Fête**
Regent's Park, p99
www.innocentvillagefete.com
Two days of music and posh food stalls.

**Greenwich & Docklands
International Festival**

The word on the street

Sure, the capital's new taste for cabaret has brought impressive diversity to our nightlife options – an evening programme offering briskly whipped breast tassles as a taster for virtuoso balalaika-playing barely raises an eyebrow these days – but literature isn't the most likely beneficiary of our love of variety. It's true, though: we've never had such a vital and imaginative spoken word scene.

If you're here in February or early March, the three-week **Word Festival** (p41; pictured) is great place to start. Beardie agit-rhymster Scroobius Pip appeared this year with comedians Robin Ince and Alexei Sayle, publisher Neil Astley, Monica Ali, and even novelist Toby Litt with a panel discussing French avant-gardists.

There are loads of regular events too. Patrick Neate's pioneering and always fabulous

Book Slam (www.bookslam.com) continues put on performances from the likes of Dave Eggers and Kate Nash, but a number of new events are taking its club-lit template and twisting it to their own devious ends. Try a radio play performed in 1930s-style for **Fitzrovia Radio Hour** (fitzrovia radio.com/index.html) at Bourne & Hollingsworth (p135), or **Polari**, the gay literary salon run at Green Carnation (p124).

Significantly, **Apples & Snakes** (www.applesandsnakes.org) – key live lit movers for over 25 years – chose spring 2008 to move to the Albany (www.thealbany.org.uk), an arts centre making spoken word central to its schedule. Their launch brought key 1960s poet Michael Horovitz together with a slam poet, Joel Stickley, young enough to be his son – another sign of a healthy scene.

early Aug **Underage Festival**
Victoria Park
www.underagefestivals.com
A hip and immensely popular music
festival for 14- to 18-year-olds.

early-late Aug
Portobello Film Festival
www.portobellofilmfestival.com

30-31 **Notting Hill Carnival**
www.nottinghillcarnival.biz
Europe's biggest street party.

31 **Summer Bank Holiday**

September 2009

Ongoing Marble Hill House
Concerts (see July); BBC
Sir Henry Wood Promenade
Concerts (see July)

6 **Regent Street Festival**
See above Sept 2008.

early Sept **Brick Lane Festival**
See above Sept 2008.

early Sept **Tour of Britain**
See above Sept 2008.

12 (tbc) **Great River Race**
See above Sept 2008.

19-20 (tbc)
Mayor's Thames Festival
See above Sept 2008.

19-20 **Open House London**
See above Sept 2008.

late Sept-early Oct **Raindance**
See above Sept 2008.

late Sept-early Nov
Dance Umbrella
See above Sept 2008.

27 (tbc) **Great Gorilla Run**
See above Sept 2008.

October 2009

Ongoing Dance Umbrella
(see Sept)

4 (tbc) **Pearly Kings &
Queens Harvest Festival**
See above Oct 2008.

15-18 **Frieze Art Fair**
See above Oct 2008.

mid Oct-early Nov
London Film Festival
See above Oct 2008.

late Oct **Diwali**
See above Nov 2008.

from late Oct **Shell Wildlife
Photographer of the Year**
See above Oct 2008.

November 2009

Ongoing Dance Umbrella (see
Sept); London Film Festival (see
Oct); Shell Wildlife Photographer
of the Year (see Oct)

5 **Bonfire Night**

6-8 (tbc) **London to Brighton
Veteran Car Run**
See above Nov 2008.

8 **Lord Mayor's Show**
See above Nov 2008.

8 **Remembrance Sunday
Ceremony**
See above Nov 2008.

mid-late Nov **London
Jazz Festival**
See above Nov 2008.

mid-late Nov
State Opening of Parliament
See above Nov 2008.

Nov-Dec **Christmas Tree & Lights**
See above Nov 2008.

December 2009

Ongoing Shell Wildlife
Photographer of the Year
(see Oct); Christmas Tree
& Lights (see Nov).

5 **VIP Day**
See above Dec 2008.

11-13 **Bankside Frost Fair**
See above Dec 2008.

mid Dec **Spitalfields Festival**
See above Dec 2008

25 **Christmas Day**

28 **Boxing Day**

31 **New Year's Eve Celebrations**
See above Dec 2008.

Itineraries

The 90p Tour

Want to see the major London sights without taking all day over it? Armed with this guide, half an hour and an Oyster card (p213) charged with 90p of credit, you're ready to receive the quintessence of tourist London. (Even without an Oyster, a single bus ticket is only £2.) You can do this tour any day and at any time, but be careful to avoid rush hour on weekdays (8-9.30am and 4.30-7pm).

Climb aboard the first no.11 to arrive at Stop B of **Liverpool Street bus station**. Head straight upstairs and do your utmost to secure one of the seats in the front window… the views simply aren't as good from anywhere else.

Tower 42 will suddenly appear straight ahead. Yes, it's boringly strait-laced in black and grey, but it towers impressively over the six-floor banks that cluster at its knees like attendant pages.

Just before the bus turns right on to Threadneedle Street, high above Pavarotti's sandwich shop, the corner building bears a grasshopper motif. This is the symbol of Sir Thomas Gresham, pioneering Tudor financier and sometime arms smuggler. He established the **Royal Exchange**, the third version of which will shortly be on your left. On your right, the **Bank of England** is squat and grey at ground level, but white and rather impressive at the height of the bus's top deck. We like those burly chaps in bas-relief, especially the last, who has had the foresight to preserve his modesty behind a huge bunch of keys.

The Duke of Wellington stares across the junction at **Mansion House**, official residence of the Lord Mayor of London (elected by Aldermen to rule the City of London, not to be confused with the plain old Mayor of London, elected by all of us). As the bus crosses the junction, glance back over your left shoulder to see the shiny metal of Sir Richard Rogers's inside-out **Lloyd's of London** building (p159). But don't look too long: at a right-angle left you can also see Nicholas Hawksmoor's **St Mary Woolnoth**. A student of Sir Christopher Wren, Hawksmoor created just six London churches, each a budget-bustin' combination of dark Gothic and elegant neo-classical styles. St Mary's starred in TS Eliot's *The Waste Land*, calling bank clerks into work with 'a dead sound on the final stroke of nine.'

Next you make an infuriatingly pointless (for commuters) and wonderfully accommodating (for tourists) loop… that brings you right up by **St Paul's** (p161). As you draw alongside, look left across the Millennium Bridge to Tate Modern (p66) – you can see why boosters called the bridge a 'blade of light'. Just after St Paul's, you'll see a statue of Queen Anne in the plaza. Beyond her is another fine work attributed to Wren: **Temple Bar**. This gate used to mark the point where the City becomes Westminster, as well as holding the heads of executed traitors on spikes. Back in 1878, the gateway was removed to facilitate traffic – and languished in the garden of a stately home for a century, before being returned to this new City location.

You now plunge down the hill to Ludgate Circus. At the crossroads, look diagonally left. The white layers of **St Bride's** 'wedding cake' spire can be seen over the grey buildings. This is another Wren creation and, as the official church to journalists, pretty much the last vestige of old **Fleet Street**. In 2005, Reuters (no.85) was the last news organisation to leave, but the

Daily Express (nos.121-128) and *Daily Telegraph* (no.135) buildings still impress. Having topped the hill, look right. See those elaborate chimes, struck by giants, and the massive clockfaces? These belong to **St Dunstan-in-the-West** (7405 1929, www.stdunstaninthe west.org), whose rector was poet John Donne. Next, on the same side, you can't miss the **Royal Courts of Justice** (p148), seeming oddly frivolous when the sun shines.

You're now on **the Strand** – location of Burlington Bertie's morning consitutional in the music hall song. To your left, enjoy flashes of the Thames. You are, though it doesn't look like it, on the riverbank. 'Strand' has the (now rather poetic) sense of 'shore of a sea, lake or river', which is exactly what this street was until 1874, when Sir Joseph Bazalgette, saviour of London from noxious sewage, completed his grand Embankment, pushing the river southwards.

St Mary-le-Strand, on your right, is as grubby as a proper city church should be, its sombre colour a perfect contrast for the lush green tree in its front courtyard. Left, note the blue railings and lamps of **Somerset House** (p149) before the buildings briefly open into the flat greyness of **Waterloo Bridge**. Here lovers Terry and Julie watch the Kinks' 'Waterloo Sunset'. Next are boarding-school trad carvery **Simpson's-in-the-Strand** (no.100), then the strange vision of a golden metal knight atop a shiny deco entrance canopy. It's the **Savoy** (p208), and you're looking down the only bit of Britain where you must drive on the right.

Here you'll probably run into traffic by McDonald's, behind black cabs queuing to pick up new fares from **Charing Cross**. As you edge along, wonder at the endless stream of people on Villiers Street.

Bank of England p48

Poking over trees is your next big money sight: **Big Ben**… or rather the clocktower that holds a vast bell called Big Ben. You're on Whitehall. Keep looking right for **Horse Guards**, where you've a good chance of seeing a sentry in his dazzling cuirass. Straight after the Women of World War II memorial glance left across the river for the London Eye, then right for **Downing Street**, home of the prime minister. You now pass the Cenotaph, memorial to the dead of both world wars, and – still looking right – an exquisite triple arch that marks King Charles Street.

If your neck doesn't already have a crick, you're about to get one. Half an hour gone, and you're in **Parliament Square**. White **Westminster Abbey** (p78), with its square double towers, will probably strike you first; in front of it, **St Margaret's Church** (p77) is quite dwarfed. Look left for the tobacco-yellow **Houses of Parliament** (p74).

The next section is a bit dull, but keep alert for a leftwards glimpse of **Westminster Cathedral** (p78), a domed, Byzantine, red-brick building, with a spire like a square minaret. Next on the left there's a glimpse of **Victoria station**, one white building with a low-slung arch alongside classic metropolitan Victorian red-and-white brick. At the next junction, just as the bus starts into a tree-laden square, look hard right on Buckingham Palace Road. Yep, that yellow-brown building in the distant park is **Buckingham Palace** (p79).

You could stay on for Sloane Street and the neo-classical squares of the King's Road, before alighting at the terminus, Fulham Town Hall. But ding the bell now and you can get the tube from Victoria – having safely ticked off London's major sights in double-quick time.

In front of the station is a roughly conical structure that contrives to look frothy despite miserably greyed stone. In 1290, after the death of his wife Eleanor, the uxorious Edward I ordered crosses to be erected to mark the 12 points at which her funeral train halted. In 1863, long after the original cross was crunched into paving, this replica was erected.

Ahead of you, **Nelson's Column** – visible from top to bottom through your big front window – marks **Trafalgar Square** (p78). Your bus now shapes to the left, passing (on your right) a statue of the mounted Charles I, set on a woozily skewed roundabout. Behind him, a little plaque marks the official centre of London. Over your shoulder are the impressive white hawsers of the pedestrian walkway over to the Southbank Centre.

End p52

24-Hour Party City

Make no mistake: London is where it's at when it comes to nightlife. No other city in the world can touch our variety or quality of venues and, now pubs and clubs can serve around the clock, it's possible to stay up for days on end. But the exigencies of local politics – suffice to say most London councils are reluctant to grant late licences where so doing would offend noise-averse residents – mean you won't be swamped with choice. So let us guide you through a massive 24-hour Saturday night. Remember to pack your most comfortable dancing shoes, charge up your Oyster card (p213) and put on the sunglasses – you'll need a bit of a disguise as the hours take their toll.

We'll start at Kilburn Park tube, with some live band leap-around action. The **Luminaire** (p174) is a gig venue adored by Londoners in the know for its customer-friendly attitude and varied bills, which usually kick off at 8pm. When you've worked up an appetite, walk back down Kilburn High Road and grab the tube 15 minutes to Piccadilly Circus. Take in the bright lights before heading up Shaftesbury Avenue and into Soho, which is starting to buzz again after a slump in the cool stakes. We love the cheap if sometimes grumpy **Hi! Sushi** (40 Frith Street, 7734 9688) for its basement of sunken tables. Last orders are officially 11pm, with the place closing at midnight, but they often take people later. If you are too late (alcohol and good tunes will do that to a timetable), join the masses for a panini and bite of the old school at the counter of 24-hour **Bar Italia** (22 Frith Street, 7437 4520), a six-decades-old nightcrawl institution.

Start to rev your night up again with cocktails at the **Soho Revue**

Bar (p125), where you'll get served a few hours of cabaret. Tiered red banquette seating and stripper dancing poles allude to the place's sleazy past, but the venue is now all swanky West End. Still, the nights are fun examples of the modern variety show: maybe All That Jazz or Gwendoline Lamour's Night of Lamour. Regardless, you're in safe post-modern hands. Appreciate this glammed-up, retro crowd, busy working quiffs, seamed stockings and plenty of under-skirt netting while you can, because soon you'll be up to your neck in sweaty old raversville.

Hail a rickshaw or, for a real taste of West End London on a Saturday night, take the walk north to Oxford Street, then turn right and keep going until the road becomes New Oxford Street. You'll find West Central Street on your right, just past the handsome old James Smith umbrella shop (p146).

Adding a whole lot of credibility to the West End's club culture, the

End (p132) hosts a rotating selection of long-running, killer underground house, techno and electro parties, so you'll be in for a treat whatever you fancy. (Since the smoking ban, though, nipping out for a cigarette has become a right pain – it's worth being judicious about when you feed the addiction.) Downstairs, the lounge and main club jump until 7am, while the attached ground-floor bar AKA usually spins house selections for a more chilled crowd.

Come kicking-out time, most folk grab the Sunday papers and make for somewhere quiet and squishy to recover. No such luck for you, my friend. You need to hammer your purse for a short taxi ride to King's Cross; to make sure you get a licensed minicab from outside the club, avoiding the dodgy and dangerous touts, speak to the official-looking bloke in the neon vest holding a clipboard. Up in King's Cross, the wittily named Breakfast at EGG (p174) is a fry-up

Luminaire p51

of techno, electro and minimal sounds over three floors. It's a riot of party people who only get going when everyone has given up. In these morning hours, smokers tend to congregate in the pretty garden to watch the sun rise. Lovely.

Around lunchtime, you'll have done enough clubbing, at least for a little bit. It's time to make tracks to London's clubbing capital: the East End. Head down the hill to King's Cross station and get on a Hammersmith & City, Metropolitan or Circle line tube east to Liverpool Street (double-check you're heading in the right direction before you board – it's been a long night already). Leave the station on to Bishopsgate, heading towards the white spike spire of Christ Church, Spitalfields, past the covered market. Turn left up Commercial Street and right at the Golden Heart pub, making your way to Corbet Place for some brunch. The **Big Chill Bar** (p182), on the corner with Dray Walk,

offers scrummy tapas-style bites, as well as full breakfasts if you can handle that amount of food. There are plenty of slouchy sofas too.

Once your feet start to twitch once again, it's over Brick Lane to **93 Feet East** (p183). The wrap-around courtyard here sees Sunday parties that were made for carrying on into, with big-name DJs heaving their record boxes through a friendly, international crowd. If and when hunger kicks in again, **Brick Lane Beigel Bake** (p179) is the very place. Leave the courtyard and turn right up Brick Lane. Walk a few blocks until, on your left, London's most famous bagel shop appears. Salt beef with mustard strong enough to sneeze by is what you want to restore those energy levels.

If you're still raring to go, head to Wet Yourself at **Aquarium** (p166), a polysexual, filthy electro and dirty bass clash not far away on Old Street. Enter the club's indoor pool at your own risk…

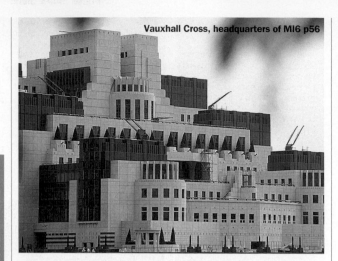
Vauxhall Cross, headquarters of MI6 p56

Being James Bond

In the century since Ian Fleming, creator of James Bond, was born in Mayfair, London has played host to numerous undercover agents, secret organisations and covert operations. Put on a comfortable pair of shoes, take this itinerary as your secret dossier and uncover the city's most secret locations, from both fact and fiction.

Choose a sunny weekday (the outdoor spaces and museums will be at their quietest) and kick off your mission at **Hyde Park Corner** tube at around 11am. Sneak out through Exit 1 (Hyde Park) and double back. Grab some takeaway liquid refreshment at the kiosk, before turning left into the park through the stone gateway. Cross the road and veer left down Rotten Row. Eager spy kids will recognise the neighbouring sand track from the horseback chase in the Alex Rider film *Stormbreaker*.

At the Serpentine, sit on one of the benches and sup your drink. Len Deighton's working-class spy, Harry Palmer, had a clandestine meeting here in *The Ipcress File*.

As a boy, Deighton is said to have witnessed a German agent's dramatic arrest in a nearby tea room, so be discreet when you set off again. You're going to take a surreptitious walk beside the lake as far as the road, cross over and turn left down Exhibition Road towards South Kensington. In the 1930s, an official handbook for communist spies recommended this area as an ideal base – you can't help but admire their style. On your right as you cross Kensington Gore, is the **Royal Geographical Society**, which has an especially long pedigree when it comes to espionage. It was a front for 19th-century spying in the era of the 'Great Game', when RGS explorers informed their superiors about imperial Russian activities in Central Asia.

A little south down Exhibition Road, also on your right, **Imperial College** counts among its alumni the enigmatic Sidney Reilly, 'Ace of Spies', thought to be the real-life inspiration for James Bond. At the **Science Museum** (p86), Alex Rider fans can relive his parachute heroics in the Making the Modern World gallery, while, just before the crossroads, the **Natural History Museum** (p86) saw service as a demonstration room for disguised radios, secret inks and exploding cowpats during World War II.

Skulk left around the Victoria & Albert Museum and, a little further along, creep into **Brompton Oratory** (p83). Before the days of wireless spy rocks, Cold War KGB agents used the war memorial immediately to the right of the entrance as a 'dubok' (dead letter box), depositing secret microfilms behind the nearby columns for later collection. But keep that strictly confidential – the Oratory aren't proud of having played an unwitting part in the history of international espionage.

Escape across the road and head right, then follow Thurloe Place left as it forks into Exhibition Road. Go left to the corner near South Kensington tube and fortify yourself with a good-value set lunch at atmospheric **Daquise** (20 Thurloe Street, 7589 6117). This restaurant, founded by a Polish fighter pilot in 1947, was a favourite hangout of East European agents: past diners include Oleg Gordievsky (the highest-ranking KGB double agent, 'exfiltrated' to this country in the mid 1980s) and three of the 'Cambridge Five'. In the 1960s, a young showgirl called Christine Keeler found herself regularly lunching here with the Soviet Embassy's Senior Naval Attaché. She must have been eager to sate her desire for fine pierogi, since she has always denied either passing on or receiving classified information from her other lover, one John Profumo, Secretary of State for War.

Appetite satisfied, duck through the arcaded main entrance to South Kensington tube and hang a left down Pelham Street (which later becomes Sloane Avenue). When you finally hit the King's Road, head right, then take the second right. At **9 Bywater Street**, the blue house is the fictional home of John le Carré's 'small and podgy' spy, George Smiley.

Back on the King's Road, you'll find **Wellington Square** almost opposite. Ian Fleming never provided an exact address, but Bond experts think no.30 is most likely the 'comfortable flat in the plane-tree'd square' which 007 called home. Further down the King's Road, drop in on Limelight Movie Art in the Antiquarius complex (nos.131-141, 7351 5353, www.antiquarius.co.uk) for Bond movie posters. Shopping done, get back on to King's Road. Keep going until you reach Oakley Street and turn down it to your left.

Just before the river, dip right into Cheyne Walk. Amble past **Cheyne Walk Brasserie** (no.50, 7376 8787, www.cheyne walkbrasserie.com) – George Smiley's local – and have a snoop at Ian Fleming's post-war home in the red-brick **Carlyle Mansions**. *Casino Royale*, intended as 'the spy novel to end all spy novels', was planned in flat no.24, although (as with every later manuscript) the text itself was written at Fleming's Jamaican home. In his teens and his twenties, Fleming lived ten minutes further on, at **Turner's House** (no.119).

ITINERARIES

Join the river and double back past Albert Bridge and the **Royal Hospital Chelsea** (7881 5200, www.chelsea-pensioners.org.uk), used as a dead letter box by 'Cambridge Five' spy Guy Burgess. The alcoholic Burgess, code-named 'Little Girl', was a flamboyant character – in exile in Moscow, he continued to get suits delivered from his Savile Row tailor. It's now time for you to do some quick reconnaissance: you're looking for the bus stop. Turn left off Chelsea Embankment up Chelsea Bridge Road and, outside the Lister Hospital, hop on to a no.360 bus (Elephant & Castle). Sit on the left.

In James Bond's day, the Secret Intelligence Service was just that: secret. Now, both MI6 and its domestic counterpart, MI5, openly operate from imposing Thameside headquarters. Once the bus is on Vauxhall Bridge sneak a peek through the glaring green glass of MI6's £240m home, **Vauxhall Cross**, believed to extend five storeys below ground on the south bank. As you shadow the river, you'll spy the long yellow roofs of **Thames House** on the far side. This is the home of MI5, sometimes known by its rather impressive postal address, 'Box 500'.

After another five minutes, disembark at the **Imperial War Museum** (p62). If you're here before March 2009, head straight for the desk at the back of the main hall and splash out on 'For Your Eyes Only', an exhibition covering Fleming's naval career and the Bond phenomenon. Look out for the author's writing desk, Halle Berry's bikini and Rosa Klebb's poison-switchblade shoes. If you're more interested in real secret agents, the first floor has a permanent Secret War gallery, which offers a free factual history of British espionage. There you'll find concealed bugs, shirt collars impregnated with invisible ink and a German Enigma code machine. Two hours can comfortably be spent wandering through both exhibitions.

From the museum, take a diagonal through the park on your left, cross Kennington Road and catch the no.59 bus (King's Cross) for the five-minute journey to Waterloo Bridge. Jump off beside the **National Theatre** (p72). Be careful, though: in 1978 Bulgarian dissident and BBC journalist Georgi Markov was stabbed with a poison umbrella as he waited here.

If the coast is clear, duck into the subway just behind you, skirting the **BFI IMAX** (p72) and proceeding towards **Waterloo** mainline station. Once you're on the main concourse, try to blend in with the crowds as you scout out the CCTV surveillance cameras that tracked another doomed hack in *The Bourne Ultimatum* movie. If you manage to spot more than 30 cameras, you've proved your worth: mission accomplished!

London by Area

BFI Southbank p72

The South Bank

Tourists have been flocking to the South Bank for centuries, but the entertainments they're expecting have changed a little. Sure, occasional plays are still premièred at **Shakespeare's Globe**, but if you're looking for the prostitutes, gamblers and bear baiting that occupied visitors to this once-insalubrious site, you'll be needing a time machine.

Instead, enjoy the wonderfully refurbished **Southbank Centre**, **BFI Southbank** cinema complex and **Hayward Gallery**, a cluster of national cultural institutions on which logic has finally been imposed. Or join the multitude strolling along the broad riverside walkway that takes you from Tower Bridge to Westminster Bridge and beyond. This strings together fine views and must-see

attractions like **Tate Modern**, the **London Eye** and the Millennium and Hungerford Bridges. Cheeky new venues keep cropping up: the **London Bridge Experience** and **Movieum** are worth checking out, as is the quirky **Topolski Studio**. But it's still-fab **Borough Market**, foodie central, that typifies the South Bank's appeal: visitors find it charming, but locals love it too.

Sights & museums

Bramah Museum of Tea & Coffee

40 Southwark Street, Bankside, SE1 1UN (7403 5650/www.bramahmuseum. co.uk). London Bridge tube/rail. **Open** 10am-6pm daily. **Admission** £4; £3.50 reductions. **Map** p61 D2 **1**
This delightful museum was founded by former tea-taster Edward Bramah, who died in early 2008. His collection

displays pots, caddies and ancient coffee makers. The exhibition doesn't take long to work round, but it's tempting to linger in the café, where a pianist often tinkles away in the early afternoon. Pre-book for afternoon cream teas (£7).

City Hall

Queen's Walk, Bankside, SE1 2AA (www.london.gov.uk). London Bridge tube/rail. **Open** 8am-8pm Mon-Fri; usually 10am-5pm Sat, Sun. **Map** p61 F2 ②

Designed by Lord Foster, this eco-friendly rotund glass structure leans squiffily away from the river. Home to London's municipal government, the building has the Photomat (a huge aerial photo of the city you can walk on), a café, an information desk and the Scoop, an outdoor amphitheatre for free entertainments and sunbathing.

Dalí Universe

County Hall Gallery, County Hall, Riverside Building, Queen's Walk, South Bank, SE1 7PB (7620 2720/ www.daliuniverse.com). Westminster tube/Waterloo tube/rail. **Open** 10am-6.30pm daily. **Admission** £12; £10 reductions. **Map** p60 A3 ③

Trademark attractions such as the Mae West Lips sofa and the *Spellbound* painting enhance the main exhibition here, curated by long-term Dalí friend Benjamin Levi. There are sculptures, watercolours, etchings and lithographs, all exploring his favourite themes. Don't miss the interesting series of Bible scenes by the Catholic-turned-atheist-turned-Catholic again.

Design Museum

Shad Thames, Bermondsey, SE1 2YD (7403 6933/www.designmuseum.org). Tower Hill tube/London Bridge tube/rail. **Open** 10am-5.45pm daily. **Admission** £7; free-£4 reductions. **Map** p61 F2 ④

Exhibitions in this white 1930s-style building focus on modern and contemporary design. The Tank is a small outdoor gallery of constantly changing installations by leading contemporary designers, while the smart Blueprint Café overlooks the Thames.

Event highlights 'Design Cities' (5 Sept 2008-4 Jan 2009).

Fashion & Textile Museum

NEW *83 Bermondsey Street, Borough, SE1 3XF (7407 8664/www.ftmlondon. org). London Bridge tube/rail.* **Open** 11am-5pm Wed-Sun. **Admission** £7; free-£4 reductions. **Map** p61 F4 ⑤

Flamboyant as its founder, fashion designer Zandra Rhodes, this pink and orange museum reopened in 2008

Fashion & Textile Museum

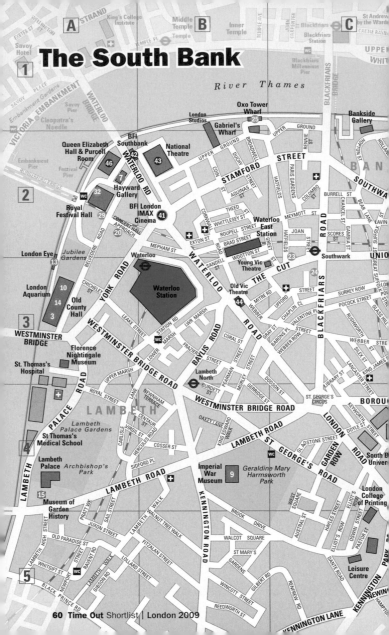

The South Bank

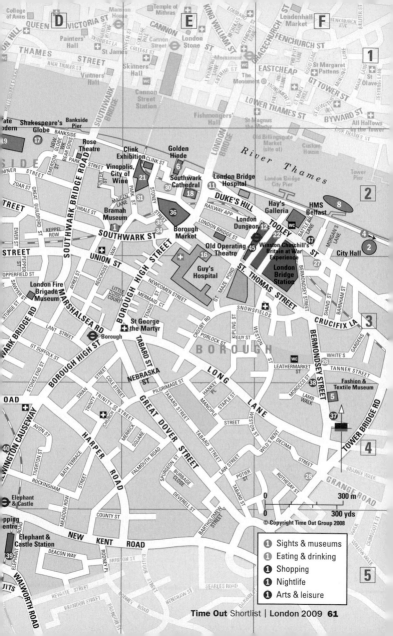

Time Out Shortlist | London 2009 **61**

under the auspices of Newham College. It holds 3,000 of Rhodes' garments, some on permanent display, along with her archive of paper designs, sketchbooks, silk screens and show videos. Temporary exhibits run all year, and a café should now be open.

Golden Hinde

St Mary Overie Dock, Cathedral Street, Bankside, SE1 9DE (0870 011 8700/ www.goldenhinde.org). Monument tube/ London Bridge tube/rail. **Open** 10am-6pm daily. **Admission** £6; £4.50 reductions. **Map** p61 E2 ⑥

Weekends see this reconstruction of Sir Francis Drake's little 16th-century flagship swarming with children dressed up as pirates for birthday dos. The meticulously recreated ship is fascinating to explore. Thoroughly seaworthy, this replica has even reprised Drake's circumnavigatory voyage. As well as the pirate parties, the 'Living History Experiences' (some overnight) are a huge hit with kids.

Hayward Gallery

Belvedere Road, South Bank, SE1 8XX (information 7921 0813/box office 0870 169 1000/www.hayward.org.uk). Embankment tube/Waterloo tube/rail. **Open** 10am-6pm Mon-Thur, Sun; 10am-10pm Fri, Sat. **Admission** £8; free-£7 reductions. **Map** p60 A2 ⑦

In the Hayward's foyer extension and its mirrored, elliptical glass Waterloo Sunset Pavilion, casual visitors can watch cartoons on touch screens in between taking in superb exhibitions. **Event highlights** Andy Warhol: Other Voices, Other Rooms (8 Oct 2008-11 Jan 2009).

HMS Belfast

Morgan's Lane, Tooley Street, Bankside, SE1 2JH (7940 6300/www.iwm.org. uk). London Bridge tube/rail. **Open** *Mar-Oct* 10am-6pm daily. *Nov-Feb* 10am-5pm daily. **Admission** £9.95; free-£6.15 reductions. **Map** p61 F2 ⑧

This 11,500-ton battlecruiser, a floating branch of the Imperial War Museum, is the last surviving big gun World War II ship in Europe. It makes an unlikely playground for children, who tear around its cramped complex of nine decks, boiler, engine rooms and gun turrets. Built in 1938, the *Belfast* was instrumental in the Normandy Landings, among many other missions.

Imperial War Museum

Lambeth Road, SE1 6HZ (7416 5320/ www.iwm.org.uk). Lambeth North tube/ Elephant & Castle tube/rail. **Open** 10am-6pm daily. **Admission** free. **Map** p60 B4 ⑨

Tanks, aircraft and artillery occupy the main hall (as well as a climb-in sub), while the lower floor is devoted to the two World Wars. There's some levity in the smelly Trench Experience and stalwart Blitz Experience, but the third floor's Holocaust Exhibition is gutwrenching – and not recommended for under-14s. Upstairs, Crimes Against Humanity runs a film about ethnic violence and contemporary genocide on loop (unsuitable for under-16s). **Event highlights** 'For Your Eyes Only: Ian Fleming and James Bond' (until 1 Mar 2009).

London Aquarium

County Hall, Riverside Building, Westminster Bridge Road, South Bank, SE1 7PB (7967 8000/tours 7967 8007/www.londonaquarium. co.uk). Westminster tube/Waterloo tube/rail. **Open** 10am-6pm daily. **Admission** £13.25; free-£11.50 reductions. **Map** p60 A3 ⑩

The aquarium, one of Europe's largest, displays its inhabitants according to geographical origin, so there are tanks of bright fish from the coral reefs and the Indian Ocean, freshwater fish from the rivers of Europe and North America, and shoreline crustaceans. Tanks are devoted to jellyfish, sharks, piranhas and octopuses, there's a touch pool with giant rays in it.

London Bridge Experience

NEW *2-4 Tooley Street, Bankside, SE1 2PF (0800 043 4666/www.thelondon bridgeexperience.com). London Bridge tube/rail.* **Open** *July-Oct* 10am-7pm daily. *Nov-June* 10am-6pm daily. **Admission** £19.95; £14.95 reductions. **Map** p61 E2 ⑪

Paint the town Tate

Tate Modern's Rothko Room (pictured) has, since it opened in 2006, proved one of the most popular spaces in the behemoth at Bankside. It contains nine of the abstract expressionist murals that Mark Rothko painted in the late 1950s for the Four Seasons restaurant in the Seagram Building in New York.

Rothko donated these immense, uncompromisingly austere panels to the Tate in 1960, after dining at the Four Seasons and deciding that he'd failed in his stated ambition of 'ruining the appetite of every son of a bitch who ever eats in that room'. The Rothko Room at Tate Modern, by contrast, follows very closely the artist's instructions on how the paintings should be hung – close to the floor and with as much natural light as possible. The effect is stunning and vaguely sepulchral.

Tate Modern's forthcoming major Rothko retrospective unites these nine paintings with others from the Seagram commission that have been loaned specially from museums both in Japan and in the United States. While the 15 Seagram murals will form the core of the show, a number of substantial gouaches will also be on display, as well as archival material that relates to Rothko's original bequest of the paintings to the Tate and to the opening of the first Rothko Room at Tate Britain in 1970.

The exhibition's curators have also acquired some of Rothko's *Blackform* and *Black on Grey* paintings, as well as a number of his works on paper. Placing these alongside the more celebrated murals will, they suggest, 'challenge standard preconceptions of Rothko as a painter focused primarily on the effect of colour.'

■ 'Rothko' is at Tate Modern (p66) from 26 September 2008 to 1 February 2009

LONDON BY AREA

The experience is split level: first, a fun-for-all-the-family history lesson that takes the choicest cuts from the bridge's 2,000-year past, with visitors invited to meet the dead souls (Sir John Rennie, a bloodied Roman soldier, William Wallace, a lighterman's widow) trapped within the haunted bridge's foundations; second, a London Dungeon-style visit to the tombs and catacombs that will frighten the pants off you with animatronics and torture scenes. It's all splendidly kitsch.

London Dungeon

28-34 Tooley Street, Bankside, SE1 2SZ (7403 7221/www.thedungeons. com). London Bridge tube/rail. **Open** *Sept-June* 10.30am-5.30pm daily. *July, Aug* 9.30am-7.30pm daily. **Admission** £19.95; £13.95-£14.95 reductions. **Map** p61 F2 ⑫

A jokey celebration of torture, death and disease under the Victorian railway arches of London Bridge. Visitors are led through a dry-ice fog past gravestones and hideously rotting corpses to experience nasty symptoms from the Great Plague exhibition: an actor-led medley of corpses, boils, projectile vomiting, worm-filled skulls and scuttling rats. Other OTT revisions of horrible London history include the Great Fire and the Judgement Day Barge, where visitors play the part of prisoners (death sentence guaranteed).

London Eye

Riverside Building, next to County Hall, Westminster Bridge Road, South Bank, SE1 7PB (0870 500 0600/www.london eye.com). Westminster tube/Waterloo tube/rail. **Open** *Oct-May* 10am-8pm daily. *June-Sept* 10am-9pm daily. **Admission** £14.50; free-£11 reductions. **Map** p60 A3 ⑬

It's hard to believe that this giant wheel was originally intended to turn beside the Thames for only five years: it has proved so popular that no one wants it to come down, and it's now scheduled to keep spinning for another 20 years. The 443ft frame, whose 32 glass capsules each hold 25 people, commands superb views over the heart of London and beyond during each 30-minute 'flight'. You can book in advance (although you're taking a gamble with the weather), or just turn up and queue for a ticket on the day. Night flights offer a more twinkly experience. There can be long queues in summer.

Movieum

NEW *County Hall, Riverside Building, South Bank, SE1 7PB (7202 7040/ www.themovieum.com). Westminster tube/Waterloo tube/rail.* **Open** 10am-5pm daily. **Admission** £12; £9 reductions. **Map** p60 A3 ⑭

Dedicated to British film since the 1950s (films made in Britain, that is, so blockbusters like *Star Wars* can sneak in), the 30,000sq ft Movieum is focused more on fun than painstaking historical reconstruction – although the story of Pinewood Studios is told. Among thousands of artefacts, you can see the Rank gong and sets from *Star Wars*, while techniques from the *Superman* films allow visitors to take part in one of more 200 films.

Museum of Garden History

Lambeth Palace Road, Lambeth, SE1 7LB (7401 8865/www.museumgarden history.org). Lambeth North tube/ Waterloo tube/rail. **Open** 10.30am-5pm Tue-Sun. **Admission** free. Suggested donation £3; £2.50 reductions. **Map** p60 A4 ⑮

John Tradescant, intrepid plant hunter and gardener to Charles I, is buried here at the world's first museum of horticulture. Topiary and box hedging, old roses, herbaceous perennials and bulbs give all-year interest, and a magnificent stone sarcophagus in the graveyard garden contains the remains of HMS *Bounty* captain William Bligh. Inside the museum are displays of ancient tools, exhibitions about horticulture, a shop and a wholesome café.

Old Operating Theatre, Museum & Herb Garret

9A St Thomas's Street, Bankside, SE1 9RY (7188 2679/www.thegarret. org.uk). London Bridge tube/rail. **Open** 10.30am-5pm Mon-Wed, Fri-Sun;

10.30am-7pm Thur. **Admission** £5.25; free-£4.25 reductions. No credit cards. **Map** p61 E2 🔟

The tower that houses this salutary revelation of antique surgical practice used to be part of the chapel of St Thomas's Hospital. The centrepiece is a pre-anaesthetic Victorian operating theatre dating from 1822, but just as disturbing are the displays of operating equipment, strangulated hernias, leech jars and amputation knives.

Shakespeare's Globe

21 New Globe Walk, Bankside, SE1 9DT (7902 1400/box office 7401 9919/www.shakespeares-globe.org). Mansion House or Southwark tube/ London Bridge tube/rail. **Open** 10am-5pm daily. **Admission** £9; £6.50-£7.50 reductions. **Map** p61 D2 🔟

The original Globe Theatre, where many of William Shakespeare's plays were first staged and which he co-owned, burned down in 1613 during a performance of *Henry VIII*. Nearly 400 years later, it was rebuilt not far from its original site using authentic construction methods and materials. In the UnderGlobe beneath the theatre is a fine exhibition (open year-round) on the history of the reconstruction, Bankside and its Elizabethan theatres. You can tour the theatre itself outside the May to September performance season; when the theatre is in use, the tour is around the Rose Theatre site instead (56 Park Street, SE1 9AR, 7593 0026, www.rosetheatre.org.uk).

Southwark Cathedral

London Bridge, Bankside, SE1 9DA (7367 6700/tours 7367 6734/www. dswark.org/cathedral). London Bridge tube/rail. **Open** 8am-6pm daily. **Admission** £2.50. **Map** p61 E2 🔟

The oldest bits of this building, one of the few places south of the river that Dickens had a good word for, date back more than 800 years. The retro-choir was where the trials of several Protestant martyrs took place during the reign of Mary Tudor. After the Reformation, the church fell into disrepair; in 1905 it became a cathedral.

An interactive museum called the Long View of London, a refectory and a lovely garden are some of the millennial improvements. There are memorials to Shakespeare, John Harvard (benefactor of the US university) and Sam Wanamaker (the force behind Shakespeare's Globe), as well as stained-glass windows with images of Chaucer, who set his pilgrims off to Canterbury from Borough High Street.

Tate Modern

Bankside, SE1 9TG (7401 5120/7887 8888/www.tate.org.uk). Blackfriars tube/rail. **Open** 10am-6pm Mon-Thur, Sun; 10am-10pm Fri, Sat. **Admission** free. **Map** p61 D2 🔟

A powerhouse of modern art, Tate Modern is awe inspiring even before you step inside thanks to its industrial architecture. It was built as Bankside Power Station in the 1950s and designed

Tate Modern

by Sir Giles Gilbert Scott, architect of Battersea Power Station and designer of the famous British red telephone box. Bankside was shut down in 1981 and opened as an art museum in 2000. The original cavernous turbine hall is used to jaw-dropping effect as the home of the large-scale, temporary Unilever Series installations. The permanent collection draws from the Tate organisation's deep reservoir of modern art (international works from 1900 and on) and features heavy-hitters such as Matisse, Rothko, Giacometti and Pollock. In 2006, the galleries were completely rehung, with the artworks grouped according to movement (Surrealism, Minimalism) rather than theme. If you don't know where to start, take one of the guided tours (ask at the information desk). The Tate-to-Tate boat service (7887 8888, £4.30 adult) links with Tate Britain (p78); it runs every 20 minutes and also stops at the Eye.

Event highlights Dan Graham: Greek Meander Pavilion (until 2 Nov 2008); Rothko (see box p63); Unilever Series: Dominique Gonzalez-Foerster (14 Oct 2008-13 Apr 2009).

Topolski's Studio & Memoir of the Century

NEW *Hungerford Bridge Arch 158, Concert Hall Approach, behind the Royal Festival Hall, South Bank, SE1 8XU (www.felikstopolski.com). Waterloo tube/rail.* **Open/admission** check website. **Map** p60 A2 ⑳

Occupying the curious spot underneath the arches at Waterloo station, *Memoir of the Century* is a massive mural depicting all the major events and personalities of the 20th century. It's the work of Feliks Topolski, a Polish-born artist who made his name as a war artist in World War II and then settled in the UK, working from his cramped studio. The mural, which was left unfinished when Topolski died in 1989, shows an extraordinary, semi-deranged vision of the world, via a fantastic jumble of figures: Winston Churchill, Bob Dylan, Elvis, Kennedy

and Khrushchev... Long closed for restoration work, the museum is scheduled to reopen in early 2009; until then private tours can be arranged.

Vinopolis, City of Wine

1 Bank End, Bankside, SE1 9BU (0870 241 4040/www.vinopolis.co.uk). London Bridge tube/rail. **Open** noon-10pm Mon, Thur, Fri; 11am-9pm Sat; noon-6pm Sun. **Admission** £17.50-£32.50; free under-16s. **Map** p61 E2 ㉑

This glossy attraction is more of an introduction to wine-tasting than a resource for oenophiles, but you do need to have some interest to get a kick out it. Participants are furnished with a wine glass and an audio guide. Exhibits are set out by country, with five opportunities to taste wine or champagne from different regions. Gin crashes the party courtesy of a Bombay Sapphire cocktail, and there's also a whisky-tasting area and the Brew Wharf microbrewery.

Winston Churchill's Britain at War Experience

64-66 Tooley Street, Bankside, SE1 2TF (7403 3171/www.britainatwar. co.uk). London Bridge tube/rail. **Open** Apr-Sept 10am-6pm daily. Oct-Mar 10am-5pm daily. **Admission** £9.95; free-£5.75 reductions. **Map** p61 F2 ㉒

This old-fashioned exhibition recalls the privations endured by the British during World War II. Visitors descend from street level in an ancient lift to a reconstructed tube station shelter that doubles as a movie theatre showing documentaries from the period. The experience continues with displays about London during the Blitz, including real bombs, rare documents, photos and reconstructed shopfronts. The displays on rationing, food production and Land Girls are fascinating, and the walk-through bombsite is disturbing.

Eating & drinking

The classy chains clustered around the refurbished Southbank Centre – including Brit-foodie **Canteen** (0845 686 1122, www.canteen.co.uk), **Ping**

Arts across the ocean

One of the first things London's newly elected mayor – Boris Johnson – did, was get himself photographed shaking hands on a pledge of cooperation with New York City mayor Michael Bloomberg. A mile upriver, Oscar-winning director Sam Mendes had beaten him to it.

After six years away, Mendes is to return to the London stage with the first instalment of a transatlantic collaboration with Joseph V Melillo's Brooklyn Academy of Music. Employing both British and American actors, the **Bridge Project** was to launch in spring 2008, but principal actor, Stephen Dillane, was unable to perform due to family illness. Summer 2009 should see things back on track with Simon Russell Beale in Shakespeare's *The Winter's Tale* and Chekhov's *The Cherry Orchard* at the Old Vic (p72).

Boris and Sam aren't alone in looking west. A highlight of the London dance year was the first **Morphoses** (www.morphoses. org) show at Sadler's Wells (p175). The bespoke company of choreographer Christopher Wheeldon combines 20 of the world's best dancers – including Alina Cojocaru (Royal Ballet) and Wendy Whelan (New York City Ballet). It is the first ballet company to split its personnel and creative energies between London and New York. 'I want to bring new audiences into the theatre and help them to fall in love with the art form,' says Wheeldon. We'll shake on that.

Pong (see below), child-friendly **Giraffe** (7928 2004, www.giraffe. net), **Wagamama** noodle bar (www.wagamama.com, 7021 0877) and pizza-joint **Strada** (7401 9126, www.strada.co.uk) – pretty much all hit the spot, while snacking your way around **Borough Market** (p71) is always a treat – just a shame it's not open all week.

Anchor & Hope
36 The Cut, Waterloo, SE1 8LP (7928 9898). Southwark tube or Waterloo tube/rail. **Open** 5-11pm Mon; 11am-11pm Tue-Sat; 12.30-5pm Sun. **££**. **Gastropub**. Map p60 C3 ㉓
With no bookings taken, customers happily wait ages for a table, such is the reputation of the rustic, Med-slanted food here. The worn floorboards and high ceilings are appealing too. It even works as a boozer, with real ales and classic cocktails treated with proper respect. Come in the afternoon or after 9pm if you hope to avoid the crowds.

Baltic
74 Blackfriars Road, South Bank, SE1 8HA (7928 1111/www.balticrestaurant. co.uk). Southwark tube. **Open** noon-3pm, 6-11pm Mon-Sat; noon-3pm, 6-10pm Sun. **££**. **East European**. Map p60 C3 ㉔
London's most glamorous East European restaurant, with high ceilings and a chandelier aglow with hundreds of amber shards. The place can be noisy, but the food is an excellent modern take on such dishes as nutty buckwheat blinis and kaszanka (Polish black pudding). The bar has more than a dozen clear varieties of vodka.

Bincho
NEW *2nd floor, Oxo Tower Wharf, Barge House Street, South Bank, SE1 9PH (7803 0858/www.bincho.co.uk). Blackfriars or Waterloo tube/rail.* **Open** noon-3pm, 5-11.30pm Mon-Fri; noon-11.30pm Sat; noon-10.30pm Sun. **£**. **Japanese**. Map p60 B1 ㉕
This new restaurant is a handsome interpretation of a yakitori-ya – a casual restaurant where office workers

slug beer or saké while noshing hot snacks. The long dining room is done out in a mini-forest of wood and bamboo, the windows giving great Thames views. Chefs at open charcoal grills prepare the meat and fish skewers.

Garrison

99-101 Bermondsey Street, Borough, SE1 3XB (7089 9355/www.thegarrison. co.uk). London Bridge tube/rail. **Open** 8am-11pm Mon-Fri; 9am-11pm Sat; 9am-10.30pm Sun. **££**. **Gastropub**. **Map** p61 F3 26

More like a bistro than a gastropub, the bustling Garrison is so full of tall rickety tables and chairs there's no real standing room. Within the quirky interior, strings of hops remind you there's booze available, but it's the mod British food and 50-strong wine list that catch the eye. Much loved for brunch too.

Magdalen

NEW *152 Tooley Street, Bankside, SE1 2TU (7403 1342/www.magdalen restaurant.co.uk). London Bridge tube/ rail.* **Open** noon-2.30pm, 6.30-10.30pm Mon-Fri; 6.30-10.30pm Sat. **££**. **British**. **Map** p61 F3 27

Magdalen's very civilised interior – all dark wood, aubergine paintwork and florally accessorised elegance – leads

you to suspect that its food will be as well mannered as its staff. A pleasant surprise, then, to be ambushed by spirited flavours on the daily changing menu of modern British food. Try the likes of rump of Hereford beef.

M Manze

87 Tower Bridge Road, Borough, SE1 4TW (7407 2985/www.manze.co.uk). Bus 1, 42, 188. **Open** 11am-2pm Mon; 10.30am-2pm Tue-Thur; 10am-2.15pm Fri; 10am-2.45pm Sat. No credit cards. **£**. **Pie & mash**. **Map** p61 F4 28

Manze's is London's oldest pie shop, established in 1902. It's also austerely beautiful, with its original tiled interior and marble-topped tables. Expect mashed potatoes, minced beef pies and liquor (a kind of parsley sauce); braver souls should try the stewed eels.

Ping Pong

NEW *Festival Terrace, Southbank Centre, Belvedere Road, South Bank, SE1 8XX (7960 4160/www.pingpongdimsum.com). Embankment tube/Waterloo tube/rail.* **Open** noon-midnight Mon-Wed; noon-1am Thur-Sat; noon-10.30pm Sun. **££**. **Dim sum**. **Map** p60 A2 29

The Ping Pong chain now has half a dozen branches in the capital. Putting a sleek, chic and slightly sanitised face

Magdalen

on dim sum, the combination of snacky food and creative cocktails make it a good choice for a fun night out.

Rake

NEW *Winchester Walk, Bankside, SE1 9AG (7407 0557). London Bridge tube/rail.* **Open** noon-11pm Mon-Fri; 10am-11pm Sat. **Pub. Map** p61 E2 ㉚

The streets around Borough Market have never been short of places to drink, but this new pub has a few characteristics that help it stand out from the pack. For one thing, it's tiny, with a canopied, heated patio adjunct. And for another, it's run by the folks behind the Utobeer stall in the market; the list of brews is therefore varied and enticing.

Shipp's Tea Rooms

NEW *4 Park Street, Bankside, SE1 9AB (7407 2692). London Bridge tube/rail.* **Open** 9.30am-5.30pm Mon-Fri; 10am-7pm Sat; 11am-5pm Sun. No credit cards. **£. Café. Map** p61 E2 ㉛

Shipp's caters perfectly for Borough Market shoppers with its nostalgic feel. Electrical contractor's premises have become a shrine to last-century tea sets, scones and victoria sponge cake, evoking an era when shoppers had time to nibble cakes over a cuppa.

Skylon

Royal Festival Hall, Belvedere Road, South Bank, SE1 8XX (7654 7800/ www.danddlondon.com). Waterloo tube/rail. **Open** *Bar* 11am-1am daily. *Brasserie* noon-11.45pm daily. *Restaurant* noon-2.30pm, 5.30-10.45pm daily. **£££. Modern European. Map** p60 A2 ㉜

Set at the front of the refurbished Royal Festival Hall, this lofty space – with fantastic river view – is divided into three: a central raised bar separates the formal restaurant from the brasserie. The room is dominated by five huge bronze chandeliers, while the menu features the likes of Swedish classic jansson's temptation. Staff are friendly too.

Table

83 Southwark Street, Borough, SE1 0HX (7401 2760/www.thetablecafe. com). Southwark tube/London Bridge

Skylon

tube/rail. **Open** 7.30am-8.30pm Mon-Thur; 7.30am-11pm Fri; 9am-4pm Sat. **£**. **Café**. **Map** p60 C2 ③③
Based in the ground floor of a Bankside architecture company, the Table is a cut above your regular office canteen. Mix and match a salad or choose from hot meals that include flans, a daily risotto and sardines, then hope to find a seat at the shared solid wood tables. Multifunctional, cheap and stylish.

Tapas Brindisa

18-20 Southwark Street, Bankside, SE1 1TJ (7357 8880/www.brindisa.com). London Bridge tube/rail. **Open** noon-3pm, 5.30-11pm Mon-Thur; 9-11am, noon-4pm, 5.30-11pm Fri, Sat. **£**. **Spanish**. **Map** p61 E2 ③④
The restaurant arm of the renowned Spanish deli turns out first-rate tapas, marrying fine imported ingredients with fresh, seasonal produce from closer to home. With its auspicious Borough Market location, the small space soon gets rammed – be prepared to wait, as no bookings are taken.

Wine Wharf

Stoney Street, Borough Market, Bankside, SE1 9AD (7940 8335/www.winewharf.com). London Bridge tube/rail. **Open** 11.30am-11pm Mon-Sat. **Wine bar**. **Map** p61 E2 ③⑤
Located between Vinopolis (p67) and Borough Market under the railway arches, this industrial-chic wine bar has a 100-glass selection, and the buzz it creates is fun and foxy. No aged noses sniffing into goblets here, but busy post-work chatter and coupley entwinement. Helping the wine along are Med delights from the deli. Jazz plays from 7.30pm on a Monday and you can buy takeaway bottles for a picnic. Beer-lovers should check out the adjoining Brew Wharf (7378 6601, www.brewwharf.com).

Shopping

There are some great design and crafts shops (such as Bodo Sperlein) in the **Oxo Tower**, between Blackfriars and Waterloo Bridges.

Borough Market

Southwark Street, Bankside, SE1 (7407 1002/www.boroughmarket.org.uk). London Bridge tube/rail. **Open** 11am-5pm Thur; noon-6pm Fri; 9am-4pm Sat. **Map** p61 E2 ③⑥
The foodie's favourite market occupies a sprawling site near London Bridge, but campaigners are currently battling a threat in the form of a rail viaduct planned for above the space. Gourmet goodies run the gamut from Flour Power City Bakery's organic loaves to chorizo and rocket rolls from Spanish specialist Brindisa, plus rare-breed meats, fruit and veg, cakes and all manner of preserves, oils and teas – head out hungry to take advantage of the numerous free samples. The market is now open on Thursdays, when it tends to be quieter than at always-mobbed weekends.

167 Bermondsey Street

NEW *167 Bermondsey Street, Borough, SE1 3UW (7407 3137/www.bermondsey167.com). London Bridge tube/rail*. **Open** 11am-8pm Tue-Sat; noon-4pm Sun. **Map** p61 F4 ③⑦
This slick concept store mixes impeccable interior design and furniture with highbrow fashion, watches and jewellery. Products come from all over the world, but Latin America is a major source of inspiration.

Terra Plana

124 Bermondsey Street, Borough, SE1 3TX (7407 3758/www.terraplana.com). London Bridge tube/rail. **Open** 11am-7pm daily. **Map** p61 F3 ③⑧
A purveyor of eco fashion long before it was trendy, the Terra Plana mini-chain has an original range of shoes for both sexes. Artisanal approaches and recycled materials are the focus.

Nightlife

Corsica Studios

NEW *Units 4/5, Elephant Road, Newington, SE17 1LB (7703 4760/www.corsicastudios.com). Elephant & Castle tube/rail*. **Open** varies. **Map** p61 D5 ③⑨

Set up by an independent, not-for-profit arts organisation, Corsica runs a cracking programme of music – over the last year we've really appreciated the likes of a festival of out-there Japanese psychedelia and a warehouse all-nighter that fused Italo disco, techno and Simian Mobile Disco.

Ministry of Sound

103 Gaunt Street, off Newington Causeway, Newington, SE1 6DP (7740 8600/www.ministryofsound .com). Elephant & Castle tube/rail. **Open** 10.30pm-5am Fri; 11pm-7am Sat. **Map** p61 D4 ⓴

Promoters spend a pretty penny booking talent for the London base of this mega-successful clubbing brand. The superpopular Gallery night offers hard house and trance, while other nights bring mainstream urban and superstar DJs to an international crowd. Brand-new Martin Audio soundsystem too.

Arts & leisure

Free-standing Pit tickets are excellent value at **Shakespeare's Globe** (p66), where artistic director Dominic Dromgoole showcases new writing alongside the Bard from May to Sept.

BFI London IMAX Cinema

1 Charlie Chaplin Walk, Waterloo, SE1 8XR (0870 787 2525/www.bfi. org.uk/imax). Waterloo tube/rail. **Map** p60 B2 ㉛

Made-for-IMAX children's fare and wow-factor documentaries are usually what's on offer at the biggest screen in the country, but watch out for monster-sized versions of mainstream films too. The seating is set so you feel like you're inside the screen.

BFI Southbank

South Bank, SE1 8XT (information 7928 3535/bookings 7928 3232/www. bfi.org.uk/nft). Embankment tube/ Waterloo tube/rail. **Map** p60 A2 ㉜

A London institution, with an unrivalled programme of retrospective seasons and previews, with regular director

and actor Q&As. The Thameside seating outside the rather underpowered main café is hugely popular in good weather, and museum-caterers Benugo run a handsome new cocktail bar/ restaurant on the other side of the building alongside the terrific Mediatheque.

National Theatre

South Bank, SE1 9PX (information 7452 3400/box office 7452 3000/ www.nationaltheatre.org.uk). Embankment or Southwark tube/ Waterloo tube/rail. **Map** p60 B2 ㊸

Nicholas Hytner's artistic directorship, with landmark successes such as Alan Bennett's *The History Boys*, has shown that the state-subsidised home of British theatre can turn out quality drama at a profit. An upcoming collaboration between hip choreographer Akram Khan and Juliet Binoche provides extra youth appeal, as does the Travelex season, for which two-thirds of the seats are offered for £10. During summer the free outdoor performing arts stage is a great way to see booty-shaking bhangra or fire-swallowing avant-gardists by the Thames.

Old Vic

Waterloo Road, Waterloo, SE1 8NB (0870 060 6628/www.oldvictheatre. com). Waterloo tube/rail. **Map** p60 B3 ㊹

The combination of double-Oscar winner Kevin Spacey and top producer David Liddiment at this 200-year-old theatre continues to be a commercial success, if not a critical one. Sam Mendes's Bridge Projects, in collaboration with Spacey and the Brooklyn Academy of Music is the big news. **Event highlights** The Bridge Project (see box p68).

Shunt

Joiner Street, Bankside, SE1 (7378 7776/www.shunt.co.uk). London Bridge tube/rail. **Open** 6-11pm Wed-Fri. **Map** p61 E2 ㊺

Set in the damp bowels of London Bridge station and run by an artists' and performers' collective, Shunt isn't your average members' bar. For a start,

Borough Market p71

everyone is welcome – non-members pay at the door, and can stay until closing time in the lovely bar. The space is interesting too: vast musty arches, part church and part dungeon. The programme is also unique: every week a different member of the collective decides what will happen, and, given the flexibility of the space, this could be cabaret, film, theatre – you name it.

Southbank Centre

Belvedere Road, South Bank, SE1 8XX (switchboard 0871 663 2501/bookings 0871 663 2500/www.rfh.org.uk). Embankment tube/Waterloo tube/ rail. **Map** p60 A2 **46**
The 3,000-capacity Royal Festival Hall reopened in 2007 after a £90m renovation. Access has been made easier, but the real meat of the project is the acoustic refurbishment of the main hall itself. The RFH's free foyer gigs have also been expanded to include concerts in the ballroom. Showcase events include Meltdown (where guest directors such as Morrissey, Scott Walker

and David Bowie curate a two-week programme), and the Shell Classic International Season. Next door is the 900-seat Queen Elizabeth Hall, a rather uninviting space that also houses pop and jazz gigs, and the much smaller Purcell Room (capacity just 365), which is used as a venue for everything from chamber concerts to poetry readings. The foyer also hosts free concerts.
Event highlights 'Klang: A Stockhausen Festival (from 1 Nov 2008).

Unicorn Theatre

Tooley Street, Bankside, SE1 2HZ (7645 0560/www.unicorntheatre.com). London Bridge tube/rail/Tower Hill tube. **Map** p61 F2 **47**
The design of this sleek arts centre was the result of a three-year collaboration with local schoolchildren (note the child-height windows). The 300-seat Weston Theatre is its large performance space, the Clore a more intimate studio for education and new work.
Event highlights 'Sleeping Beauty', for over-5s (2 Dec 2008-24 Jan 2009).

Routemaster bus p77

Westminster & St James's

Westminster

More imposing than atmospheric, Westminster is for many the heart of London. Home to the **Houses of Parliament**, the area has been the seat of power for 1,000 years; Britain's first Parliament met in **Westminster Abbey**.

Sights & museums

Banqueting House
Whitehall, SW1A 2ER (0870 751 5178/ www.hrp.org.uk). Westminster tube/ Charing Cross tube/rail. **Open** 10am-5pm Mon-Sat. **Admission** £4.50; free-£3.50 reductions. **Map** p75 C2 ①
Designed by Inigo Jones in 1622, this was London's first true Renaissance building. The austerity of the exterior belies the sumptuous Rubens ceiling in the first-floor hall (call to check it's open before you visit). Charles I was beheaded just outside in 1649.

Cabinet War Rooms & Churchill Museum
Clive Steps, King Charles Street, SW1A 2AQ (7930 6961/www.iwm.org.uk). St James's Park or Westminster tube. **Open** 9.30am-6pm daily. **Admission** £11; free-£8.50 reductions. **Map** p75 C2 ②
This was Churchill's bunker during World War II. Every book, chart and pin in the map room remains where it was in August 1945, as does the microphone he used for broadcasts.

Houses of Parliament
Parliament Square, SW1A 0AA (tours 0870 906 3773/www.parliament.uk). Westminster tube. **Open** phone for

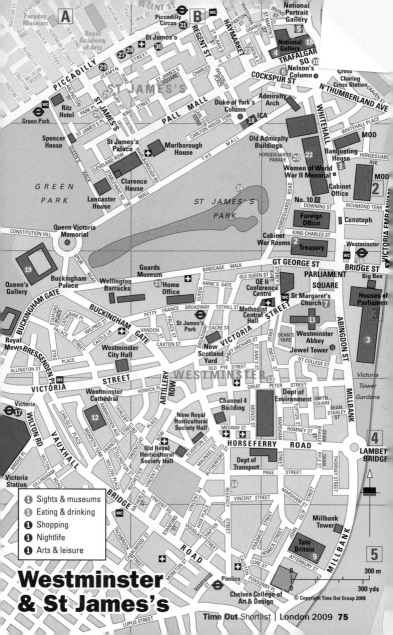

Westminster
& St James's

Legend:
- Sights & museums
- Eating & drinking
- Shopping
- Nightlife
- Arts & leisure

Watch this space

With the new Fourth Plinth commission due to be installed in 2009, we introduce the contenders.

In 2009, London welcomes the newest work in an unusual artistic tradition. Left empty when all the other areas of Trafalgar Square (p78) got their allotted martial and regal statues in the 1840s, the plinth in the north-west corner has become a showcase for contemporary sculpture. In 1999 some bright spark realised the so-called **Fourth Plinth** would be ideal for temporary installations: work by Mark Wallinger, Bill Woodrow, Rachel Whiteread, Marc Quinn and, at the time of writing, Thomas Schütte has since occupied the prestigious site. Judging by the six new nominations, displayed in the National Gallery (p77) through spring 2008, the forthcoming sculpture could be the best yet.

Our two favourites (pictured above) are Yinka Shonibare's scale model – in a glass bottle – of Nelson's flagship and Anish Kapoor's *Sky Plinth*, which is an assemblage of five concave mirrors designed to reflect the sky and upside down earth. Jeremy Deller's *The Spoils of War* – a burnt-out car, the result of an attack on civilians in Iraq – would certainly provide an interesting counterpoint to the square's militaristic vainglory, while Antony Gormley's notion that the plinth be occupied 24 hours a day by volunteers (8,760 in all, standing for an hour each over the year) takes interactivity to the max. The sun- and wind-powered contraption *Faîtes L'Art, pas La Guerre (Make Art, Not War)* by Bob & Roberta Smith holds a kind of middle ground: polemical fun, perhaps. Over Tracey Emin's contribution, a family group of meerkats, we choose quietly to draw a veil.

As we go to print, a committee is deliberating on which of these will win; check the web for details.

■ www.fourthplinth.co.uk

details. **Admission** *Visitors' Gallery* free. *Tours* £7; free-£5 reductions. **Map** p75 C3 ❸

Completed in 1860, this neo-Gothic extravaganza was created by Charles Barry, who won an architectural competition to replace the original Houses of Parliament. Barry was assisted on the interiors by Augustus Pugin. The only parts of the original palace to survive a fire in 1834 were the Jewel Tower and Westminster Hall, one of Europe's finest medieval buildings. Visitors can watch the Commons or Lords in session from the galleries. Parliament goes into recess in summer, when there are tours of Westminster Hall and the two houses.

National Gallery

Trafalgar Square, WC2N 5DN (7747 2885/www.nationalgallery. org.uk). Leicester Square tube/Charing Cross tube/rail. **Open** 10am-6pm Mon, Tue, Thur-Sun; 10am-9pm Wed. **Admission** free. **Map** p75 C1 ❹

Founded in 1824, this is now one of the world's greatest art collections, with more than 2,000 works, starting with 13th-century religious pieces and heading towards modernity via gems such as Holbein's *Ambassadors* and Velázquez's *Rokeby Venus*. There are also important works by Turner and Constable, but the real crowd-pullers are the likes of Monet's *Water-Lilies*, Van Gogh's *Chair* and Seurat's *Bathers at Asnières*. The National Dining Rooms and National Café (p79) are exemplary. **Event highlights** 'Renaissance Faces: Van Eyck to Titian' (15 Oct 2008-18 Jan 2009); 'Sisley in England and Wales' (12 Nov 2008-15 Feb 2009).

National Portrait Gallery

2 St Martin's Place, WC2H 0HE (7306 0055/www.npg.org.uk). Leicester Square tube/Charing Cross tube/rail. **Open** 10am-6pm Mon-Wed, Sat, Sun; 10am-9pm Thur, Fri. **Map** p75 C1 ❺

Subjects of the portraits here range from Tudor royalty to current celebs. The gallery's manageable size and attractive design make it wonderfully personable, and the rather average top-floor restaurant has great views. **Event highlights** Photographic Portrait Prize (until 24 Feb 2009); BP Portrait Award (June-Sept 2009).

Routemaster buses

Cockspur Street, Stops B & (opposite) S. **Map** p75 C1 ❻

The iconic red double-deckers were withdrawn from service in 2005, but beautifully refurbished Routies run Routes 9 (Stop B) and 15 (Stop S) every 15 minutes, 9.30am to 6.30pm. No.9 goes west to the Royal Albert Hall, no.15 east via St Paul's to Tower Hill.

St Margaret's Church

Parliament Square, SW1P 3JX (7654 4840/www.westminster-abbey.org/ stmargarets). St James's Park or Westminster tube. **Open** 9.30am-3.45pm Mon-Fri; 9.30am-1.45pm Sat; 2-5pm Sun. **Admission** free. **Map** p75 C3 ❼

Originally founded in the 12th century, St Margaret's houses some of the most impressive pre-Reformation stained glass in London. Later windows celebrate Sir Walter Raleigh, executed in Old Palace Yard, and poet John Milton, who married his second wife here.

St Martin-in-the-Fields

NEW *Trafalgar Square, WC2N 4JJ (7766 1100/box office 7839 8362/ www.stmartin-in-the-fields.org). Leicester Square tube/Charing Cross tube/rail.* **Open** 8am-6pm daily. **Admission** free. **Map** p75 C1 ❽

A church has stood here 'in the fields' between Westminster and the City since the 13th century; this version was built in 1726 by James Gibbs. It's the parish church for Buckingham Palace, but is better known for classical music concerts. Major refurbishment was completed in early 2008; the bright interior has been fully restored, with Victorian additions carefully removed and the addition of a controversial altar window that shows a stylised Cross as if it is rippling on water. The crypt, its fine café and the London Brass Rubbing Centre have all been modernised.

Tate Britain

Millbank, SW1P 4RG (7887 8000/ www.tate.org.uk). Pimlico tube. **Open** 10am-5.50pm daily. **Admission** free. **Map** p75 C5 ❾

Younger, sexier Tate Modern (p66) gets the wolf whistles, but the collection at Tate Britain is at least as strong – for historical art in London, it is second only to the National (p77). Displays span five centuries of British art from the 16th century, taking in Hogarth, Gainsborough, the Blakes (William and Peter), Constable, Reynolds, Bacon and Moore; Turner has the Clore Gallery all to himself. Nor does Tate Britain skimp on more recent artists: Howard Hodgkin, Lucian Freud and David Hockney are all represented. The Tate-to-Tate boat service (7887 8888, £4.30 adult) is great fun too. **Event highlights** Francis Bacon (11 Sept 2008-4 Jan 2009); Turner Prize (30 Sept 2008-18 Jan 2009); Tate Triennial (4 Feb-26 May 2009).

Trafalgar Square

Charing Cross tube/rail. **Map** p75 C1 ❿
The centrepiece of London, Trafalgar Square was conceived in the 1820s by the Prince Regent, who commissioned John Nash to create a grand square to pay homage to Britain's naval power. It has always been a natural gathering point – especially since it was semi-pedestrianised in 2003. The focus is Nelson's Column, a Corinthian pillar topped by a statue of naval hero Horatio Nelson, but the Fourth Plinth (see box p76) gives things a more modern cast.

Westminster Abbey

20 Dean's Yard, SW1P 3PA (7222 5152/tours 7654 4900/www. westminster-abbey.org). St James's Park or Westminster tube. **Open** 9.30am-3.45pm Mon, Tue, Thur, Fri; 9.30am-7pm Wed; 9.30am-1.45pm Sat. *Abbey Museum* 10.30am-4pm Mon-Sat. *Cloisters* 8am-6pm Mon-Sat. *Garden* Apr-Sept 10am-6pm Tue-Thur. Oct-Mar 10am-4pm Tue-Thur. **Admission** £10; free-£7 reductions. **Map** p75 C3 ⓫
Westminster Abbey has been synonymous with British royalty since the 11th century, when Edward the Confessor built a new church on the site just in time for his own funeral. Since then, the British monarchy have almost all been crowned and buried here. Of the original abbey, only the Pyx Chamber (once the royal treasury) and Norman undercroft remain. The Gothic nave and choir were rebuilt in the 13th century; the Henry VII Chapel, with its spectacular fan vaulting, was added in 1503-1512, and Nicholas Hawksmoor's west towers in 1745. The interior is cluttered with monuments to statesmen, scientists, musicians and poets. The Little Cloister garden offers some respite – as well as free lunchtime concerts.

Westminster Cathedral

42 Francis Street, SW1P 1QW (7798 9055/www.westminstercathedral.org.uk). Victoria tube/rail. **Open** 7am-7pm Mon-Fri, Sun; 8am-7pm Sat. **Admission** free. *Campanile* £5; £3 reductions. No credit cards. **Map** p75 A4 ⓬
This neo-Byzantine confection is Britain's premier Catholic cathedral, built between 1895 and 1903. The inside is still unfinished, but you get a taste of what's planned from the magnificent columns and mosaics. Eric Gill's Stations of the Cross (1914-18) are justly famous, and the view from the bell tower is superb. Much-needed renovation work should begin in 2008.

Eating & drinking

Cinnamon Club

Old Westminster Library, 30-32 Great Smith Street, SW1P 3BU (7222 2555/ www.cinnamonclub.com). St James's Park or Westminster tube. **Open** 7.30-9.30am, noon-2.30pm, 6-10.45pm Mon-Sat. **£££. Indian**. **Map** p75 C4 ⓭
Destination of choice for power brokers and politicians, Cinnamon Club's spacious dining hall has the feel of a grand colonial club. The modern Indian food runs from dressed-up rustic staples to regal stalwarts. Indian breakfasts too.

Millbank Lounge

City Inn Westminster, 30 John Islip Street, SW1P 4DD (7932 4700/

www.millbanklounge.com). Pimlico or Westminster tube. **Open** 11am-11pm Mon-Sat; noon-10.30pm Sun. **Cocktail bar**. Map p75 B4 ⑭

Hidden away down a backstreet, this quality hotel bar is criminally under-used. You'll have no trouble finding a comfy chair in the expansive bar area – but you'll need to take your time over the long drinks menu.

National Café

East Wing, National Gallery, Trafalgar Square, WC2N 5DN (7747 2525/www. thenationalcafe.com). Charing Cross tube/rail. **Open** 8am-11pm Mon-Sat; 10am-6pm Sun. **££. Brasserie. Map** p75 C1 ⑮

This relaxed café-cum-brasserie is an informal alternative to its British elder sister in the Sainsbury Wing (National Dining Rooms, 7747 2525). Service is less reliable, but longer opening hours are a boon. It's an attractive space, with dark wood panels and a marble-topped counter running the length of one wall. Adjoining the main room is a self-service area for salads and sandwiches.

St Stephen's Tavern

10 Bridge Street, SW1A 2JR (7925 2286). Westminster tube. **Open** 10am-11.30pm Mon-Thur, Sat; 10am-midnight Fri; 10.30am-10.30pm Sun. **Pub. Map** p75 C3 ⑯

A restored gem of a pub opposite Big Ben. The decor is all carved wood and etched glass, with towering displays of flowers reaching to the high ceilings.

Nightlife

Pacha

Terminus Place, SW1E 5NE (0845 371 4489/www.pachalondon.com). Victoria tube/rail. **Open** 10pm-5am Fri, Sat. **Map** p75 A4 ⑰

Join the sleek and minted for glammed-up house nights. The refurbed Pacha has a knock-'em-dead Martin Audio soundsystem, and fabulous plans for a roof garden – although nothing is likely to happen until the new, superclassy, four-floor Pacha Terrace opens in King's Cross, perhaps in summer 2008.

Arts & leisure

St Martin-in-the-Fields (p77) and the elegant, 18th-century church of **St John's Smith Square** (7222 1061, www.sjss.org.uk) both host regular classical concerts.

Institute of Contemporary Arts (ICA)

Nash House, the Mall, SW1Y 5AH (7930 6393/bookings 7930 3647/ www.ica.org.uk). Piccadilly Circus tube/ Charing Cross tube/rail. **Open** noon-11pm Mon; noon-1am Tue-Sat; noon-10.30pm Sun. **Admission** *Daily membership* £2-£3, £1.50-£2 reductions. **Map** p75 B1 ⑱

Founded in 1948, the ICA still revels in a remit that challenges traditional notions of art. Its cinema screens hard-to-find world and experimental cinema, its theatre stages performance art and quality gigs, and its gallery is avid in pursuit of the controversial.

St James's

Traditional, quiet and terribly exclusive, St James's is where **Buckingham Palace** presides over lovely **St James's Park**. There are signs of a change of pace, however: destination restaurants are opening (**Sake no hana**) and even upper-crust **Fortnum & Mason** has been given a spruce-up.

Sights & museums

The lavishly restored, 18th-century **Spencer House** (27 St James's Place, SW1A 1NR, 7499 8620, www.spencerhouse.co.uk) opens most Sundays, and you can visit Prince Charles's home, **Clarence House** (The Mall, SW1A 1AA, 7766 7303, www.royalcollection. org.uk) in summer – book ahead.

Buckingham Palace & Royal Mews

The Mall, SW1A 1AA (7766 7300/ Royal Mews 7766 7302/www.royal

collection.org.uk). *Green Park or St James's Park tube/Victoria tube/rail.* **Open** *State Rooms* late July-Sept 9.45am-6pm (last entry 3.45pm) daily. *Queen's Gallery* 10am-4.30pm daily. *Royal Mews* Oct-July 11am-4pm daily. Aug, Sept 10am-5pm daily. **Admission** £14; free-£12.50 reductions. *Queen's Gallery* £8; free-£7 reductions. *Royal Mews* £7; free-£6 reductions. **Map** p75 A3 ⑲

Built in 1703, the world-famous palace started life as a grand house for the Duke of Buckingham, but George III liked it so much he bought it, in 1761, for his young bride Charlotte. His son, George IV, hired John Nash to convert it into a palace, and construction of the 600-room building began in 1825. But the project was beset with problems; Nash was dismissed in 1830 and the unimaginative Edward Blore had to finish the job. The Queen's Gallery contains highlights of Elizabeth's fine art and decorative collection, including the Diamond Diadem, and visitors can see the State Apartments when the royals are on their hols. The Royal Mews (further along Buckingham Palace Road) has royal carriages, the official Rolls-Royces and the royal horses.

Changing of the Guard

Horse Guards Parade, Horse Guards Road, SW1A 2AX. Embankment tube/Charing Cross tube/rail. **Parade** 11am Mon-Sat; 10am Sun. **Admission** free. **Map** p75 C2 ⑳

The Changing of the Foot Guards (11.30am alternate days) takes place at Buckingham Palace. For us, though, the daily cavalry version is better. The crowds are smaller, and you get shiny armour, swords and beautiful horses.

Guards Museum

Wellington Barracks, Birdcage Walk, SW1E 6HQ (7414 3428/www.the guardsmuseum.com). St James's Park tube. **Open** 10am-4pm daily. **Admission** £3; free-£2 reductions. **Map** p75 B3 ㉑

This museum presents the 350-year history of the Foot Guards, using uniforms, medals, paintings and such

memorabilia as their mascot Jacob the Goose, run over by a van in barracks.

Household Cavalry Museum

NEW *Horse Guards, Whitehall, SW1A 2AX (7414 2392/www.household cavalry.co.uk). Embankment tube/ Charing Cross tube/rail.* **Open** 10am-6pm daily. **Admission** £6; £4 reductions. **Map** p75 C2 ㉒

This excellent museum allows visitors to peer at medals and cuirasses and view video diaries of serving soldiers, but the best bit is a simple glass screen, through which you can see the magnificent horses in their stables.

Eating & drinking

In the reborn Fortnum's (p82), check out the ice-cream at **Parlour** and excellent wine bar **1707**.

Brumus Bar

NEW *Haymarket Hotel, 1 Suffolk Place, SW1Y 4BP (7470 4000/www.firmdale. com). Piccadilly Circus tube.* **Open** 11am-midnight daily. **Cocktail bar**. **Map** p75 B1 ㉓

As you'd expect of the main bar at London's most talked-about new hotel, Brumus is a handsome chap. More surprising, it isn't a bit snobbish, attracting its fair share of unhip post-theatre types. The pricey cocktails are imaginative, and there's cabaret on Fridays at 6pm.

Inn The Park

St James's Park, SW1A 2BJ (7451 9999/www.innthepark.com). St James's Park tube. **Open** 8am-9pm Mon-Fri; 9am-9pm Sat, Sun. **££**. **Café/British**. **Map** p75 B2 ㉔

Oliver Peyton's all-day lakeside café has everything going for it: a stunning park location, a beautiful modern building and a varied British menu. There are famous poached egg and soldiers breakfasts and a summer barbecue (on the long terrace until 9pm); the restaurant à la carte is less reliable.

Red Lion

2 Duke of York Street, SW1Y 6JP (7321 0782). Piccadilly Circus tube.

Sweet little somethings

Everyone knows the buttoned-up Brits go a bit crazy over afternoon tea. You might be more surprised to discover how much we've taken to uninhibited kitsch retro settings in which to indulge the habit. Forget lack-lustre self-service catering in the park, forget greasy caffs, forget the pomp of posh hotel tearooms – currently the best exponents of the art of the mid-afternoon treat are exactly where the fairy cake fetish of the shopping classes meets the foodie love of gourmet teas.

Start at the renewed Fortnum & Mason (p82), but not in the Eastbourne retirement home sobriety of the St James's Restaurant on the fourth floor. Instead, head down to the first floor and **Parlour** (pictured). Here the focus is on floats, sundaes, cakes, shakes and ice-cream cocktails, the walls look like undulating layers of chocolate and vanilla, and the counter is a pink and white mosaic. Expect to pay a prodigious £25 for sundaes and coffee for two, but the David Collins interior is a wow.

For home comforts, **Shipp's** (p70) by Borough Market is a kitsch delight – just check out the hanging tea cups. The cakes, kept under giant glass cloches, and leaf teas are of very high quality, and sandwiches are served too. Afternoon tea costs £17.50, but is pretty much a full meal. While you scoff, admire retro teapots, tablecloths and bone china sourced from the owner's antiques shop.

Finally, after the crisp furniture and elegant accessories of Heal's, Oliver Peyton's **Meals** (p145) comes as something of a surprise: cut-out cupboards suggest a fairy-tale landscape of foliage and stars, while the fake wooden 'tablecloths' and marshmallow pink chairs could be from a pantomime set. Try the fab-a-roony retro 'jaffa cake' and you'll be hooked.

Open noon-11.30pm Mon-Sat. **Pub**.
Map p75 A1 ㉕

Established in the 1600s and given an ornate makeover by the Victorians, the Red Lion is a timeless English pub with classic dark wood decor. Two narrow bar areas are straddled by a carved, etched-glass island bar dispensing fine real ale and generic food.

Sake no hana

NEW *23 St James's Street, SW1A 1HA (7925 8988). Green Park tube.* **Open** noon-3pm, 6pm-midnight Mon-Sat. **££££. Japanese**. Map p75 A1 ㉖

Alan Yau has here turned his attention to Japanese fine dining, approaching it in a typically unorthodox way. Award-winning architect Kengo Kuma has transformed a dull interior with cedar, clever lighting and screens. The pick 'n' mix menu features both home-style and creatively modern dishes, but the results are uniformly thrilling.

Shopping

Fortnum & Mason

181 Piccadilly, W1A 1ER (7734 8040/ www.fortnumandmason.co.uk). Green Park or Piccadilly Circus tube. **Open** 10am-6.30pm Mon-Sat; noon-6pm Sun (food hall only). Map p75 A1 ㉗

London's oldest department store had a major – but sensitive (the courtly tail-coated staff remain) – upgrade for its 300th birthday in 2007. The famed biscuits, confectionery, jams, coffee and tea are still sold on the ground floor, while downstairs you'll find game, fish and traiteur dishes. The extended roster of eating and drinking choices now includes Parlour, an exquisite setting for a pricey knickerbocker glory, and 1707, a terrific wine bar. The upper floors are essentially a classy gift shop – antique teacups, Lulu Guinness bags, leather backgammon sets and select perfumes (Miller Harris, Clive Christian).

Hatchards

187 Piccadilly, W1J 9LE (7439 9921/ www.hatchards.co.uk). Piccadilly Circus tube. **Open** 9.30am-7pm Mon-Sat; noon-6pm Sun. Map p75 A1 ㉘

London's oldest bookshop (1797) has counted Disraeli, Byron and Wilde among its customers. Excellent for travel, biography and signed editions.

Jeffery-West

16 Piccadilly Arcade, SW1Y 6NH (7499 3360/www.jeffery-west.co.uk). Green Park or Piccadilly Circus tube. **Open** 10am-6pm Mon-Wed, Fri, Sat; 10am-7pm Thur. Map p75 A1 ㉙

With its playboy vampire's apartment feel – red walls, objets d'art, a skeleton in the window – this shop is the perfect showcase for Marc Jeffery and Guy West's trad men's shoes, much loved by modern-day dandies.

Jermyn Street

Green Park or Piccadilly Circus tube. Map p75 B1 ㉚

This anachronistic street is London's centre for traditional shirtmaking. Turnbull & Asser (nos.71-72, 7808 3000, www.turnbullandasser.co.uk) was the first, but Harvie & Hudson (nos.96-97, 7839 3578, www.harvieandhudson. com) and Emma Willis (no.66, 7930 9980, www.emmawillis.com) also craft fine bespoke shirts. With its wonderful sign and old-fashioned interior, Bates the Hatter (no.21A, 7734 2722, www. bates-hats.co.uk) is another gem, albeit with a different speciality. The appetite can be sated at cossetting British dining room Wiltons (no.55, 7629 9955, www.wiltons.co.uk) or cheesemongers Paxton & Whitfield (no.93, 7930 0259, www.paxtonandwhitfield.co.uk).

Nightlife

Pigalle Club

215-217 Piccadilly, W1J 9HN (0845 345 6053/www.thepigalleclub.com). Piccadilly Circus tube. **Open** 7pm-2am Mon-Wed; 7pm-3am Thur-Sat. Map p75 B1 ㉛

With low lighting, antique fittings and diamond-shaped mirrors, this chic basement supper club is all about 1940s-style glamour. Tables for diners cluster round the stage, where jazz, jive and cabaret crooners perform. Food is pricey, but non-diners are welcome.

King's Road p93

South Kensington & Chelsea

South Kensington

South Kensington isn't the most exhilarating part of London in many ways, but it is thoroughly unmissable. Why? This is the location of the majority of London's world-class museums: the **Natural History Museum**, **Science Museum** and **Victoria & Albert Museum** are clustered together, but such is the wealth of exhibits in each you'd be foolish to try to 'do' more than one of them in a single day. The enormous **Royal Albert Hall** and similarly overblown **Albert Memorial** pay homage to the man behind it all, with **Kensington Gardens** as a refreshing green backdrop.

Sights & museums

Albert Memorial

Kensington Gardens (opposite Royal Albert Hall), SW7 (tours 7495 0916). South Kensington tube. **Tours** 2pm, 3pm 1st Sun of mth. **Tickets** £4.50; £4 reductions. No credit cards. **Map** p84 B2 ❶
One of the great sculptural achievements of the Victorian period centres on a gilded Prince Albert (the man responsible for setting up the area's three extraordinary museums), attended by a marble frieze of artists, architects and musicians. The 180ft spire is inlaid with semi-precious stones.

Brompton Oratory

Thurloe Place, Brompton Road, SW7 2RP (7808 0900/www.brompton oratory.com). South Kensington tube.

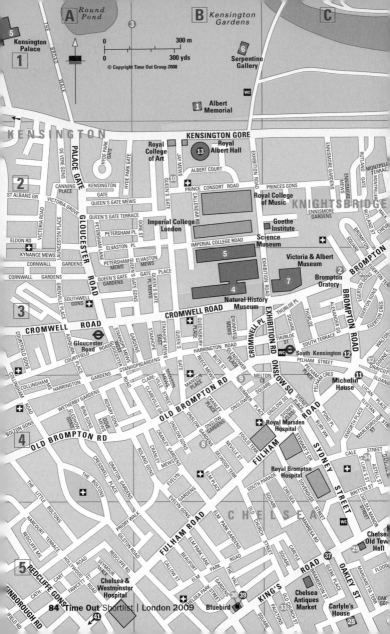

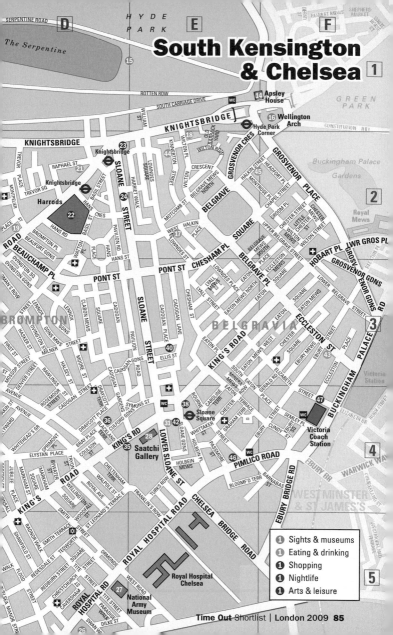

South Kensington & Chelsea

D SERPENTINE ROAD
E HYDE PARK
F SHEPHERD MARKET · MARKET MEWS

The Serpentine

GREEN PARK

ROTTEN ROW
SOUTH CARRIAGE DRIVE
WC **14** Apsley House
16 Wellington Arch
CONSTITUTION HILL

KNIGHTSBRIDGE
Hyde Park Corner

23 Knightsbridge
21 Knightsbridge

Buckingham Palace Gardens

BELGRAVE SQUARE

Royal Mews

Harrods
22

BELGRAVE PL

HOBART PL · LWR GROS PL

BROMPTON

GROSVENOR GDNS

BELGRAVIA

ECCLESTON ST

PONT ST
CHESHAM PL

KING'S ROAD

40

SLOANE STREET

47
Victoria Coach Station

WC **38** Sloane Square

Victoria Station

31 **42**

28
35 Saatchi Gallery

KING'S RD

LOWER SLOANE ST

WC **46** PIMLICO ROAD

EBURY BRIDGE RD

WARWICK WAY

WEST MINSTER & ST JAMES'S

CHELSEA BRIDGE ROAD

ROYAL HOSPITAL ROAD

Royal Hospital Chelsea

27
National Army Museum

| ● Sights & museums |
| ● Eating & drinking |
| ● Shopping |
| ● Nightlife |
| ● Arts & leisure |

Open 6.30am-8pm daily. **Admission** free; donations appreciated. **Map** p84 C3 ❷

The second-biggest Catholic church in the country (after Westminster Cathedral) was completed in 1884, but feels older – partly because many of the marbles, mosaics and statuary pre-date the structure. The vast main space culminates in a magnificent Italian altarpiece. The Solemn Mass sung in Latin at 11am on Sundays is enchanting, as are the Vespers, sung at 3.30pm.

Kensington Gardens & Kensington Palace

(7298 2117/recorded information 7298 2141/www.royalparks.gov.uk). **Map** p84 A/B1 ❸

When asthmatic William III, averse to the dank air of Whitehall Palace, relocated to Kensington Palace (Kensington Gardens, W8 4PX, 0844 482 7777, www.hrp.org.uk, admission £12; free £10 reductions), a corner of Hyde Park (p88) was sectioned off to make grounds for the palace. Some of the palace – a Wren-adapted Jacobean mansion – is open to the public. Apart from the grand King's Apartments, the feel is rather intimate. The Royal Ceremonial Dress Collection includes 14 dresses worn by Diana, Princess of Wales, the palace's most famous former resident. Other points of interest in the Gardens are the Peter Pan statue by the Long Water, the Diana, Princess of Wales Memorial Playground (a real youngsters' wonderland) and the Princess Diana Memorial Fountain.

Natural History Museum

Cromwell Road, SW7 5BD (information 7942 5725/www.nhm.ac.uk). South Kensington tube. **Open** 10am-5.50pm daily. **Admission** free. No credit cards. **Map** p84 B3 ❹

This cathedral to the Victorian passion for knowledge is every bit as impressive as the giant cast of a *Diplodocus* skeleton in the main hall. If you've come with children, you may not see much more than the Dinosaur gallery, with its animatronic Tyrannosaurus

rex. But there's much more – millions of plants, animals, fossils, rocks and minerals. Some of the galleries still have the sober feel of the Victorian era; others, like Creepy Crawlies, are so beloved of children you can hardly get near the exhibits. Entry to the Earth Galleries is dramatic: you pass through a giant suspended globe and twinkling images of the star system.

Event highlights 'Darwin', 200th anniversary (14 Nov 2008-31 Mar 2009).

Science Museum

Exhibition Road, SW7 2DD (7942 4000/booking & information 0870 870 4868/www.sciencemuseum.org.uk). South Kensington tube. **Open** 10am-5.45pm daily. **Admission** free. **Map** p84 B3 ❺

The Science Museum demonstrates how science is interwoven with daily life, using engines, cars, planes, ships, medicine, computers and domestic exhibits. Landmark inventions such as Stephenson's *Rocket*, Arkwright's spinning machine, Whittle's turbojet and the Apollo 10 command module are celebrated in the Making the Modern World gallery. The Who Am I? gallery in the Wellcome Wing explores discoveries in genetics, brain science and psychology, while the Launchpad gallery has all sorts of absorbing experiments for kids. There's an IMAX cinema too.

Serpentine Gallery

Kensington Gardens, W2 3XA (7402 6075/www.serpentinegallery.org). Lancaster Gate or South Kensington tube. **Open** 10am-6pm daily. **Admission** free. **Map** p84 B1 ❻

This secluded, airy gallery features a rolling programme of exhibitions showcasing up-to-the-minute artists, while the annual Serpentine Pavilion project commissions a renowned architect to design and build a new pavilion.

Victoria & Albert Museum

Cromwell Road, SW7 2RL (7942 2000/www.vam.ac.uk). South Kensington tube. **Open** 10am-5.45pm Mon-Thur, Sat, Sun; 10am-10pm Fri. **Admission** free. No credit cards. **Map** p84 C3 ❼

Natural History Museum

The 150-year-old V&A dazzles: its grand galleries contain four million pieces of furniture, ceramics, sculpture, paintings, posters, jewellery and metalwork from across the world. The museum boasts the finest collection of Italian Renaissance sculpture outside Italy, while home-grown treasures – the Great Bed of Ware, Canova's *The Three Graces*, Henry VIII's writing desk – are housed in the British Galleries, where you'll also find interactive exhibits for children. Don't miss the Fashion galleries or the museum's famous photography collection. The Jameel Gallery houses Islamic art.
Event highlights 'Cold War Modern: Design 1945-1970' (27 Sept 2008-11 Jan 2009); 'International Baroque' (4 Apr-19 July 2009).

Eating & drinking

Anglesea Arms

15 Selwood Terrace, SW7 3QG (7373 7960/www.capitalpubcompany.com). South Kensington tube. **Open** 11am-11pm Mon-Sat; noon-10.30pm Sun. **Pub**. **Map** p84 B4 ⑧

Dickens and DH Lawrence both frequented this splendid free house. There's a sympathetically dated feel to the sturdy wood interior but the drinks are bang up to date (ales are a forte).

Hummingbird Bakery

NEW *47 Old Brompton Road, SW7 3JP (7584 0055/www.hummingbirdbakery. com). South Kensington tube.* **Open** 10.30am-7pm daily. **£**. **Café**. **Map** p84 B4 ⑨

At this cosy café/shop, all-American cup cakes are lined up in the display case, while heavyweights such as New York cheesecake and devil's food cake command centre-stage on the sideboard. Counter service can be chaotic.

190 Queensgate

Gore Hotel, 190 Queensgate, SW7 5EX (7584 6601/www.gorehotel.co.uk). Gloucester Road or South Kensington tube. **Open** noon-1am Mon-Wed, Sun; noon-2am Thur-Sat. **Cocktail bar** **Map** p84 B2 ⑩

The perfect pub, cocktail bar and destination lounge. Upholstered seating and carved dark wood surround the bar, and DJs play on Saturday nights.

Shopping

Conran Shop

*Michelin House, 81 Fulham Road, SW3
6RD (7589 7401/www.conran.com).
South Kensington tube.* **Open** 10am-
6pm Mon, Tue, Fri; 10am-7pm Wed,
Thur; 10am-6.30pm Sat; noon-6pm
Sun. **Map** p84 C4 ⓫

Conran's flagship store in the beautiful
1909 Michelin Building showcases furniture and design for the house and
garden; expect plenty of accessories,
gadgets, books, stationery and toiletries.

Library

*268 Brompton Road, SW3 2AS (7589
6569). South Kensington tube.* **Open**
10am-6.30pm Mon, Tue, Thur-Sat;
10am-7pm Wed; 12.30-5.30pm Sun.
Map p84 C3 ⓬

Designer labels and literature may
seem an unlikely combination, but
this fantastic emporium will convince
you otherwise. For men, stock from
seasoned greats like McQueen and
Westwood hangs alongside that of
newer fashion stars. There's also gift-
friendly womenswear (such as cashmere and Balenciaga bags). Staff are
knowledgeable and ever-helpful.

Arts & leisure

Royal Albert Hall

*Kensington Gore, SW7 2AP
(information 7589 3203/box office
7589 8212/www.royalalberthall.com).
South Kensington tube/9, 10, 52, 452
bus.* **Map** p84 B2 ⓭

This 5,000-capacity rotunda is best
known as the key BBC Proms venue.
Classical concerts are occasionally held
here (look out for recitals on the Willis
pipe organ), plus pop and rock gigs,
boxing matches and opera.

Knightsbridge

Knightsbridge is about be-seen-in
restaurants and designer shops, but
that doesn't mean it's particularly
stylish: we're talking old-school
money – which can mean terrific
people-watching opportunities.

Sights & museums

Apsley House

*149 Piccadilly, W1J 7NT (7499 5676/
www.english-heritage.org.uk). Hyde
Park Corner tube.* **Open** *Nov-Mar*
10am-4pm Tue-Sun. *Apr-Oct* 10am-
5pm Tue-Sun. **Admission** £5.30; £4
reductions. Joint ticket with Wellington
Arch £6.90; £5.20 reductions; £17.30
family. **Map** p85 F1 ⓮

Built by Robert Adam in the 1770s,
Apsley House was home to the Duke of
Wellington for 35 years. Rooms hold
interesting trinkets and paintings,
including a fine Velázquez and a
Correggio, which hang near Goya's
portrait of the Iron Duke after he
defeated the French in 1812.

Hyde Park

*Hyde Park Corner (7298 2000/www.
royalparks.gov.uk) Lancaster Gate or
Queensway tube.* **Map** p85 E1 ⓯

At 1.5 miles long and about a mile wide,
Hyde Park is the largest of London's
Royal Parks. There's plenty of picnick-
ing and outdoor activity: in summer,

Hummingbird Bakery p87

rowing boats and pedaloes can be hired on the Serpentine, London's oldest boating lake, and year-round the park is populated with roller-skaters and bike- and horse-riders.

Hyde Park has long been a focal point for freedom of speech. The legalisation of public assembly in the park led to the establishment of Speakers' Corner in 1872 (close to Marble Arch tube), where ranters have the floor.

Wellington Arch

Hyde Park Corner, W1J 7JZ (7930 2726/www.english-heritage.org.uk). Hyde Park Corner tube. **Open** *Apr-Oct* 10am-5pm Wed-Sun. *Nov-Mar* 10am-4pm Wed-Sun. **Admission** £3.20; free-£2.40 reductions. Joint ticket with Apsley House £6.90; £5.20 reductions. **Map** p85 F1 ⑯
Built in the late 1820s to mark Britain's triumph over Napoleonic France, the arch has three floors of displays. There are views of the Houses of Parliament and Buckingham Palace, though trees obstruct much of the view in summer.

Eating & drinking

Amaya

19 Motcomb Street, Halkin Arcade, SW1X 8JT (7823 1166/www.real indianfood.com). Knightsbridge tube. **Open** 12.30-2.15pm, 6.30-11.15pm Mon-Sat; 12.45-2.30pm, 6.30-10.15pm Sun. **££. Indian. Map** p85 E2 ⑰
Amaya puts a dressy Indian spin on the tapas formula. The darkly seductive decor with chandeliers and terracotta statues attracts a mix of expense-accounters and couples. You can watch the chefs in action too.

Blue Bar

The Berkeley, Wilton Place, SW1X 7RL (7235 6000/www.the-berkeley.co.uk). Hyde Park Corner tube. **Open** 4pm-1am Mon-Sat; 4-11pm Sun. **Cocktail bar. Map** p85 E2 ⑱
With its glass walls and watery blue interior, the David Collins-designed Blue Bar feels rather like an aquarium. Seating is limited to 50, so each new entry halts conversations as heads

crane to rate celebrity status. Cocktails are well crafted, but people don't come here for the drinks.

Leon

136 Brompton Road, SW3 1HY (7589 7330/www.leonrestaurants.co.uk). Knightsbridge tube. **Open** 8am-6pm Mon-Fri. **£. Café. Map** p85 D2 ⑲
Set up in 2003 by celebrity chef Allegra McEvedy, Leon (now with eight outlets in London) emphasises careful sourcing and seasonal produce in its fast food. The results can vary, however.

Racine

239 Brompton Road, SW3 2EP (7584 4477). Knightsbridge or South Kensington tube/14, 74 bus. **Open** noon-3pm, 6-10.30pm Mon-Sat; 6-10pm Sun. **££. French. Map** p84 C3 ⑳
Push aside the heavy velvet curtains shielding the entrance and you enter a lost world, where well-padded gents and their female consorts revel in bourgeois French cooking. Try the likes of calves' brains with black butter and capers.

Zuma

5 Raphael Street, SW7 1DL (7584 1010/www.zumarestaurant.com). Knightsbridge tube. **Open** *Bar* noon-11pm Mon-Fri; 12.30-11pm Sat; noon-10pm Sun. *Restaurant* noon-2.15pm, 6-10.45pm Mon-Fri; 12.30-3.15pm, 6-10.45pm Sat; 12.30-2.45pm, 6-10.15pm Sun. **££££. Japanese. Map** p85 D2 ㉑
Despite the 'modern izakaya' tag, this is high-end dining, and an exciting spot for schmoozing. Zuma also has one of the best saké lists in town, complete with saké sommelier. The two-hour sittings are strictly enforced.

Shopping

Harrods

87-135 Brompton Road, SW1X 7XL (7730 1234/www.harrods. com). Knightsbridge tube. **Open** 10am-8pm Mon-Sat; noon-6pm Sun. **Map** p85 D2 ㉒
One of London's top tourist attractions, this cathedral to consumerism is by turns tasteful and tacky. The food halls

LONDON BY AREA

are spectacular; the meat and game room retains its original Edwardian tiling. The two Rooms of Luxury cover accessories by the likes of Vuitton and Chloé, and there are more deluxe names in the fashion and beauty sections.

Harvey Nichols

109-125 Knightsbridge, SW1X 7RJ (7235 5000/www.harveynichols.com). Knightsbridge tube. **Open** *Store* 10am-8pm Mon-Sat; noon-6pm Sun. *Café* 8am-10.30pm Mon-Sat; 8am-6pm Sun. *Restaurant* noon-3pm, 6-11pm Mon-Fri; noon-4pm, 6-11pm Sat; noon-4pm Sun. **Map** p85 D2 **㉓**

Harvey Nicks is a stylish receptacle of well-sourced labels, with a restaurant (the Fifth Floor, 7235 5250) that knocks spots off every other department store eaterie. Fashion is the real forte, with less ubiquitous names such as David Szeto and California label Rodarte featuring alongside catwalk supremos. The women's shoe department includes a Louboutin boutique, while the food hall boasts a Daylesford Organic concession and café.

Sloane Street

Knightsbridge tube. **Map** p85 D2 **㉔**
If high-end, international designer salons are your bag (or shoe or even scent), then the Knightsbridge end of Sloane Street is very heaven: Fendi, Prada, Vuitton, Farhi and Ferragamo are just the start.

Chelsea

It's been more than four decades since *Time* magazine declared that London – by which was principally meant **King's Road** – was swingin'. These days you're more likely to find suburban swingers wondering where it went than the next Jean Shrimpton, but places like **Daylesford Organic** and **Shop at Bluebird** have improved the retail opportunities. Chelsea proper begins with Sloane Square, spoiled by traffic and redeemed by the edgy **Royal Court Theatre**.

Sights & museums

Carlyle's House

24 Cheyne Row, SW3 5HL (7352 7087/www.nationaltrust.org.uk). Sloane Square tube/11, 19, 22, 49, 211, 239, 319 bus. **Open** *Apr-Oct* 2-5pm Wed-Fri; 11am-5pm Sat, Sun. **Admission** £4.75; £2.40 reductions. **Map** p84 C5 **㉕**

Thomas Carlyle and his wife Jane moved to this house in 1834. After his death, it was preserved as a museum, offering a snapshot of Victorian life.

Chelsea Physic Garden

66 Royal Hospital Road (entrance on Swan Walk), SW3 4HS (7352 5646/ www.chelseaphysicgarden.co.uk). Sloane Square tube/11, 19, 239 bus. **Open** *Apr-Oct* noon-dusk Wed; noon-5pm Thur, Fri; noon-6pm Sun. **Admission** £7; free-£4 reductions. No credit cards. **Map** p85 D5 **㉖**

The grounds of this lovely botanic garden, founded in 1673, are full of healing herbs and vegetables, rare trees and dye plants. The tours trace their history.

National Army Museum

Royal Hospital Road, SW3 4HT (7730 0717/www.national-army-museum. ac.uk). Sloane Square tube/11, 137, 239 bus. **Open** 10am-5.30pm daily. **Admission** free. No credit cards. **Map** p85 D5 **㉗**

Eccentric displays make this museum far more entertaining than the exterior suggests. The collection runs up to the American War of Independence. Major Michael Lane, conqueror of Everest, donated his frostbitten fingertips.

Saatchi Gallery

NEW *Duke of York's HQ, off King's Road, SW3 4RY (www.saatchi-gallery. co.uk). Sloane Square tube.* **Open** 10am-10pm Mon-Sat; 10am-8pm Sun. **Map** p85 E4 **㉘**
See box opposite.

Eating & drinking

Apartment 195

195 King's Road, SW3 5ED (7351 5195/www.apartment195.co.uk). Sloane

The art of the now

When Charles Saatchi does contemporary art, he does it with a splash. His new gallery – located in a former barracks in Chelsea – is certainly substantial. There will be more than a dozen rooms spread over three floors, making over 50,000 square feet of gallery space available for a series of temporary exhibitions.

Given his fame as a purchaser and promoter of what became known in the 1990s as the YBAs (Young British Artists) – Damien Hirst and Tracey Emin are famous former protégés – it will surprise many that the new Saatchi Gallery will exhibit little YBA work. Saatchi has shrewdly already sold most of those holdings.

Instead, his new gallery is to open in summer 2008 with 'The Revolution Continues: New Chinese Art', an exhibition of paintings that is likely to include Zhang Xiaogang's *A Big Family* (pictured). Future exhibitions should feature artists from the United States and from India. Those who visited his former St John's Wood and County Hall galleries will be delighted, however, to hear that Richard Wilson's *20:50* – a huge, walk-in installation made of a shallow, reflective pool of sump oil – is planned to be one of the few pieces on permanent view.

Admission to Saatchi's new gallery, unlike its predecessors, should be free, thanks to a sponsorship deal with a New York-based art auction house. This moves it into the territory of that titan of contemporary art, Tate Modern (p66), which only charges for special exhibitions. But while the Tate shows work produced since the early 1900s – the broadest possible definition of 'contemporary' art – Saatchi's contemporary is firmly focused on the art of right now.

■ www.saatchi-gallery.co.uk

Square tube then 11, 22 bus. **Open** 6-11pm Mon-Sat. **Bar**. **Map** p84 C5 29
You have to press a buzzer to gain entry here, but a warm welcome awaits. The decor is Vivienne Westwood meets laid-back gentlemen's club. Cocktails are the thing: the mojitos are sublime.

Bluebird

350 King's Road, SW3 5UU (7559 1000/www.danddlondon.com). Sloane Square tube then 11, 19, 22, 49, 319 bus. **Open** *Bar* noon-midnight Mon-Thur; noon-1am Fri, Sat; noon-11.30pm Sun. *Restaurant* 12.30-2.30pm, 6-11pm Mon-Fri; noon-3.30pm, 6-11pm Sat; noon-3.30pm, 6-10pm Sun. **££**. **Modern European**. **Map** p84 B5 30
Bluebird recently unveiled a new look: the restaurant and bar now occupy a single, glorious upper room. Service is bouncy and the revamped menu places an emphasis on local producers.

Botanist

NEW *7 Sloane Square, SW1W 8EE (7730 0077/www.thebotanistonsloane square.com). Sloane Square tube.* **Open** 8am-11.30pm Mon-Fri; 9am-11.30pm Sat, Sun. **££**. **Gastropub**. **Map** p85 E4 31
We anticipate great things here, given that the Botanist's owners, the Martin brothers, have already made a success of a string of London gastropubs (the Gun, p179, being a prime example). The Botanist promises eat-in and take-away food all day, as well as swanky cocktails with a Caribbean theme – in honour of Sir Hans Sloane, the pioneering botanist after whom it is named.

Itsu

118 Draycott Avenue, SW3 3AE (7590 2400/www.itsu.com). South Kensington tube. **Open** 11am-10.30pm Mon-Sat; 11am-9.30pm Sun. **£**. **Sushi**. **Map** p84 C3 32
Waiting for a seat at the sushi counter or a booth at the back is no hardship here, thanks to the chic first-floor bar. Dishes have a real spring in their step (the simpler items work best), but the colour-coded plates are quickly cleared away, so it's easy to lose track of how much you've eaten – and spent.

Chelsea Physic Garden p90

Pig's Ear

35 Old Church Street, SW3 5BS (7352 2908/www.thepigsear.co.uk). Sloane Square tube then 11, 22 bus. **Open** noon-11pm Mon-Sat; noon-10.30pm Sun. **££**. **Gastropub**. **Map** p84 C5 33
Brimming with bohemian London character, this Chelsea treat does indeed serve tasty, deep-fried porcine ears (as well as the excellent Pig's Ear ale from Gloucestershire). The food is adventurous, and the crowd mixed.

Tom's Place

NEW *1 Cale Street, SW3 3QP (7351 1806/www.tomsplace.org.uk). Sloane Square or South Kensington tube.* **Open** 11am-11pm Mon-Wed, Sun; 11am-midnight Thur-Sat. **££**. **Fish 'n' chips**. **Map** p84 C4 34
This posh fish and chip shop is the latest project from acclaimed young British chef Tom Aikens – who runs a relaxed Brit-French restaurant on the same street (no.27, SW3 3QP, 7349 0202, www.tomskitchen.co.uk), as

well as a nearby haute cuisine place (43 Elystan Street, 7584 2003, www. tomaikens.co.uk). Fish is mostly line-caught from Marine Stewardship Council-approved sources, and while the food is excellent, portions are small for the prices. See also box p94.

Shopping

Duke of York Square

King's Road, SW3 4LY. Sloane Square tube. **Map** p84 D4 **35**
West London's first new public square for over a century is a former barracks transformed into a landscaped pedestrian area with fountains and stone benches. Among high-end high-street clothes shops and cafés, the flagship store of Liz Earle Naturally Active Skincare (no.53, 7730 9191, www.liz earle.com) and ultra-modern Michel Guillon Vision (no.35, 7730 2142, www. michelguillon.com) are stand-outs.

John Sandoe

10 Blacklands Terrace, SW3 2SR (7589 9473/www.johnsandoe.com). Sloane Square tube. **Open** 9.30am-5.30pm Mon, Tue, Thur-Sat; 9.30am-7.30pm Wed; noon-6pm Sun. **Map** p85 D4 **36**
This 50-year-old independent looks just as a bookshop should, with the stock literally packed to the rafters. Of the 25,000 books here, 24,000 are a single copy – so there's serious breadth.

King's Road

Sloane Square tube then 11, 19, 22 bus/49 bus. **Map** p84 C5 **37**
These days you don't come to the King's Road, centre of 1960s Swingin' London, expecting to find psychedelic minis, either skirt or car, nor punk rockers of any stripe. Still, after some time seemingly destined for chain-store mediocrity, it is again beginning to collect fine one-off stores. The decorative jewellery at Les Néréides (no.166, 7376 6270, www.lesnereides.com), the feminine styles at Austique (no.330, 7376 3663, www.austique.co.uk) or the modern and vintage-inspired prints on everything from wallpaper to wash-bags at Cath Kidston (no.322, 7351

7335, www.cathkidston.co.uk) should sate the style conscious, and antiques-lovers need look no further than the dozens of dealers who are housed in Antiquarius (nos.131-141, 7351 5353, www.antiquarius.co.uk). The gorgeous squares that open up on either side of the street are always a pleasure to see.

Ortigia

NEW *55 Sloane Square, SW1W 8AX (7730 2826/www.ortigia-srl.com). Sloane Square tube.* **Open** 10am-6pm Mon-Sat. **Map** p85 E4 **38**
This new flagship store has a sleek monochrome interior that perfectly sets off divinely packaged original perfumes and bathroom goodies, with designs inspired by crests from opulent Italian palazzos, ancient Greek tiles and Roman mosaics. Each fragrance is designed to be unisex: think orange blossom, lime and fico d'India.

Shop at Bluebird

350 King's Road, SW3 5UU (7351 3873/www.theshopatbluebird.com). Sloane Square tube. **Open** 9am-7pm Mon-Sat; noon-6pm Sun. **Map** p84 B5 **39**
Sharing the landmark art deco garage with Terence Conran's café/restaurant/deli complex, the Shop at Bluebird is part lifestyle boutique, part design gallery. The 10,000sq ft space is a shifting showcase of clothing by non-ubiquitous designers from Britain and abroad, plus lingerie, accessories, furniture, books and gadgets. Ole Henriksen Face/Body, one of only two spas in the world dedicated to treatments by the celebrity facialist, opened at the end of 2007.

Arts & leisure

Cadogan Hall

5 Sloane Terrace, SW1X 9DQ (7730 4500/www.cadoganhall.com). Sloane Square tube. **Map** p85 E3 **40**
This former church was transformed into an auditorium in 2004. The Royal Philharmonic Orchestra is resident, but the hall also hosts smaller ensembles, plus a handful of lunchtime BBC Proms.

LONDON BY AREA

Fish 'n' chips deluxe

Welcome to the new chip supper. It seems the gentrification of working-class food has reached its conclusion: breaded scampi for £20 and £2.50 for five – that's five – onion rings. When, back in 1995, Fergus Henderson started serving frowned-upon former staples, notably offal, to paying customers at St John (p156), it marked a sea change in attitudes. What granny had cooked only because it was cheap was now rare and hence valuable, much as oysters were once no more than filler to eke out the pricey beef in a pie.

Of course, posh new chippie **Tom's Place** (p92; pictured) can justify these prices. For one thing, the food is excellent. For another, it has impeccable eco-credentials: the fish are mostly line-caught (rather than trawled), we're assured they are from Marine Stewardship Council-approved sources, and they are caught

using small family-run boats. The types served include gurnard, pollock, ray, Pacific cod (which, unlike Atlantic cod, is OK to eat), sardines, mackerel, monkfish and line-caught sea bass.

Owner Tom Aikens isn't alone in suddenly seeing the potential in luxury battered fish. Local chip shop **Geales** (2 Farmer Street, Notting Hill, W8 7SN, 7727 7528, www.geales.com) has been turned into a suave fish restaurant. Its roots aren't totally forgotten, though: ketchup comes in a porcelain jug rather than a squeezy bottle, but the core of the menu is still fish in batter. And you still pay a 15p cover.

Traditionalists might prefer to head further afield: **Faulkner's** (424-426 Kingsland Road, Dalston, E8 4AA, 7254 6152) or **Fish Club** (189 St John's Hill, Battersea, SW11 1TH, 7978 7115, www.thefishclub.com) are both excellent.

Chelsea Football Club

Stamford Bridge, Fulham Road, SW6 1HS (0870 300 1212/www.chelseafc. com). Fulham Broadway tube. **Map p84 A5 ㊶**

The capital's most recent Premiership winners were pipped to top place by Manchester United in 2008. You can forget about seeing Chelsea in Premiership action, but you might get tickets for cup games, and the stadium tours are fun.

Royal Court Theatre

Sloane Square, SW1W 8AS (7565 5000/www.royalcourttheatre.com). Sloane Square tube. **Map p85 E4 ㊷**

The emphasis here has always been on new voices in British theatre – from John Osborne's *Look Back in Anger* in the inaugural year, 1956, to numerous discoveries over the past decade.

Belgravia

Belgravia is characterised by the embassies clustered at Belgrave Square. Entertain yourself with a stroll through tiny mews, then settle into some plush dining, drinking or shopping.

Eating & drinking

Boisdale

13 Eccleston Street, SW1W 9LX (7730 6922/www.boisdale.co.uk). Victoria tube/rail. **Open/food served** noon-1am Mon-Fri; 7pm-1am Sat. **Admission** £4.50-£12. **Whisky bar.** Map p85 F3 ㊸

There's nowhere quite like this Scottish-themed enterprise. The range of single malts is unrivalled; another nice touch is the heated cigar terrace (you may need to book in advance). Live jazz is played from 10pm.

Nag's Head

53 Kinnerton Street, SW1X 8ED (7235 1135). Hyde Park Corner or Knightsbridge tube. **Open** 11am-11pm Mon-Sat; noon-10.30pm Sun. No credit cards. **Pub.** Map p85 E2 ㊹

No mobiles and no credit cards at this charming time warp of a pub – the Nag's Head echoes a time when National Service was a given and glam destinations could only be glimpsed in crank-up machines like the one here.

Nahm

The Halkin, Halkin Street, SW1X 7DJ (7333 1234/www.nahm.como.bz). Hyde Park Corner tube. **Open** noon-2.30pm, 7-10.45pm Mon-Fri; 7-10.45pm Sat; 7-9.45pm Sun. **£££.** **Thai.** Map p85 E2 ㊺

David Thompson may not always be in the kitchen, but his influence at this understated hotel dining room is as strong as ever. Recently, he revamped lunch to include more 'street food'. Thai food is rarely this thrilling.

Shopping

Daylesford Organic

44B Pimlico Road, SW1W 8LP (7881 8060/www.daylesfordorganic. com). Sloane Square tube. **Open** 8am-8pm Mon-Sat; 11am-5pm Sun. Map p85 E4 ㊻

This impressive, three-floor offshoot of Lady Carole Bamford's Cotswolds-based farm shop includes a café. Goods include ready-made dishes, cakes and breads, charcuterie and cheeses.

Elizabeth Street

Sloane Square tube. Map p85 F4 ㊼

Conveniently central but often overlooked, Elizabeth Street lies between the grotty bedsits of Victoria and swanky Sloane Street – a combination that, oddly, has attracted unusual and high-quality boutiques: luxury streetwear at Lucien Pellat-Finet (no.51, 7259 9995, www.lucienpellat-finet.com), cute kiddie footwear at Papillon (no.43, 7730 6690, www.papillon4children.com) and fine works from the legendary headware specialist at Philip Treacy (no.69, 7730 3992, www.philiptreacy. co.uk). For gorgeous personalised stationery, try the Grosvenor Stationery Company (no.30, 7730 4515, www. grosvenorstationerycompany.com). A hot chocolate at the delightful Chocolate Society (no.36, 7259 9222, www.chocolate.co.uk) will restore you.

Berwick Street p121

The West End

Marylebone

Given how much money goes through the tills along Oxford Street, clogged pavements and busy shops make it a surprisingly unpleasant place for shopping, although it is home to the always-impressive **Selfridges**, doughty **John Lewis** and worthwhile chain flagships such as **Primark** and **Uniqlo**, both good for cheap basics. To escape the crowds, make like the locals and head north into Marylebone's quiet squares and pretty high street, where you can browse the lovely independent boutiques. In terms of sightseeing, the **Wallace Collection** is a real gem, and far too often overlooked, while **Regent's Park** is one of the city's finest and most popular green spaces.

Sights & museums

Madame Tussauds

Marylebone Road, NW1 5LR (0870 400 3000/www.madame-tussauds.com). Baker Street tube. **Open** 9.30am-6pm daily. **Admission** £25; £10-£22.50 reductions. **Map** p97 A1 ❶

Madame Tussauds compensates for its inherently static attractions with a flurry of attendant activity. As you enter the first room, you're dazzled by fake paparazzi flashbulbs. Starry-eyed kids can take part in a 'Divas' routine with Britney, Beyoncé and Kylie. Figures are constantly being added – the latest include Leonardo DiCaprio, Bollywood heart-throb Shah Rukh Khan and *Pirates of the Caribbean* stars Orlando Bloom and Keira Knightley. Other rooms contain public figures past and present, from Henry and his six wives to the Beatles, Blair and Bush. The Planetarium has been

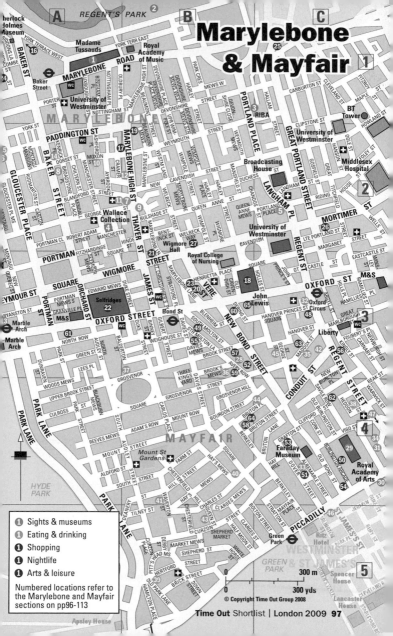

Marylebone & Mayfair

Legend:
- **1** Sights & museums
- **1** Eating & drinking
- **1** Shopping
- **1** Nightlife
- **1** Arts & loisure

Numbered locations refer to the Marylebone and Mayfair sections on pp96-113

© Copyright Time Out Group 2008

replaced by the Wonderful World of Stars, a 360-degree animated take on celebrity – as viewed by aliens – from Wallace and Gromit creators Aardman.

Regent's Park

Baker Street or Regent's Park tube.
Map p97 B1 ❷
Regent's Park (open 5am-dusk daily) was originally a hunting ground of Henry VIII, and only opened to the public in 1845. Now it's a spectacular place to while away an entire day, with attractions such as London Zoo (p171), a lake with rowing boats for hire, spectacular rose gardens, ice-cream stands and the Garden Café (7935 5729, www.thegardencafe.co.uk). At the lovely Open Air Theatre (p175), performances of Shakespeare plays are an integral part of London summers.

Royal Institute of British Architects

66 Portland Place, W1B 1AD (7580 5533/www.architecture.com). Great Portland Street tube. **Map** p97 C1 ❸
Temporary exhibitions are held in RIBA's Grade II-listed HQ, which houses a bookshop, café and library, and hosts an excellent lecture series.

Wallace Collection

Hertford House, Manchester Square, W1U 3BN (7935 0687/www.wallacecollection.org). Bond Street tube. **Open** 10am-5pm daily. **Admission** free.
Map p97 A2 ❹
This handsome late 18th-century house holds a collection of furniture, paintings, armour and objets d'art. It all belonged to Sir Richard Wallace, who, as the illegitimate offspring of the fourth Marquess of Hertford, inherited the treasures amassed by his father. Room after grand room contains Louis XIV and XV furnishings and Sèvres porcelain, and the galleries are hung with paintings by Titian, Velázquez, Gainsborough and Reynolds; Franz Hals's *Laughing Cavalier* is one of the best known. There are also regular temporary exhibitions. The lovely Wallace restaurant, in the glass-roofed courtyard, is run by Oliver Peyton.

Eating & drinking

Artesian

Langham Hotel, 1C Portland Place, W1B 1JA (7636 1000/www.artesianbar.co.uk). Oxford Circus tube. **Open** 7.30am-2am Mon-Fri; 8am-2am Sat; 8am-midnight Sun. **Bar**. **Map** p97 C2 ❺
Some of the design features at this bar – reopened after a makeover by David Collins – sail close to OTT, but a subdued colour scheme makes the total effect soothing. The grand cocktails, expertly made, are served in remarkably beautiful glassware.

Duke of Wellington

NEW *94A Crawford Street, W1H 2HQ (7224 9435). Marylebone tube/rail.* **Open** noon-11pm daily. **££**.
Gastropub. **Map** p97 A2 ❻
The ground floor of this scrubbed-up pub, run by the same people behind the Pig's Ear in Chelsea (p92), now has sputnik light pendants, stargazer lilies and framed Banksy postcards on the walls. The beer's still the real thing, and now the food is too. The bar menu includes the likes of crab bisque and char-grilled steak; similar dishes are available in the small, cosy first-floor dining room (open evenings only). If you're looking for a proper contemporary gastropub, you'll be delighted.

Fairuz

3 Blandford Street, W1U 3DA (7486 8108/8182/www.fairuz.uk.com). Baker Street or Bond Street tube. **Open** noon-11.30pm Mon-Sat; noon-11pm Sun. **££**.
Middle Eastern. **Map** p97 B2 ❼
Fairuz distinguishes itself from other top-tier Lebanese restaurants in London with a very different vibe. Instead of the usual smart-international look, it resembles a generic Med-taverna, with rough white walls and a fold-back frontage for fine weather. It's a relaxed, pleasant spot, although tables are tightly spaced. Food is excellent. Book for dinner.

Galvin Bistrot de Luxe

66 Baker Street, W1U 7DJ (7935 4007/www.galvinrestaurants.com). Baker Street tube. **Open** noon-2.30pm,

LONDON BY AREA

Regent's Park p99

6-11pm Mon-Sat; noon-3pm, 6-10.30pm Sun. **£££**. **French**. Map p97 A2 ❽
The location, on a bleak stretch of Baker Street, is unpromising. Yet the Galvin brothers (Chris and Jeff) have created a phenomenon: an outstanding restaurant, packed with enthusiastic diners even midweek. Service can be frantic, but doesn't detract from the exceptional cooking. The wine list is interesting too, with an additional, exclusive selection for the deep-pocketed.

Golden Hind

73 Marylebone Lane, W1U 2PN (7486 3644). Bond Street tube. **Open** noon-3pm, 6-10pm Mon-Fri; 6-10pm Sat. **£**. **Fish & chips**. Map p97 B2 ❾
Run by a group of Greek guys, this café-style chippie – established in 1914 – has the feel of a traditional English gaff, despite a couple of Greek touches on the menu. The small, no-frills dining room gets packed out by locals, drawn by reliable grub at cheap-for-the-area prices.

La Fromagerie

2-6 Moxon Street, W1U 4EW (7935 0341/www.lafromagerie.co.uk). Baker Street or Bond Street tube. **Open** 10.30am-7.30pm Mon; 8am-7.30pm Tue-Fri; 9am-7pm Sat; 10am-6pm Sun. **££**. **Café**. Map p97 A2 ❿
It's all about the ingredients in the 'tasting café' of this gourmet shop. The attractively skylit space is packed at weekends, when foodies and shoppers cram the central communal table. The cheese plate dominates a daily changing menu with selections from the walk-in cheese room (you can also take out), but don't ignore the house ploughman's: the pork and veal pie comes from the fine butcher next door.

L'Autre Pied

NEW *5-7 Blandford Street, W1U 3DB (7486 9696/www.lautrepied.co.uk). Bond Street tube.* **Open** noon-3pm, 6-10.45pm Mon-Fri; 6-10.45pm Sat. **£££**. **Modern European**. Map p97 A2 ⓫
The reason for the instant popularity of L'Autre Pied isn't immediately obvious. It's a good-looking restaurant, for sure, but the unclothed wooden tables and noise levels are more reminiscent of a canteen chain. It must be that the chef is Marcus Eaves, formerly at Pied à Terre. Here, he has taken haute cuisine techniques and scaled them back. The results include some impressive dishes, but portions are small for the prices. One to watch, nonetheless.

Providores & Tapa Room

109 Marylebone High Street, W1U 4RX (7935 6175/www.theprovidores.co.uk). Baker Street or Bond Street tube. **Open** *Providores* noon-2.45pm, 6-10.30pm Mon-Sat; noon-2.45pm, 6-10pm Sun. *Tapa Room* 9-10.30am, noon-10.30pm Mon-Fri; 10am-3pm, 4-10.30pm Sat; 4-10pm Sun. **£££** Providores. **££** Tapa Room. **Global**. Map p97 B2 ⓬
Executive chef and co-owner Peter Gordon's fusion cooking (South-east Asia meets New Zealand) remains an inspiration. The Tapa Room is a buzzy drop-in for the pretty and privileged, who enjoy refined, complex tapas, while the more grown-up Providores upstairs serves complicated yet well-balanced dishes.

Rhodes W1

Cumberland, Great Cumberland Place, W1H 7DL (7479 3737/www.garyrhodes.co.uk). Marble Arch tube. **Open** noon-2.30pm, 7-10.30pm Tue-Fri; 7-10.30pm Tue-Sat. **£££**. **British**. Map p97 A3 ⓭
Here, a forbidding black door opens on to a darkened cellar-cum-foyer, through which you enter a sparkly world of fun – every table has a Swarovski chandelier. The food is equally stunning; not as flag-waving as you'd expect from the man who started the British food renaissance, but local ingredients are treated with light brilliance.

Royal China Club

40-42 Baker Street, W1U 7AJ (7486 3898/www.royalchinaclub.co.uk). Baker Street or Marble Arch tube. **Open** noon-11pm Mon-Thur; noon-11.30pm Fri, Sat; noon-10.30pm Sun. **£££**. **Dim sum**. Map p97 A2 ⓮
The sleek dining room, well-stocked bar and polite servers are all very well and

LONDON BY AREA

good, but they're nothing extraordinary – unlike the food. Royal China Club serves some of the best and most interesting dim sum in London, featuring intelligent combinations and delicate flavours. Shellfish is a forte, while the wide range of teas is a further highlight.

Windsor Castle

29 Crawford Place, W1H 4LJ (7723 4371). Edgware Road tube. **Open** 11am-11pm Mon-Sat; noon-10.30pm Sun. **Pub**. **Map** p97 A2 ⑮

Every spare inch of wall space inside this delightful pub is plastered with patriotic memorabilia: a ceiling of Royal Family plates, souvenir mugs, portraits of royals past and present, a photo of the Queen Mum pulling a pint. It should be awful, but it's actually rather charming.

Shopping

Alfie's Antique Market

13-25 Church Street, NW8 8DT (7723 6066/www.alfiesantiques.com). Edgware Road tube/Marylebone tube/rail. **Open** 10am-6pm Tue-Sat. **Map** p97 A1 ⑯

Church Street has blossomed into antiques row, its growing cluster of shops centred on Alfie's Antique Market, which boasts over 100 dealers in vintage furniture and fashion, art, accessories, books, maps and more. Highlights include Dodo Posters, selling 1920s and '30s ads, and the Girl Can't Help It (7724 8984, www.thegirl-canthelpit.com), run by exuberant New Yorker Sparkle Moore and her partner Jasja Boelhouwer (AKA Cad Van Swankster). This snapshot of vintage Hollywood covers everything from glamorous red-carpet gowns, 1950s circle skirts and leopardprint shoes for the ladies to Hawaiian shirts, slick '40s and '50s suits, gabardine jackets and camp accessories for men.

Daunt Books

83-84 Marylebone High Street, W1U 4QW (7224 2295/www.dauntbooks.co.uk). Baker Street tube. **Open** 9am-7.30pm Mon-Sat; 11am-6pm Sun. **Map** p97 B2 ⑰

A lovely Edwardian bookshop (part of a mini-chain) known for its travel section: books – related literature as well as guides – are arranged by country in the expansive, three-floor back room complete with oak galleries and conservatory ceiling. The children's range is also excellent.

John Lewis

278-306 Oxford Street, W1A 1EX (7629 7711/www.johnlewis.co.uk). Bond Street or Oxford Circus tube. **Open** 9.30am-7pm Mon-Wed, Fri, Sat; 9.30am-8pm Thur; noon-6pm Sun. **Map** p97 B3 ⑱

The renovators of the John Lewis flagship didn't give the owners much change from £60m, but they left them with new transparent-sided escalators and a partly glazed roof, allowing in plenty of natural light. Renowned for solid reliability and the courtesy of its staff, John Lewis also deserves a medal for its breadth of stock. The spacious ground-floor cosmetics hall, for example, has glam Crème de la Mer and Eve Lom, but also natural brands like Neal's Yard and Burt's Bees. Well-informed hand-holding and after-sales care make buying electronics here a breeze, but the greatest tension-soother is the floor dedicated to children: the shoe department even has computer games and CBBC on the telly.

Kabiri

37 Marylebone High Street, W1U 4QE (7224 1808/www.kabiri.co.uk). Baker Street tube. **Open** 10am-6.30pm Mon-Sat; noon-5pm Sun. **Map** p97 B2 ⑲

The work of more than 100 jewellery designers, both little-known and established, is showcased here. Innovation and a sense of humour are linking themes; with Miss Bibi and Dima two names to look out for. There's also a concession in Selfridges.

KJ's Laundry

74 Marylebone Lane, W1U 2PW (7486 7855/www.kjslaundry. com). Bond Street tube. **Open** 10am-7pm Mon-Wed, Fri, Sat; 10am-8pm Thur; 11am-5pm Sun. **Map** p97 B3 ⑳

This unintimidating, understated boutique is a good bet for highly wearable clothes with an edge. Jane Ellis and Kate Allden have worked hard to source lines you won't see all over town, such as Lee Mathews' feminine, handmade slip dresses and Hiromi Tsuyoshi's buttonless cardigans. Great beauty buys include vegan skincare from San Francisco's Fresh Body Market.

Mint

70 Wigmore Street, W1U 2SF (7224 4406/www.mintshop.co.uk). Bond Street tube. **Open** 10.30am-6.30pm Mon-Wed, Fri, Sat; 10.30am-7.30pm Thur. **Map** p97 B3 ㉑

Surprising and inspirational, Mint is a compact two-level space full of globally sourced homewares from established designers and recent graduates alike. As well as contemporary statement furniture, there are plenty of smaller, more affordable items here too.

Selfridges

400 Oxford Street, W1A 1AB (0800 123400/www.selfridges.com). Bond Street or Marble Arch tube. **Open** 9.30am-8pm Mon-Wed, Fri, Sat; 9.30am-9pm Thur; noon-6pm Sun. **Map** p97 A3 ㉒

Selfridges' innovative displays, concessions and themed events have brought a sense of theatre to shopping. The latest addition to the ground floor's glut of luxury accessories and beauty products is the Wonder Room – a very flashy jewellery hall featuring an 'arcade' of perimeter boutiques, as well as rarefied gadgets and trinkets. You can sample a cornucopia of international delicacies in the food hall and browse a branch of famed Foyles bookshop in the basement, while the exhaustive fashion collections cover every taste and budget, from the best of the high street to big international names and emerging British-based designers.

Tracey Neuls

29 Marylebone Lane, W1U 2NQ (7935 0039/www.tn29.com). Bond Street tube. **Open** 11am-6.30pm Mon-Fri; noon-5pm Sat. **Map** p97 B3 ㉓

Tracey Neuls' TN_29 label has gathered a cult following from Seattle to Sydney, but the Cordwainers-trained Canadian designer is based in this small shop/studio. The idiosyncratic designs play on historical styles such as brogues and 1930s-style button shoes in worn-looking, muted leathers, complete with deliberate 'imperfections'. Her newer line is handmade in Italy using more luxurious materials.

Weardowney Get-Up Boutique

9 Ashbridge Street, NW8 8DH (7725 9694/www.weardowney.com). Edgware Road tube/Marylebone tube/rail. **Open** 10am-6pm Mon-Wed, Fri, Sat; 10am-9pm Thur. **Map** p97 A1 ㉔

This boutique, owned by ex-models Gail Downey and Amy Wear, sells modern, hand-knitted creations that embrace such fashion-forward styles as capes, minidresses and even knickers with frills. The complex, set in a converted pub, also contains a school for knitting and hand-sewing courses and a guesthouse (p207).

Nightlife

Lowdown at the Albany

240 Great Portland Street, W1W 5QU (7387 5706/www.lowdownatthealbany. com). Great Portland Street tube. **Map** p97 C1 ㉕

This rough-around-the-edges basement venue hosts very cool comedy nights. Our personal recommendation is the monthly Clark's at Lowdown: a reliable roster of smart, young, left-field comedians is MCed by the thoroughly genial Dan Clark. Excellent for Edinburgh previews as well.

Social

5 Little Portland Street, W1W 7JD (7636 4992/www.thesocial.com). Oxford Circus tube. **Open** noon-midnight Mon-Wed; 1pm-midnight Thur-Sat; 5pm-midnight Sun. **Map** p97 C2 ㉖

A discreet, opaque front still hides this daytime diner and DJ bar of supreme quality, established by Heavenly Records in 1999. It remains popular with music industry workers, minor alt-rock celebs and other sassy trendies who, after drinks upstairs, descend to an intimate basement space rocked by DJs six nights a week.

Arts & leisure

Wigmore Hall

36 Wigmore Street, W1U 2BP (7935 2141/www.wigmore-hall.org.uk). Bond Street tube. **Map** p97 B2 ㉗

With its perfect acoustics, art nouveau decor and excellent basement restaurant, the Wiggy is one of the world's top concert venues for chamber music and song. The Monday lunchtime recitals and Sunday morning coffee concerts are excellent value.

Mayfair

South of Oxford Street, Mayfair has been home to an elite of international toffs ever since it was conceived as an elegant residential suburb, arranged around squares with service mews tucked behind them. Rarefied restaurants (**Hibiscus** the newest sensation), shops (cutting-edge **Luella**), hotel bars (**Donovan**) and galleries serve every whim of the wealthy, but this is England: don't expect the wealth to be ostentatious, just remember that a tiny mews home – once merely the stables – these days would cost multiple racehorses. You might not fancy going shopping without at least a platinum card to protect your assets, but the quieter streets are fascinating for their architecture, atmosphere and the voyeuristic pleasure of spying on how the other half lives.

Sights & museums

Handel House Museum

25 Brook Street (entrance in Lancashire Court), W1K 4HB (7495 1685/www.handelhouse.org). Bond Street tube. **Open** 10am-6pm Tue, Wed, Fri,

Sat; 10am-8pm Thur; noon-6pm Sun. **Admission** £5; free-£4.50 reductions. **Map** p97 B3 ㉘

George Frideric Handel lived in this Mayfair house for 36 years, until his death in 1759. It has been beautifully restored with original and recreated furnishings, paintings and a welter of the composer's scores (in the same room as photos of Jimi Hendrix, who once lived next door). The surprisingly dynamic programme includes recitals every Thursday.

Royal Academy of Arts

Burlington House, Piccadilly, W1J 0BD (7300 8000/www.royalacademy.org.uk). Green Park or Piccadilly Circus tube. **Open** 10am-6pm Mon-Thur, Sat, Sun; 10am-10pm Fri. **Admission** varies. **Map** p97 C4 ㉙

Britain's first art school was founded in 1768 and moved to the extravagantly Palladian Burlington House a century later. It is now best known for the galleries, which stage populist temporary exhibitions. Those in the John Madejski Fine Rooms are drawn from the RA's holdings – ranging from Constable to Hockney – and are free. The popular Summer Exhibition draws on works entered by the public.

Event highlights Summer Exhibition (early June-mid Aug 2009).

St James's Piccadilly

197 Piccadilly, W1J 9LL (7734 4511/www.st-james-piccadilly.org). Piccadilly Circus tube. **Open** 8am-6.30pm daily. **Admission** free. **Map** p97 C4 ㉚

Consecrated in 1684, St James's is the only church Sir Christopher Wren built on an entirely new site. A calming building, with few architectural airs or graces, it was bombed to within an inch of its life in World War II but painstakingly reconstructed. Grinling Gibbons's delicate limewood garlanding around the sanctuary survived and is one of the few real frills. This is a busy church, staging regular classical concerts and hosting markets outside: antiques (Tue) and arts and crafts (Wed-Sat). There's also a handy café tucked into a corner by the quiet garden.

Bentley's Oyster Bar & Grill

11-15 Swallow Street, W1B 4DG (7734 4756/www.bentleysoysterbarandgrill. co.uk). Piccadilly Circus tube. **Open** *Oyster Bar* noon-midnight Mon-Sat; noon-10pm Sun. *Restaurant* noon-3pm, 6-11pm Mon-Sat; noon-3pm, 6-10pm Sun. **£££**. **Fish**. Map p97 C4 ③①

Irish chef Richard Corrigan (of Soho veteran restaurant Lindsay House) relaunched this old-timer a couple of years ago, and it's been a great success. Housed in the same lovely Victorian building for more than 90 years, the ground-floor oyster bar is more relaxed; there's also a smarter first-floor grill, with oak floor and crisp linen. Prices are Mayfair, but the food is first-rate.

Chisou

4 Princes Street, W1B 2LE (7629 3931/ www.chisou.co.uk). Oxford Circus tube. **Open** noon-2.30pm, 6-10.15pm Mon-Sat. **£££**. **Japanese**. Map p97 C3 ③②

This bright and orderly establishment is deservedly full most nights. Plain cream walls, black slate accents and stylish air-con ovoids don't fit the description of a typical Japanese tavern, but the menu explains Chisou's hybrid identity: 'traditional dishes with a modern twist, served izakaya style'. From salt-grilled fish, sushi, tempura and noodles to specials like saké-steamed clams, the choices are plentiful and delicious.

Donovan Bar

Brown's Hotel, 33-34 Albemarle Street, W1S 4BP (7493 6020/www.roccoforte collection.com). Green Park tube. **Open** 11am-1am Mon-Sat; noon-11.30pm Sun. **Bar**. Map p97 C4 ③③

The polarised black and whiteness of the diminutive Donovan Bar is a fitting testament to its muse, Stepney-born photographer Terence Donovan, whose monochrome prints of swinging 1960s London pepper the walls. Live jazz plays every evening except Sundays. It's the epitome of nostalgia-chic, but the cocktail list is surprisingly forward-thinking.

Gaucho Piccadilly

25 Swallow Street, W1B 4DJ (7734 4040/www.gauchorestaurants.co.uk). Piccadilly Circus tube. **Open** noon-midnight Mon-Sat; noon-11pm Sun. **££**. **Steakhouse**. Map p97 C4 ③④

Steakhouse chic is what the Gaucho flagship branch is all about – from its well-stocked wine shop to a pitch-dark cocktail bar and penchant for cowskin wallpaper and pouffes. The steaks? Good, with the *bife de lomo* (fillet) often outstanding. Service is a touch too slick, but that's the nature of smart chains.

Hibiscus

NEW *29 Maddox Street, W1S 2PA (7629 2999/www.hibiscusrestaurant. co.uk). Oxford Circus tube.* **Open** noon-2.30pm, 6.30-10pm Mon-Fri. **££££**. **Haute cuisine**. Map p97 C3 ③⑤

After seven years in Shropshire, Claude and Claire Bosi moved their acclaimed restaurant to London. The understated little space is offset by Claude's thrilling cooking: no wonder it earned a Michelin star within months of opening. Of course, food (or wine) like this doesn't come cheap (although set menus soften the blow), but Hibiscus is that rare thing – an epicurean restaurant that takes a serious interest in flavour, texture, appearance and quality, without a hint of snobiness.

La Petite Maison

54 Brooks Mews, W1K 4EG (7495 4774). Bond Street tube. **Open** noon-3pm, 7-11.30pm Mon-Sat. **££££**. **French**. Map p97 B3 ③⑧

Imported from a Nice original by the boss of Zuma (p89) and Roka (p139), La Petite Maison serves dishes to share, tapas-style – maybe courgette flowers or anchovies deep-fried with sage. There's not much space, but the linen curtains and frosted glass block out the ugly road and draw in daylight.

Maze

13-15 Grosvenor Square, W1K 6JP (7107 0000/www.gordonramsay.com). Bond Street tube. **Open** noon-midnight daily. **£££**. **Modern European**. Map p97 B3 ③⑦

Sat lazily on a sunny afternoon, cocktail in hand, surrounded by buff leather, zebrano wood and lustrous glass panels, gazing out across the plane trees, you might conclude that Maze has one of London's loveliest locations. The name on the door is Gordon Ramsay, but the kitchen belongs to his protégé Jason Atherton, who has a similar eye for perfection. You're free to order as much or as little as you like of the perfect tapas – a real treat. Alternatively, try the well-priced set lunch.

Momo

25 Heddon Street, W1B 4BH (7434 4040/www.momoresto.com). Piccadilly Circus tube. **Open** noon-2.30pm, 6.30-11pm Mon-Sat; 6.30-10.30pm Sun. **££**. **North African**. Map p97 C4 ❸

London's most high-profile Moroccan restaurant celebrated its tenth anniversary in 2007 with one hell of a party. But most nights here are a party, thanks to sexy decor, even sexier staff and excellent music. The food's not bad either. Moroccan isn't the most sophisticated of cuisines, but here it seems exotic: think wood pigeon pastilla (filo pastry pie) dusted with a star-and-crescent design in icing sugar. Booking is essential at weekends.

Nobu

1st floor, the Metropolitan, 19 Old Park Lane, W1K 1LB (7447 4747/www.nobu restaurants.com). Hyde Park Corner tube. **Open** noon-2.15pm, 6-10.15pm Mon-Thur; noon-2.15pm, 6-11pm Fri, Sat; 12.30-2.30pm, 6-9.30pm Sun. **££££**. **Japanese**. Map p97 B5 ❸

The Nobu chain extends from Hawaii to Tokyo, with three branches in London alone. This one is no longer the celeb-magnet it used to be, but the modern Japanese dishes still dazzle. Service is charming and the restaurant is even quite child-friendly during the day. Panoramic views over Hyde Park give you something to gaze at even when the famous people fail to show up.

Only Running Footman

NEW *5 Charles Street, W1J 5DF (7499 2988/www.themeredithgroup.co.uk). Green Park tube.* **Open** 7.30am-11.30pm Mon-Fri; 9am-11.30pm Sat, Sun. **££-£££**. **Gastropub**. Map p97 B4 ❹

This long-standing Mayfair favourite has reopened after a huge refurb. The ground floor still looks like a proper pub, with jolly chaps propping up the mahogany bar, decent ales on draught and a bar food menu, including full

Bentley's Oyster Bar & Grill

Sketch

Lecture Room's haute-beyond-haute cuisine – the Glade is the most egalitarian. The lunchtime brasserie (in which, horrors, the staff wear jeans) threatens to jar with Sketch's finely honed sensibilities, but the menus are appropriately artful and not unreasonably priced for the quality. But nothing can prepare you for the loos, each housed in a gleaming white egg.

Tamarind

20-22 Queen Street, W1J 5PR (7629 3561/www.tamarindrestaurant.com). Green Park tube. **Open** noon-2.45pm, 6-11.30pm Mon-Fri; 6-11.30pm Sat; noon-2.45pm, 6-10.30pm Sun. **£££**. **Indian**. **Map** p97 B5 ❸

The large basement interior is looking scuffed – despite a nouveau riche gilding and bronzing refurb a few years back – but a lily lies beneath. Chef Alfred Prasad produces consistently excellent north and south Indian dishes. Prices are high, but the food is great and the service friendly and attentive.

Umu

14-16 Bruton Place, W1J 6LX (7499 8881/www.umurestaurant.com). Bond Street or Green Park tube. **Open** noon-2.30pm, 6-11pm Mon-Fri; 6-11pm Sat. **££££**. **Japanese**. **Map** p97 C4 ❹

Michelin-starred Umu lets its customers in through a sliding portal at the touch of a pad. Within the low-lit, dark-timbered, mirror-lined dining room, carefully choreographed staff proffer drinks from a list covering more than 80 saké labels and 300 wines. Set menu courses tickle the taste buds at every turn: this is the kind of place where you'll find sea urchin roe and pine nuts folded into deep-fried scorpion fish. Exceptional.

Wild Honey

NEW *12 St George Street, W1S 2FB (7758 9160). Oxford Circus or Bond Street tube.* **Open** noon-2.30pm, 5.30-10.30pm Mon-Sat; 12.30-3.30pm, 5.30-9.30pm Sun. **££**. **Modern European**. **Map** p97 C3 ❺

Anthony Demetre and Will Smith, owners of Arbutus (p116), have the

English breakfasts. On the first floor there's a quieter, more formal dining room serving British dishes; they're pricey, but the wine list is affordable.

Red Lion

1 Waverton Street, W1J 5QN (7499 1307). Green Park tube. **Open** noon-11pm Mon-Fri; 6-11pm Sat. **Pub**. **Map** p97 B4 ❹

A slice of the English countryside in the bowels of Mayfair, the Red Lion exudes rural bonhomie. Age-old pub ephemera hangs from hooks and sits on shelves, while an affable bunch of drinkers sup a well-kept range of ales and chow down on familiar pub grub.

Sketch

9 Conduit Street, W1S 2XZ (0870 777 4488/www.sketch.uk.com). Oxford Circus tube. **Open** noon-2.30pm, 7-10.30pm Tue-Fri; 7-10.30pm Sat. **£££-££££**. **Modern European**. **Map** p97 C3 ❷

Of the three bits of Pierre Gagnaire's Sketch – including extravagant destination dining at the Gallery and the

magic touch. Winner of our 2007 award for Best New Restaurant, Wild Honey feels very different from the Soho original – this is a convivial oak-panelled yet modern space that's made for lingering. But the combination of exceptionally good food at fair prices (especially for the set lunch) and a user-friendly wine list are the same. Booking is essential.

Wolseley

160 Piccadilly, W1J 9EB (7499 6996/ www.thewolseley.com). Green Park tube. **Open** 7am-midnight Mon-Fri; 8am-midnight Sat; noon-11pm Sun. **£££. Modern European. Map** p97 C5 ㊻

The Wolseley has the commodity money can't buy: glamour. It emanates from the gorgeous 1920s room, the battalions of waiters, and the sense that everyone in here (yourself included) could be in a 1950s film. The European grand-café schtick means a variety of eating and drinking options are offered: crustacea and caviar, cocktails and coffee, breakfast and dinner and sundaes. Fabulous for afternoon tea.

Yoshino

3 Piccadilly Place, W1J 0DB (7287 6622/www.yoshino.net). Piccadilly Circus tube. **Open** noon-9pm Mon-Sat. **££. Japanese. Map** p97 C4 ㊼

Maybe it's the waitresses' long, white aprons; maybe it's the clean, cool interior; maybe it's just the careful preparation that goes into the food – somehow Yoshino manages to feel posher than its prices suggest. The fully explained dinner list mainly comprises bentos and some à la carte sushi.

Shopping

Apple Store

235 Regent Street, W1B 2EL (7153 9000/www.apple.com). Oxford Circus tube. **Open** 10am-9pm Mon-Sat; noon-6pm Sun. **Map** p97 C3 ㊽

The trailblazing concept store is always bustling with visitors lured inside by the latest products and software from the electronics giant. Extras include bargain bins (which sometimes feature discount laptops among the accessories and hardware), software demonstrations and one-on-one technical support (book an appointment).

Browns

23-27 South Molton Street, W1K 5RD (7514 0000/www.brownsfashion.com). Bond Street tube. **Open** 10am-6.30pm Mon-Wed, Fri, Sat; 10am-7pm Thur. **Map** p97 B3 ㊾

Joan Burstein's venerable store has reigned supreme for nearly 40 years. Among the 100-odd designers jostling for attention among its five interconnecting shops are Chloé, Dries Van Noten and Balenciaga. As well as the superbrands, Browns champions rising stars, such as Central St Martins graduates Christopher Kane and Gareth Pugh. Across the road, Browns Focus (nos.38-39, 7514 0063) is younger and more casual, while Browns Labels for Less (no.50, 7514 0052) is loaded with the previous season's leftovers.

Burlington Arcade

Piccadilly, W1 (www.burlington-arcade.co.uk). Green Park tube. **Open** 9.30am-5.30am Mon-Fri; 10am-6pm Sat. **Map** p97 C4 ㊿

Opened in 1819, this genteel covered shopping promenade is patrolled by 'Beadles' (decked out in top hats and tailcoats). It was recently restored to its Regency glory and has attracted some stylish new tenants among the traditional purveyors of cashmere and jewellery. Highlights include Globe-Trotter and Mackintosh (iconic British luggage and rainwear), Parisian pâtisserie Ladurée and Jimmy Choo-trained shoe designer Beatrix Ong.

Dover Street Market

17-18 Dover Street, W1S 4LT (7518 0680/www.doverstreetmarket.com). Green Park tube. **Open** 11am-6pm Mon-Wed, Fri, Sat; 11am-7pm Thur. **Map** p97 C4 (51)

Comme des Garçons designer Rei Kawakubo's ground-breaking six-storey space combines the edgy energy of London's indoor markets – concrete floors, tills housed in corrugated-iron

Posh scoff, nice price

It wasn't an announcement that attracted a great deal of notice, but this year **L'Atelier de Joël Robuchon** (pictured; p129), one of London's sleekest fine-dining establishments, began to offer two courses of its fabulously finicky food, served up amid £5m-worth of darkly stunning, Tokyo-style interior, for just £27 a head.

Since London's nomination as the culinary capital of world by *Restaurant* magazine a few years back, it's been clear that this is a city in which you can eat very well indeed. The problem is everyone knows it – hence, you can expect inflated prices and ludicrous waiting times for any of London's hot new tables. Never fear – if you know how, even this food-crazed town accommodates human-scale budgets and holiday-proportioned timescales. The trick is simple: do lunch.

Take one of London's most highly praised new openings, **Hibiscus** (p106). Here dining à la carte costs in the region of £80 each, but you can get two courses for just £21.50 a head – when

you visit for lunch. Ditto the Joël Robuchon deal. And a two-course lunch of brilliantly elaborate food in the gorgeous new **Landau** (p138) can be experienced for just £20 a head.

If you really can't kick the evening habit, **Arbutus** (p116; £13.50 for two courses) and new sister-restaurant **Wild Honey** (p108; £15.50-£17.50 for three courses) offer meal deals both for lunch and pre-theatre. Each of them has a Michelin star and, far more impressively, both have won our Best New Restaurant award. All their wines can be served in a 250ml carafe – the perfect size for exploring the winelist without destroying either wallet nor liver.

There's also an instance of catch-it-while you can. **Hakkasan** (p138) has long been one of our favourite lunchtime deals – £20 a head for pretty much the finest Chinese food in town, served in a sexy, Shanghai-decadent setting. But since Alan Yau sold up in January 2008 (see box p126), we wonder if pricing changes are on the way? Get in while you can.

shacks, Portaloo dressing rooms – with rarefied labels. All 14 of the Comme collections are here, alongside exclusive lines such as Azzedine Alaïa and Veronique Branquinho and outposts of interesting shops such as Shoreditch's Labour and Wait and LA vintage-couture emporium Decades. The theatrical displays make it fun to browse, and there's an outpost of Parisian fave Rose Bakery on the top floor.

Elemis Day Spa

2-3 Lancashire Court, W1S 1EX (7499 4995/www.elemis.com). Bond Street tube. **Open** 9am-9pm Mon-Sat; 10am-6pm Sun. **Map** p97 B3 🟡

This leading British spa brand's exotic, unisex retreat is tucked away down a cobbled lane off Bond Street. The elegantly ethnic treatment rooms are a lovely setting in which to relax and enjoy a spot of pampering, from wraps to results-driven facials.

Garrard

24 Albemarle Street, W1S 4HT (0870 871 8888/www.garrard.com). Bond Street or Green Park tube. **Open** 10am-6pm Mon-Fri; 10am-5pm Sun. **Map** p97 C4 🟡

Whether Jade Jagger's contract as creative director will be renewed remains to be seen, but one thing's for certain: she has modernised the Crown Jeweller's diamond-studded designs to appeal to a new generation of bling-seekers.

Georgina Goodman

NEW *44 Old Bond Street, W1S 4GB (7409 2929/www.georginagoodman. com). Bond Street tube.* **Open** 10am-6pm Mon-Wed, Fri, Sat; 10am-7pm Thur. **Map** p97 C4 🟡

Proudly the youngest brand on the street, the two small and perfectly formed floors of this boutique showcase Goodman's sculptural, lovingly made high heels and flats, long admired by shoe king Manolo Blahnik. Her original store (12-14 Shepherd Street, Mayfair, W1J 7JF, 7499 8599) now houses her bespoke workshop – and hosts the unmissable biannual sample sales.

Grays Antique & Grays in the N

58 Davies Street, W1K Davies Mews, W1K 5A 7034/www.graysantiqu Street tube. **Open** 10a Map p97 B3 🟡

Stalls in this smart covered market sell everything from jewellery to rare books (there are over 200 dealers), and a liveried doorman greets you as you enter from South Molton Street.

Kurt Geiger

NEW *198 Regent Street, W1B 5TP (3238 0044/www.kurtgeiger.com). Oxford Circus tube.* **Open** 10am-7pm Mon-Wed, Fri, Sat; 10am-8pm Thur; noon-6pm Sun. **Map** p97 C3 🟡

This flagship location of the shoe store opened as part of a massive expansion that shows no sign of diluting the designs. It isn't quite cutting edge, but Geiger continues to offer high-quality takes on current fashions. Other upmarket labels are stocked too: Gina, Chloé, Marc Jacobs, Paul Smith and Church's.

Luella

NEW *25 Brook Street, W1K 4HB (7158 1830/www.luella.com). Bond Street tube.* **Open** 10am-6pm Mon-Wed, Fri, Sat; 10am-7pm Thur. **Map** p97 B3 🟡

London's first stand-alone store by anglophile designer Luella Bartley crosses deliciously horsey English aristocrat with full-throttle rock 'n' roller to come up with accessories, eyewear, it-bags, a lauded ready-to-wear collection and all manner of things unabashedly girly. Fans will find chunky patent handbags, love-heart purses, pirate stickers and Linda Farrow Vintage eyewear. A creaky, wood-panelled back room houses the main collection and an op-art staircase descends into a secret hangout parlour with dainty teacups, cute car-boot tat and a stack of vintage mags. Customisation king Noki has taken the edge off the rather posh interior, scrawling all over the Luella v Noki footwear, reworking classic prints and sprinkling dots of neon over antique fittings.

(7629). Bond **Mill**ar-Sat. Map p97 B4 ❺❾

...rained British perfumer Lyn Harris's distinctive, long-lasting scents, in their lovely decorative packaging, are made with quality natural extracts and oils. Perennial favourites include Noix de Tubéreuse, Figue Amère and Citron Citron. Candles, body washes and body lotions complete the product range, and though prices are on the steep side, they're worth every penny.

Paul Smith Sale Shop

23 Avery Row, W1X 9HB (7493 1287/www.paulsmith.co.uk). Bond Street tube. **Open** 10.30am-6.30pm Mon-Wed, Fri, Sat; 10.30am-7pm Thur; 1-5.30pm Sun. **Map** p97 B3 ❺❾
If you can't afford Smith's regular gear, come here instead, where you'll find samples and last season's stock at up to 50% off – covering clothes for men, women and children, plus accessories.

Postcard Teas

9 Dering Street, W1S 1AG (7629 3654/ www.postcardteas.com). Bond Street or Oxford Circus tube. **Open** 10.30am-6.30pm Tue-Sat. **Map** p97 B3 ❻⓪
The range in this exquisite little shop is not huge, but it is selected with care, with some real rarities in among the Darjeeling, China, Ceylon and Assam. There's a table for those who want to try a pot; downstairs are vintage postcards from the collection of art dealer Antony d'Offay, father of the shop's owner Timothy.

Primark

NEW *499-517 Oxford Street, W1K 7DA (7495 0420/www.primark.co.uk). Marble Arch tube.* **Open** 9am-9pm Mon-Fri; 9am-8pm Sat; noon-6pm Sun. **Map** p97 A3 ❻❶
There were scenes recalling the storming of the Bastille when the flagship of the trend-led, cheap-as-chips retail chain opened in 2007. The place is great for basics, but if you're lucky enough to stumble across some shoes or a top

you really like, you'll probably walk into someone else wearing the same thing the second you step out the door.

Savile Row

Green Park or Piccadilly Circus tube. **Map** p97 C4 ❻❷
Running south off Conduit Street, this is the spiritual home of bespoke British tailoring. Gieves & Hawkes (no.1, 7434 2001) should be a compulsory address for anyone interested in the history of British menswear, having operated a bespoke tailoring service for more than two centuries. At no.15, Henry Poole & Co (7734 5985, www.henrypoole.com) was the first to set up on the Row in 1806. Since then, the firm has cut suits for clients including Napoleon III, Winston Churchill and 'Buffalo Bill' Cody, and is credited with inventing the tuxedo, in 1865. Kilgour (no.8, 7734 6905, www.8savilerow.com) is one of the flashiest, most fashion-savvy of the Savile Row tailors, the choice of rock stars and James Bonds alike. The premises fuse old and new principles with a traditional English entrance but Philippe Starck decor. Those unenthused by bespoke tailoring can check out the denim at Evisu (no.9, 7734 2540) or visit the wonderful b store (no.24A, 7734 6846, www.bstorelondon.com), a wonderful platform for cutting-edge designers for both men and women.

Simon Finch Rare Books

53 Maddox Street, W1S 2PN (7499 0974/www.simonfinch.com). Oxford Circus tube. **Open** 10am-6pm Mon-Fri. **Map** p97 C3 ❻❸
Located in a narrow Mayfair townhouse, Simon Finch's era-spanning, idiosyncratic collection contains wonderful surprises, such as an original copy of Hubert Selby Jr's *Last Exit to Brooklyn*. Prices start at around £20, so it's worth popping in even if you're not a serious collector.

Timothy Everest

35 Bruton Place, W1J 6NS (7629 6236/ www.timothyeverest.co.uk). Bond Street tube. **Open** 10am-6pm Mon-Fri; 11am-5pm alternate Sat. **Map** p97 B4 ❻❹

Luella p111

One-time apprentice to the legendary Tommy Nutter, Everest is a star of the latest generation of London tailors and known for his more relaxed 21st-century definition of style.

Uniqlo

NEW *311 Oxford Street, W1C 2HP (7290 7701/www.uniqlo.co.uk). Bond Street or Oxford Circus tube.* **Open** 10am-8pm Mon-Wed; 10am-9pm Thur-Sat; noon-6pm Sun. **Map** p97 B3 ⑥₅
There are two outposts of Uniqlo, Japan's biggest clothes retailer, on Oxford Street alone – but this one is 25,000sq ft and three storeys of flag-ship. Not as cheap as Primark but more stylish, Uniqlo sells simple staples for men and women.

Soho

This hip square mile of London is the stuff of legend, etched on vinyl and captured on celluloid. Louche and libertine, it's in danger of losing its lustre with each half-baked campaign attempting to 'revitalise' it. Westminster Council, never the most enlightened of bodies, has put in motion a scheme to regenerate the most atmospheric of Soho sidewalks, **Berwick Street**. The only 'sights' listed for Soho are really locations – **Leicester Square**, **Soho Square**, **Chinatown**. It isn't that the district's unfriendly to tourists – far from it: this bit of London doesn't give a stuff where you're from or, more importantly, what you plan to do while you're here. On weekend nights, keep clear of Leicester Square (it isn't dangerous, it's just crowded with idiots) and be aware that several iconic locations (jazz institution **Ronnie Scott's** seeming eager to join them) are starting to loosen their grip. Still, if you want to drink or eat or dance, you could hardly find a better part of London to do so. Have a wander among the skinny streets that radiate off Old Compton Street, Soho's main artery – and see if you can't still find yourself a bit of mischief.

Soho & Covent Garden

© Copyright Time Out Group 2008

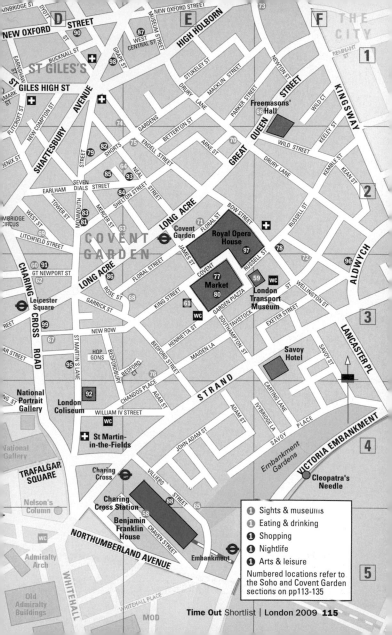

NEW OXFORD STREET

D DYOTT STREET

CAMBRIDGE ST

NEW OXFORD STREET

E HIGH HOLBORN

F THE CITY

NEW OXFORD STREET

ST GILES'S

90

87 WEST CENTRAL ST

98

ST GILES HIGH ST

BUCKNALL ST

MUSEUM STREET

GRAPE ST

STUKELEY ST

MACKLIN STREET

PARKER STREET

NEWTON STREET

KINGSWAY

REMNANT ST

FLITCROFT ST

SHAFTESBURY AVENUE

NEW COMPTON ST

74

GARDENS

BETTERTON STREET

DRURY LANE

Freemasons' Hall

66

GREAT QUEEN STREET

WILD CT

KEELEY ST

KEMBLE ST

KEAN ST

JENIX ST

SHAFTESBURY AVENUE

STREET

79 82 SHORTS

75 ENDELL STREET

ARNE ST

70

WILD STREET

DRURY LANE

RUSSELL ST

EARLHAM

SEVEN DIALS STREET

64

85 93

SHELTON STREET NEAL STREET

84

MERCER ST

83 81

WEST ST

LITCHFIELD STREET

69

63

COVENT GARDEN

LONG ACRE

71 FLORAL ST

BOW STREET

Covent Garden

Royal Opera House

97

78

RUSSELL ST

72

ALDWYCH

96

CHARING CROSS ROAD

60 91

62

GT NEWPORT ST

86

FLORAL STREET

JAMES ST

COVENT

77 Market 80

59

WC

London Transport Museum

WELLINGTON STREET

Leicester Square

99

ROSE ST

68

KING STREET

61

GARDEN PIAZZA

WC

SOUTHAMPTON ST

EXETER STREET

LANCASTER PL

SAVOY ST

GARRICK ST

NEW ROW

HENRIETTA ST

67

ST MARTIN'S LANE

HOP GDNS

BEDFORDBURY

BEDFORD STREET

MAIDEN LA

TAVISTOCK ST

Savoy Hotel

95

BEDFORD CT

76

CHANDOS PLACE

AGAR ST

STRAND

CARTING LANE

IVYBRIDGE LA

SAVOY PLACE

VICTORIA EMBANKMENT

National Portrait Gallery

92

London Coliseum

WILLIAM IV STREET

JOHN ADAM ST

ADAM ST

SAVOY

Embankment Gardens

St Martin-in-the-Fields

National Gallery

TRAFALGAR SQUARE

Nelson's Column

Charing Cross

VILLIERS STREET

88

65

Cleopatra's Needle

WC

Charing Cross Station

58

Benjamin Franklin House

CRAVEN STREET

Embankment

Admiralty Arch

NORTHUMBERLAND AVENUE

1 Sights & museums
1 Eating & drinking
1 Shopping
1 Nightlife
1 Arts & leisure

Numbered locations refer to the Soho and Covent Garden sections on pp113-135

Old Admiralty Buildings

WHITEHALL

WHITEHALL PLACE

MOD

Sights & museums

Chinatown

Gerrard Street. Leicester Square tube.
Map p114 C3 ❶
It wasn't until the 1950s that the Chinese put down roots here and the ersatz oriental gates, stone lions and pagoda-topped phone boxes suggest a Chinese theme park, but this is a close-knit residential and working enclave, a genuine focal point for London's Chinese community. The area is crammed with restaurants, Asian grocery stores and small shops selling iced-grass jelly, speciality teas and cheap air tickets to Beijing. Haozhan (p118) is our current favourite Gerrard Street restaurant, but Golden Dragon (nos.28-29, 7734 2763) and the refurbished Royal Dragon (no.30, 7734 1388) do reliable Anglo-Cantonese nosh. For pure atmosphere, drop in on one of the bustling cafés – try a 'bubble tea' (sweet, icy and full of balls of jelly slurped up with a straw) at Jen Café (4-8 Newport Place) or late-night favourite HK Diner (22 Wardour Street).

Leicester Square

Leicester Square or Piccadilly Circus tube. **Map** p114 C3 ❷
Leicester Square is reasonably pleasant by day, but by night a sinkhole of semi-undressed inebriates out on a big night 'up west'. How different it once was. Satirical painter William Hogarth had a studio here (1733-64), as did 18th-century artist Sir Joshua Reynolds; both are commemorated by busts in the small gardens that lie at the heart of the square, although it's the statue of a tottering Charlie Chaplin that gets all the attention.

Soho Square

Tottenham Court Road tube.
Map p114 C1 ❸
This tree-lined quadrangle was once King's Square – a weather-beaten statue of Charles II stands at the centre. Locked at night, by day its grass is full of canoodling couples, while snacking workers occupy its benches, one of

Leicester Square

which bears a plaque for Kirsty MacColl, singer of 'Soho Square'. Night and day, traffic cruises around it, waiting for one of the area's few parking bays to become free. The centrepiece is a little mock Tudor gardeners' hut.

Eating & drinking

Arbutus

63-64 Frith Street, W1D 3JW (7734 4545/www.arbutusrestaurant.co.uk). Tottenham Court Road tube. **Open** noon-2.30pm, 5-11pm Mon-Sat; 12.30-3.30pm, 5.30-9.30pm Sun. **££. Modern European**. **Map** p114 C2 ❹
Always full (although counter-dining means casual diners are often accommodated), Arbutus has a alluring British and Mediterranean menu that is precise but unfussy. Braised pig's head with potato purée and caramelised onions is a trademark dish. The room is minimalist but pleasant, the diners a mixed bunch, and the staff friendly and prescient. New sister-restaurant Wild Honey (p108) is also very fine.

Barrafina

*54 Frith Street, W1D 4SL (7813 8016/
www.barrafina.co.uk). Tottenham
Court Road tube.* **Open** noon-3pm,
5-11pm Mon-Sat. **££**. **Spanish**.
Map p114 C2 ❺

There's an agreeable slickness and
bustle about Sam and Eddie Hart's terrific tapas bar. Expect to queue unless
you eat outside regular mealtimes, but
once you're seated at the L-shaped
counter (which, apart from the open
kitchen and grill, is pretty much the
whole shebang), the fun really starts –
watch the chefs cook squirming mol-
luscs and perfect tortilla.

Bar Shu

*28 Frith Street, W1D 5LF (7287
6688). Leicester Square or Tottenham
Court Road tube.* **Open** noon-11.30pm
Mon-Sat; noon-11pm Sun. **££**.
Sichuan. Map p114 C2 ❻

One of a growing number of London
restaurants serving fiery Sichuan food.
Not for the faint-hearted, but great for
those in search of authentic flavours.

Café Boheme

NEW *13 Old Compton Street, W1D 5JQ
(7734 0623/www.cafeboheme.co.uk).
Leicester Square or Tottenham Court
Road tube.* **Open** 8am-3am Mon-Sat;
8am-midnight Sun. **££**. **Brasserie**.
Map p114 C2 ❼

This well-established brasserie has just
had a handsome makeover, but underneath it's still the same Boheme. The
classic French menu won't set pulses
racing, but it's competent, charmingly
served and delivered to a table on Old
Compton Street where you can sit into
the small hours.

Côte

NEW *124-126 Wardour Street, W1F
0TY (7287 9280/www.cote-
restaurants.co.uk). Oxford Circus or
Tottenham Court Road tube.* **Open**
8am-11pm Mon-Wed; 8am-midnight
Thur, Fri; 10am-midnight Sat; 10am-
10.30am Sun. **££**. **French**. Map
p114 B2 ❽

Like the original in Wimbledon Village,
the new branch of Côte is good-looking.
Expect welcoming and professional ser-

vice, and reasonably interesting, well-
made, fair-priced dishes that a modern
bistro in France would be happy with,
such as pissaladière and spatchcocked
chicken. If you're rushing, opt for a plat
rapide and be in and out in half an hour.

Dehesa

NEW *25 Ganton Street, W1F 9BP
(7494 4170). Oxford Circus tube.*
Open noon-11pm Mon-Wed; 9am-
11pm Thur, Fri; 10am-11pm Sat; 11am-
5pm Sun. **£££**. **Spanish-Italian
tapas**. Map p114 A2 ❾

Dehesa is the second restaurant of Salt
Yard (p139) owners Sanja Morris and
Simon Mullins. The menu is similar,
featuring an eclectic ensemble of
Spanish and Italian tapas, but here a
big deal is made of charcuterie, with a
special counter reserved for the slicing
of meats. The food quality is superb,
with a wine list on a par with it. Note
that reservations aren't taken, and hot
food isn't served all day, every day.

Diner

NEW *18-20 Ganton Street, W1F 7BU
(7287 8962/www.thedinersoho.com).
Oxford Circus or Piccadilly Circus tube.*
Open 8am-12.30am Mon-Fri; 9am-
12.30am Sat; 9am-11pm Sun. **£**. **North
American**. Map p114 A2 ❿

This artfully reconstructed US diner
is a calculated hotchpotch of retro styles.
A fun and friendly attitude, ample
space, great drinks and hearty, good-
quality scoff including stellar own-
made burgers are all reasons to visit.

Dog & Duck

*18 Bateman Street, W1D 3AJ (7494
0697). Tottenham Court Road tube.*
Open 11am-11pm Mon-Sat; noon-
10.30pm Sun. **Pub**. Map p114 C2 ⓫

This historic two-floor Victorian gem
has changed little since Orwell drank
here in the 1940s. The cosy bar upstairs
is named after him. Downstairs, in the
narrow space, ales are the attraction.

Fernandez & Wells

*73 Beak Street, W1F 9RS (7287 8124).
Oxford Circus or Piccadilly Circus tube.*
Open 8am-7pm Mon-Fri; 9am-7pm Sat.
£. **Café**. Map p114 B2 ⓬

LONDON BY AREA

Diner p117

LONDON BY AREA

Round the corner from its forebear – a very classy sandwich bar on Lexington Street – this espresso bar serves superb coffee and nibbles (panini, cakes) to punters perched on a handful of high stools. That's it, but that's all it needs.

French House

49 Dean Street, W1D 5BG (7437 2799/www.frenchhousesoho.com). Leicester Square or Piccadilly Circus tube. **Open** noon-11pm daily. **Pub**. **Map** p114 C2 ⑬

The famous French House pub is as popular now as when cabaret stars and a louche literary set were using it either side of the war. Most evenings you'll find yourself parked on the pavement outside, but if you make it to the bar (still sporting a photo of De Gaulle, whose Free French had their wartime offices upstairs), there's draught Kronenbourg and Breton cider.

Haozhan

8 Gerrard Street, W1D 5PJ (7434 3838). Leicester Square or Piccadilly Circus tube. **Open** noon-11.30pm Mon-Thur; noon-midnight Fri, Sat; noon-10.30pm Sun. **£££. Sichuan**. **Map** p114 C3 ⑭

This modern-looking venue's contemporary, globe-trotting menu is produced by a chef from renowned Hakkasan (p138), which means adventurous, impeccable cooking. Many dishes are textural masterpieces, staff are ultra-attentive, and the low bill is a pleasant surprise.

Hummus Bros

88 Wardour Street, W1F 0TJ (7734 1311/www.hbros.co.uk). Oxford Circus or Tottenham Court Road tube. **Open** 11am-10pm Mon-Wed; 11am-11pm Thur, Fri; noon-11pm Sat; noon-10pm Sun. **£. Café**. **Map** p114 B2 ⑮

A fine concept diner. The dip comes shaped around the inside of a bowl, which is filled with vibrant toppings (stewed beef, fava beans, guacamole). Those in the know order one of two daily changing specials. It isn't ideal for a quiet chat, but for a swift, nutritious lunch or early evening meal, the Bros are hard to beat.

Imli

167-169 Wardour Street, W1F 8WR (7287 4243/www.imli.co.uk). Tottenham Court Road tube. **Open** noon-11pm daily. **£. Indian & Pakistani**. Map p114 B2 ⑯

A branch of the fine-dining restaurant Tamarind (p108), this Soho café makes much of its affordable selection of snacks and curries. It's a spacious venue, smartly furnished with Indian artefacts, splashes of orange-themed colour and chunky wooden furniture. The tapas-style menu sometimes falls short of the mark, however.

LAB

12 Old Compton Street, W1D 4TQ (7437 7820/www.lab-townhouse.com). Leicester Square or Tottenham Court Road tube. **Open** 4pm-midnight Mon-Sat; 4-10.30pm Sun. **Cocktail bar**. Map p114 C2 ⑰

As one category of the painstakingly conceived and encyclopedic drinks menu suggests, LAB is streets ahead. The small and sexy two-floor space is invariably packed with Sohoites fuelled by London's freshest mixologists. Straight out of the London Academy of Bartending, graduates are aided by colleagues of considerable global experience in fixing some 30 original concoctions (most around £7) or 50 classics, using high-end spirits and fresh ingredients. A contemporary retro decorative and aural backdrop does the rest.

Maison Bertaux

28 Greek Street, W1D 5DQ (7437 6007). Leicester Square, Piccadilly Circus or Tottenham Court Road tube. **Open** 8.30am-11pm Mon-Sat; 8.30am-7pm Sun. **£**. No credit cards. **Café**. Map p114 C2 ⑱

Many consider the original outpost of Pâtisserie Valerie (44 Old Compton Street, 7437 3466, www.patisserie-valerie.co.uk) to be essential Soho, but café nostalgics and connoisseurs of lost afternoon melancholy do better heading to eccentric Maison Bertaux. Head up the tight staircase and take tea amid the changing artworks, or enjoy the frou-frou decor and pavement life downstairs by the counter of old-fashioned cakes.

Milk & Honey

61 Poland Street, W1F 7NU (7292 9949/www.mlkhny.com). Oxford Circus tube. **Open** *Non-members* 6-11pm Mon-Fri; 7-11pm Sat. **Bar**. Map p114 B2 ⑲

Tucked away behind unmarked Prohibition era-style black doors, this jazz-tinged speakeasy-style cocktail bar from the people behind the Player (p120) is a charming mix of semi-exclusivity and unprecedented friendliness. Non-members will need to book in advance (and leave by 11pm), but will be treated like old friends by the staff.

Mother Mash

26 Ganton Street, W1F 7QZ (7494 9644/www.mothermash.co.uk). Oxford Circus tube. **Open** 8.30am-10pm Mon-Fri; noon-10pm Sat; noon-5pm Sun. **£**. **Café**. Map p114 A2 ⑳

Sausages? Yes. Pies? Of course. Mashed spud? Now you're talking! A standard butter-and-milk mash is offered among a handful of variants, such as Irish champ. There's also a choice of gravies, including a traditional 'liquor' (parsley sauce). There are breakfast and salad options too, as well as wine and beer.

New Mayflower

68-70 Shaftesbury Avenue, W1D 6LY (7734 9207). Leicester Square or Piccadilly Circus tube. **Open** 5pm-4am daily. **££. Chinese**. Map p114 C3 ㉑

A Chinatown stalwart. The lengthy Anglo-Cantonese menu has all the familiar dishes, plus some more esoteric concoctions. The decor is a bit rough around the edges, and there's often a long wait for a table, but the very late hours are some compensation.

New World

1 Gerrard Place, W1D 5PA (7734 0396). Leicester Square or Piccadilly Circus tube. **Open** 11am-11.45pm Mon-Sat; 11am-11pm Sun. **££. Chinese**. Map p114 C3 ㉒

One of Chinatown's most popular dim sum venues – not for the rather average food or the indifferent service, but for its

LONDON BY AREA

trolley service, a disappearing custom that allows diners to glimpse dishes before they order. Reasonable prices too.

Nordic Bakery

14 Golden Square, W1F 9JF (3230 1077/www.nordicbakery.com). Oxford Circus or Piccadilly Circus tube. **Open** 8am-8pm Mon-Fri; noon-7pm Sat. **£**. **Café**. **Map** p114 B3 ㉓

The simplicity of the Nordic Bakery formula takes a lot of beating: small range of food (sandwiches, cinnamon buns, oatmeal cookies, and donuts on a Wednesday); high-ceilinged room decorated with impeccable Scandinavian good taste; good coffee.

Player

8 Broadwick Street, W1F 8HN (7292 9945/www.thplyr.com). Oxford Circus or Tottenham Court Road tube. **Open** 5.30pm-midnight Mon-Wed; 5.30pm-1am Thur, Fri; 7pm-1am Sat. **Cocktail bar**. **Map** p114 B2 ㉔

Few places hit the mark as perfectly as this subterranean cocktail lounge (open to non-members before 11pm), where the retroactively glamorous 1970s decor extends from Player-branded, turquoise carpet and sculpted wall panelling to the cluster of disco balls dangling behind the DJs, who can be relied on to crank it up from 8pm Thur-Sat (£5 entry after 9pm). Even accountants will feel like movie stars here.

Spiga

84-86 Wardour Street, W1V 3LF (7734 3444/www.vpmg.net). Leicester Square, Piccadilly Circus or Tottenham Court Road tube. **Open** noon-11pm Mon, Tue; noon-midnight Wed-Sat. **££**. **Pizza**. **Map** p114 B2 ㉕

Spiga's stablemates in the Vince Power Music Group include style bars and music venues. There are no musicians or DJs at this classy pizzeria, but a light jazz soundtrack accompanies casual daytime dining and picks up for the buzzier evening crowd. Modern decor, booth seating, a small bar and smart, black-clad Italian staff provide the good looks. As for the food, it's competently put together.

Sun & Thirteen Cantons

21 Great Pulteney Street, W1F 9NG (7734 0934). Oxford Circus or Piccadilly Circus tube. **Open** noon-11pm Mon-Fri; 6-11pm Sat. **Pub**. **Map** p114 B3 ㉖

Another pub veering from the traditional route to appeal to music fans and modern tastes in drinking. The rather smart Sun still bears the shiny wood and frosted glass of its pub heritage. Within, however, in the main bar adjoining an equally smart dining room (Thai food served throughout), you'll find pints of Kirin Ichiban and Peeterman and bottles of lager sunk to a contemporary aural backdrop. Thursday and Friday DJ sessions happen downstairs.

Two Floors

3 Kingly Street, W1R 5LF (7439 1007/www.barworks.co.uk). Oxford Circus or Piccadilly Circus tube. **Open** noon-11.30pm Mon-Thur; noon-midnight Fri, Sat. **Bar**. **Map** p114 A3 ㉗

A fine, fine bar: reasonably priced, modest, understated. There's no sign – look out for the old no.3. Inside, furniture institutional and loungey fills an informal, long bar space, each table bearing a drinks menu with a black two of diamonds on the cover. Downstairs is Handy Joe's intimate Tiki Bar.

Yauatcha

15 Broadwick Street, W1F 0DL (7494 8888). Leicester Square, Oxford Circus, Piccadilly Circus or Tottenham Court Road tube. **Open** 11am-11.45pm Mon-Sat; 11am-10.45pm Sun. **£££**. **Dim sum**. **Map** p114 B2 ㉘

Sold by founder Alan Yau in early 2008, Michelin-starred Yauatcha is still shockingly popular. At dinnertime you have to fight through crowds waiting in the entrance to reach the basement restaurant, a cacophony of music and media chat. It's worth it, though: once you're there you can eat excellent dim sum (served till late), a small range of main courses or first-class pâtisserie. The decor is noteworthy, too, blending cool minimalism with the ranked jars of a traditional Chinese teahouse.

Dehesa p117

that ended with World War II, but one Soho institution remains from the early 1960s: father-and-son tailors Mr Eddie & Chris Kerr (no.52, 7437 3727, www.eddiekerr.co.uk) turn out sharp bespoke gear in unostentatious surroundings. The fruit and veg stalls of Berwick Market (9am-6pm Mon-Sat) are a focal point, but Berwick Street is also famous for its record shops; surviving old-timers include Sister Ray (nos.34-35, 7734 3297) and Vinyl Junkies (no.94, 7439 2775). There are also the remnants of Soho's most famous industry: sex. At the southern end of the street doorways sport hand-lettered signs inviting punters to walk up the scruffy stairways within; nearby narrow Walker's Court is Soho's last remaining red-light quarter.

Shopping

Albam

NEW 23 Beak Street, W1F 9RS (3157 7000/www.albamclothing.com). Oxford Circus or Piccadilly Circus tube. **Open** noon-7pm Mon-Sat; noon-5pm Sun. **Map** p114 A3 ㉙

This fantastic menswear store opened in October 2007 and has already accumulated a cult fan base of customers who want great-looking garments at decent prices. Find items like the perfect white T-shirt in Egyptian cotton at a reasonable £25, or wear-with-everything straight-leg indigo jeans at £70.

Berwick Street

Oxford Circus or Piccadilly Circus tube. **Map** p114 B2 ㉚

While the rest of London succumbs to chains and clean-up campaigns, this amiable thoroughfare offers authenticity by the pound. Signs engraved on façades above shopfronts recall an era

COS

NEW 222 Regent Street, W1B 5BD (7478 0400/www.cosstores.com). Oxford Circus tube. **Open** 10am-8pm Mon-Wed, Fri, Sat; 10am-9pm Thur; noon-6pm Sun. **Map** p114 A2 ㉛

H&M's new upmarket sibling COS ('Collection Of Style') offers chic basics in luxurious fabrics, including cashmere and linen. Expect quality staples – shirts, trousers, blazers – for men and women, plus a good range of shoes.

Foot Patrol

16A St Anne's Court, W1F 0BG (7734 6625/www.foot-patrol.com). Oxford Circus tube. **Open** 11am-7pm Mon-Fri; 11am-6.30pm Sat. **Map** p114 B2 ㉜

Famous for its metal display cages, Foot Patrol has a special place in the little black books of trainer-heads everywhere. The rapidly changing stock mainly consists of Nike, Adidas and New Balance, with some vintage and limited-edition offerings too.

Foyles

113-119 Charing Cross Road, WC2H 0EB (7437 5660/www.foyles.co.uk). Tottenham Court Road tube. **Open** 9.30am-9pm Mon-Sat; noon-6pm Sun. **Map** p114 C2 ㉝

Independently owned and open since 1906, Foyles is London's best-known

Popstarz come to Soho

As gay scenes go, London's is one of the world's biggest, most energetic and most diverse. There's not a night of the week without something amazing on. You thought gay clubbing was all about drag shows and vogueing? Time to try gay R&B, queer metal parties, hedonistic house after-after parties... And where did this diversity come from? A lot of the credit must go to Popstarz.

Rewind 13 years to when promoter and DJ Simon Hobart was spinning tunes in London's gay bars and clubs. He looked around at the bare torsos and gurning faces and decided, as current Popstarz promoter Jamie Wilton says, 'that this isn't me, this isn't my friends'. The rest of Britain was bouncing merrily along to Britpop and Hobart wanted to set up a club that played the tunes he was into: indie, in other words. From the start it was a huge success – Popstarz's opening night in 1996 drew 500 people – and eventually the night had become so trendy Noel Gallagher and Mick Jagger, bastions of swaggering hetero attitude, turned up to find out what all the fuss was about.

Strangely, given its level of influence, Popstarz has always been tucked away from the centre of town – in Islington, in Holborn, most recently in King's Cross. Until now. Having spawned a whole scene in Soho, including a late-night bar (Trash Palace), a smaller club (Ghetto) – home of ace electro fixtures, the Cock and nagnagnag – and even its own alt-queer magazine (F*@k), the mother of them all, the original Popstarz Friday nighter, has finally joined its satellites bang in the middle of the West End. Popstarz is now held at **SIN** (p125), where a new generation of music slebs (among them Beth Ditto, pictured) have already rocked up. And Soho nightlife, which until recently had looked pretty dead, is suddenly beginning to seem vital again.
■ www.Popstarz.org

LONDON BY AREA

bookshop, revered for the volume of its stock, which is spread over five floors at this flagship location. On the first floor are a café and Ray's Jazz (7440 3205), whose predominantly CD-based stock covers the entire spectrum (blues, avant-garde, gospel, folk, world), although modern jazz is the main draw.

Kingly Court

Carnaby Street, opposite Broadwick Street, W1B 5PW (7333 8118/www. carnaby.co.uk). Oxford Circus tube. **Open** 11am-7pm Mon-Sat; noon-6pm Sun. **Map** p114 A2 ③④

Not your average shopping centre, this compact, three-floor complex brings together a funky mix of established streetwear chains, boutiques and gift shops. The vintage selection is particularly good: check out Marshmallow Mountain for immaculate vintage shoes, clothes and bags, and Twinkled, which extends the retro look to the home. Microzine brings together an entire men's mag of fashion, furnishings and gadgets under one roof, and there's also finest quality tea at Camellia Sinensis.

Liberty

Regent Street, W1B 5AH (7734 1234/www.liberty.co.uk). Oxford Circus tube. **Open** 10am-8pm Mon-Wed, Fri; 10am-9pm Thur; 10am-7pm Sat; noon-6pm Sun. **Map** p114 A2 ③⑤

Charmingly idiosyncratic, Liberty is housed in a 1920s mock Tudor structure. The main Great Marlborough Street entrance, flanked by Paula Pryke's exuberant floral concession, leads into a room devoted to the store's own label, in the middle of a galleried atrium. As well as the famous scarves, Liberty's art nouveau prints now adorn everything from silk lingerie to chic stamped-leather handbags. The ground level is great for decorative notebooks, photo albums, unusual perfumes and toiletries, and jewellery. The basement menswear department is one of London's most stylish, with an emphasis on individualistic lines rather than superbrands. Don't miss the impressive Arts and Crafts furniture on the fourth floor.

Playlounge

19 Beak Street, W1F 9RP (7287 7073/www.playlounge.co.uk). Oxford Circus or Piccadilly Circus tube. **Open** 10.30am-7pm Mon-Sat; noon-5pm Sun. **Map** p114 A3 ③⑥

This fun shop has a small but well-chosen range of action figures, gadgets, books, comics, T-shirts and clothing. Look out too for Astro Boy books, Kubrick figures and Sigikid Toys.

Nightlife

There are regular, top-quality solo comedy shows at **Soho Theatre** (p126).

Astoria & Astoria 2

157 Charing Cross Road, WC2H 0EL (information 8963 0940/box office 0871 231 0821/www.festivalrepublic. com). Tottenham Court Road tube. **Map** p114 C1 ③⑦

That this old 2,000-capacity alt-rock sweatbox may have to close in 2008 to make way for Crossrail has outraged certain sections of the rock world, even though we've long found the Astoria a disappointing place to watch bands: we can't recommend it for sound, decor or staff. Virtually an adjunct, Astoria 2 is better on all counts; on Saturdays, it hosts student-indie night Frog.

Bar Rumba

36 Shaftesbury Avenue, W1V 7DD (7287 6933/www.barrumba.co.uk). Piccadilly Circus tube. **Open** 9pm-3am Mon; 6pm-3am Tue; 8pm-3am Wed; 8pm-3.30am Thur; 7pm-4am Fri; 9pm-3.30am Sat; 8.30pm-2.30am Sun. **Map** p114 B3 ③⑧

This basement venue focuses on cool urban sounds. On Tuesdays, Barrio Latino features a salsa class followed by heavy reggaeton, and Movement is the capital's longest-running junglist jam on Thursdays. Fridays pull in a cool crowd for hip hop slam Front To Back.

Café de Paris

3-4 Coventry Street, W1D 6BL (7734 7700/www.cafedeparis.com). Piccadilly Circus tube. **Open** *Restaurant* 6-8pm Sat. *Club* 10pm-3am Fri, Sat;

(special events) 7pm-2am Mon-Thur.
Map p114 C3 ❸❾
There aren't many London clubs that drip with as much glamour as the Café de Paris. It's increasingly popular for one-off events and cabaret shows (Flash Monkey is always outstanding), so dust off your most fabulous frock first.

Candy Bar

4 Carlisle Street, W1D 3BJ (7494 4041/ www.thecandybar.co.uk). Tottenham Court Road tube. **Open** 5-11.30pm Mon-Thur; 3pm-2am Fri, Sat; 5-11pm Sun. **Map** p114 B2 ❹❶

The biggest and best lesbian bar in town also hosts erotic dancers and karaoke nights. It's not women-only but the door policy is selective. More pole dancing than pool playing.

Comedy Camp

Barcode, 3-4 Archer Street, W1D 7AP (7483 2960/www.comedycamp.co.uk). Leicester Square or Piccadilly Circus tube. **Shows** 8.30pm Tue. **Map** p114 B3 ❹❶

Jo Caulfield and Scott Capurro are the caustic regulars at what is currently one of our favourite weekly comedy nights, with consistently great line-ups and a brilliant atmosphere.

Comedy Store

1A Oxendon Street, SW1Y 4EE (Ticketmaster 0870 060 2340/ www.Thecomedystore.co.uk). Leicester Square or Piccadilly Circus tube. **Map** p114 C3 ❹❷

The legendary Store still has some of the best bills on the circuit. The venue is purpose-built for serious punters, with a semicircle of seats, and favours trad stand-up. Wednesdays feature top improv outfit the Comedy Store Players.

Green Carnation

5 Greek Street, W1D 4DD (7434 3323/www.greencarnationsoho.co.uk). Tottenham Court Road tube. **Open** 4pm-2.30am Mon-Sat; 3pm-11.30pm Sun. **Map** p114 C2 ❹❸

This gay bar has been refitted to spectacular effect. Head upstairs for posh cocktails under chandeliers, to the sound of live piano and cabaret tunes.

100 Club

100 Oxford Street, W1D 1LL (7636 0933/www.the100club.co.uk). Oxford Circus or Tottenham Court Road tube. **Map** p114 B1 ❹❹

Perhaps the most adaptable venue in London, this wide, 350-capacity basement room has provided a home for trad jazz, pub blues, northern soul and punk (the venue staged a historic show in 1976 that featured the Sex Pistols, the Clash and the Damned).

Madame Jo Jo's

8-10 Brewer Street, W1S 0SP (7734 3040/www.madamejojos.com). Leicester Square or Piccadilly Circus tube. **Open** 8pm-3am Tue, Thur; 10pm-3am Wed, Fri; 7pm-3am Sat; 9.30pm-2am Sun. **Map** p114 B3 ❹❺

Virtually all those who sample this Soho stalwart love it. The sumptuous, slightly shabby red decor makes it stand out from the local crowd, and it spins several entertainment plates (cabaret, comedy and club). Saturday evening brings a riot of feathers and hen parties for Kitsch Cabaret, before the doors are thrown open for rockabilly and ska night Lost & Found. Other highlights include Keb Darge's Deep Funk, a worthy survivor of the capital's 1980s rare groove scene.

Pizza Express Jazz Club

10 Dean Street, W1D 3RW (club 7439 8722/restaurant 7437 9595/www.pizza express.co.uk). Tottenham Court Road tube. **Map** p114 B1 ❹❻

The upstairs restaurant is jazz-free, but the 120-capacity basement has become one of the most important modern jazz venues in Europe. It peaked a few years back, but you can still find excellent residencies from the likes of Scott Hamilton and Peter White, running the gamut through swing, mainstream, modern, contemporary and fusion.

Punk

14 Soho Street, W1D 3DN (7734 4004/ www.fabbars.com). Tottenham Court Road tube. **Open** 5pm-2am Mon-Wed; 5pm-3am Thur, Fri; 9pm-3am Sat. **Map** p114 C1 ❹❼

When regulars include Kate Moss, Lily Allen and Mark Ronson, it seems there's little this basement space can do wrong. It accommodates 270 at a squeeze, and the Mapplethorpe-style flower prints and Rock Galpin furniture suit the mix of high-heeled girls and indie mash-ups from the Queens of Noize at their fab Smash 'n' Grab parties on Thursdays.

Ronnie Scott's

47 Frith Street, W1D 4HT (7439 0747/ www.ronniescotts.co.uk). Leicester Square or Tottenham Court Road tube. **Map** p114 C2 ⓭

This legendary institution, opened by the saxophonist Ronnie Scott in 1959, was taken over in 2006 by a theatre impresario, who closed it down for a mammoth refit under the auspices of Parisian designer Jacques Garcia. They tarted up the furniture, moved the main bar, expanded capacity to 250 and revamped the kitchen. It looks good – and the food is rather better – but it's come at a cost. Shows are expensive and the 'jazz' definition got controversially loose (Alexander O'Neal? Craig David?). You'll still find lots of excellent jazz, though, including the Mingus Big Band, Wynton and Branford Marsalis, and Georgie Fame.

Shadow Lounge

5 Brewer Street, W1F 0RF (7287 7988/www.theshadowlounge.com). Piccadilly Circus tube. **Open** 10pm-3am Mon, Wed; 9pm-3am Tue, Thur-Sat. **Map** p114 B2 ⓭

For professional cocktail waiters, celebrity sightings, suits, cuties and fancy boots, this gay cocktail lounge is your venue. Expect to pay a hefty cover charge and to queue at weekends, but it's worth it once you're inside.

SIN

144 Charing Cross Road, WC2H 0LB. Tottenham Court Road tube. **Open** 10pm-4am Fri, Sat. **Map** p114 C1 ⓾

The new home of the still wonderful Popstarz (see box p122) hosts rockin' metal night Decadence & Disorder each Saturday (www.s8uk.com).

Candy Bar

Soho Revue Bar

11-12 Walkers Court, W1F 0ED (7734 0377/www.sohorevuebar.com). Piccadilly Circus tube. **Open** 8pm-3am Tue-Sun. **Map** p114 B3 ⓭

The Raymond Revue Bar was a 1960s cabaret club, notorious for its strip shows. Today, girls are still taking their clothes off, but in the much more middle-class guise of burlesque, at variety nights like Sunday's All That Jazz or the Hurly Girly Show on first Saturdays. The main room has tiered seating for gawping from, while a piano bar offers more intimate gigs upstairs. Drag queen du jour Jodie Harsh hosts the Friday night Circus, and Trannyshack encourages a mostly gay crowd to 'release the woman within' every Wednesday.

Arts & leisure

Curzon Soho

99 Shaftesbury Avenue, W1D 5DY (information 7292 1686/bookings 0870 756 4620/www.curzoncinemas.com). Leicester Square tube. **Map** p114 C2 ⓾

LONDON BY AREA

Chain me up

Alan Yau has shaped the way Londoners eat. A bold claim, but it's no exaggeration to say that the basement restaurant he opened in 1992, Wagamama (p146), completely shook up our ideas of oriental food, canteen dining and – of course – noodle dishes. After losing this first chain, Yau scored another major hit with Busaba Eathai (p145), then moved upmarket with Chinese fine dining at Hakkasan (p138) and all-day dim sum at Yauatcha (p120), both of which won Michelin stars. Still roaringly successful, both restaurants were sold in January 2008 – so what is Yau doing with the dosh?

Two very different things, as it happens. He has opened a superb and terribly posh spin on Japanese bar food, Sake no hana (p82), and, at the same time, laid the groundwork for **Cha Cha Moon**. Cha Cha Moon takes him back full circle to Wagamama: it's a noodle bar, but this time it's Yau's take on Hong Kong's wonderful mein dong (noodle stalls).

This time he may not have everything his own way. At the moment there are some other very serious culinary types also developing modern 'street food'. Urban Turban (p190) comes from Vineet Bhatia, a pioneer of haute Indian cuisine for 15 years, while Thai maestro David Thompson – Yau's collaborator in the development of Busaba – is planning to open the first of his planned Long Chim chain some time in 2008.
■ 15-21 Ganton Street, Soho, W1F 9BN (7297 9800).

All the cinemas in the Curzon group programme a superb range of shorts, rarities, double bills and mini-festivals, but the Curzon Soho is the best – not least because it also has a great ground-floor café and decent basement bar.

Odeon Leicester Square

Leicester Square, WC2H 7LQ (0871 224 4007/www.odeon.co.uk). Leicester Square tube. **Map** p114 C3 **⑤**
This art deco masterpiece is London's archetypal red-carpet star-studded site for premières. Catch one of the occasional silent movie screenings with live organ music if you possibly can; otherwise, get a comfy but pricey sight of a current blockbuster.

Prince Charles

7 Leicester Place, Leicester Square, WC2H 7BY (bookings 0870 811 2559/www.princecharlescinema.com). Leicester Square tube. **Map** p114 C3 **⑤**
The best value in town for releases that have ended their first run elsewhere. Watch good-quality screenings from raked seating that has perhaps seen a bit too much action during the popular weekend singalong sessions.

Prince Edward Theatre

28 Old Compton Street, W1D 4HS (0870 040 0046). Piccadilly Circus or Leicester Square tube. **Map** p114 C2 **⑤**
The London home for *Jersey Boys*, the story of Frankie Valli and the Four Seasons. The pace is lively, the sets gritty and the doo-wop standards ('Big Girls Don't Cry', 'Fallen Angel', 'Can't Take My Eyes Off You') superbly performed. Production subject to change.

Soho Theatre

21 Dean Street, W1D 3NE (7478 0100/box office 0870 429 6883/ www.sohotheatre.com). Tottenham Court Road tube. **Map** p114 C2 **⑤**
Its cool blue neon lights, front-of-house café and occasional late-night shows attract a younger, hipper crowd than most theatres. The Soho brings on aspiring writers through regular workshops, and has regular solo comedy shows and drag performances.

tkts

Clocktower Building, Leicester Square, WC2H 7NA (www.officiallondon theatre.co.uk). Leicester Square tube. **Open** 10am-7pm Mon-Sat; noon-3pm Sun. **Map** p114 C3 ⑤⑦

This non-profit organisation sells cut-price tickets for West End shows on a first come, first served basis on the day of performance. The branch at Canary Wharf DLR (platforms 4/5) opens 11.30am-6pm Mon-Sat.

Covent Garden

Covent Garden Market is sneered at by many locals for being touristy, but that's unfair. Sure the the Piazza gets overrun, but it is also a handsome galleried space with lots of outdoor restaurant seating, a few decent shops and no traffic. The street entertainment (quality-vetted but, yes, living statues make it through) takes place under the portico of **St Paul's** (the Actors' Church), which has a lovely garden. For proper boutiques, though, turn left out of the tube station away from the market. You're in the heart of theatreland, of course, and close to both of London's opera houses, but there's one treat that beats all others in our view: the wonderful, brand spanking new **London Transport Museum**.

Sights & museums

Benjamin Franklin House

36 Craven Street, WC2N 5NF (7925 1405/www.benjaminfranklinhouse.org). Charing Cross tube/rail. **Open** pre-book tours by phone or online. *Box office* 10.30am-5pm Wed-Sun. **Admission** £7; free-£5 reductions. **Map** p115 E5 ⑤⑧

The house where Franklin – scientist, diplomat, philosopher, inventor and Founding Father of the United States – lived between 1757 and 1775 was reopened as a centre for academic research on Franklin in 2006. The

public can explore it too through well-run, pre-booked tours that last a short but intense 45 minutes (at noon, 1pm, 2pm, 3.15pm, and 4.15pm Wed-Sun). These are led by an actress in character as Franklin's landlady, Margaret Stevenson, using projections and sound to conjure up the world and times in which Franklin lived.

London Transport Museum

NEW *The Piazza, WC2E 7BB (7379 6344/www.ltmuseum.co.uk). Covent Garden tube.* **Open** 10am-6pm Mon-Thur, Sat; 11am-9pm Fri. **Admission** £8; free-£6.50 reductions. **Map** p115 F3 ⑤⑨

Two years of the most thorough refurbishment since the museum moved to this magnificent old flower market building in 1980 have provided more display space, much easier chronological navigation, and a more confident focus on social history and design (a new gallery is dedicated to posters and such classics as the original Harry Beck tube map). The place is still a huge amount of fun: a climb-aboard replica of the first bus (Shillibeer's horse-drawn carriage from 1829) is just the first of an extraordinary array of vehicles – trams, buses, trains and tubes. The famous tube-driving simulator remains, but has been joined by a purpose-built, computerised exhibit called Connections, incorporating some 55,000 model buildings in its depiction of the countless individual journeys made throughout the city every day. **Event highlights** 'The Art of the Poster: Century of Design for London's Transport' (17 Oct 2008-Mar 2009).

Photographers' Gallery

5 & 8 Great Newport Street, WC2H 7HY (7831 1772/www.photonet.org.uk). Leicester Square tube. **Map** p115 D3 ⑥⓪

Home of the annual £30,000 Deutsche Börse Photography Prize, this gallery also hosts a diverse range of exhibitions, as well as running an excellent events programme. It occupies two almost adjacent spaces at the moment, but there are plans to relocate it to new premises in 2010.

LONDON BY AREA

St Paul's Covent Garden

St Paul's Covent Garden

Bedford Street, WC2E 9ED (7836 5221/www.actorschurch.org). Covent Garden or Leicester Square tube. **Open** 9am-4.30pm Mon-Fri; 9am-12.30pm Sun. **Admission** free. **Map** p115 E3 ⑥
Known as the Actors' Church for its association with Covent Garden's theatres, this magnificently spare building was designed by Inigo Jones in 1631. Actors commemorated on its walls range from those lost in obscurity – 'Pantopuck the Puppetman' – to those destined for immortality – Vivien Leigh and, yes, Boris Karloff. George Bernard Shaw set the first scene of *Pygmalion* under the church's rear portico, and the first known plague victim, Margaret Ponteous, is buried in the delicious churchyard outside.

Eating & drinking

Abeno Too

17-18 Great Newport Street, WC2H 7JE (7379 1160/www.abeno.co.uk). Leicester Square tube. **Open** noon-11pm Mon-Sat; noon-10.30pm Sun. **£**. **Japanese**. **Map** p115 D3 ⑥
Okonomiyaki is fun, cheap comfort food – ingredients are added to a batter that is cooked and combined with noodles on a table-top hotplate in front of you. There are also more familiar noodle dishes and desserts.

Bullet

3rd floor, Snow & Rock, 4 Mercer Street, WC2H 9QA (7836 4922/ www.bullet-coffee.com). Covent Garden tube/Charing Cross tube/rail. **Open** 10am-6pm daily. **£**. **Café**. **Map** p115 D2 ⑥
A jewel of a café, three flights of stairs up in a branch of outdoor specialists Snow & Rock. It's worth the climb for superb coffee and wonderful own-made cakes – and the location keeps it quiet.

Food for Thought

31 Neal Street, WC2H 9PR (7836 9072). Covent Garden tube. **Open** noon-8.30pm Mon-Sat; noon-5pm Sun. **£**. No credit cards. **Vegetarian**. **Map** p115 E2 ⑥
This long-standing veggie hotspot is always packed. Rainbow hippie trousers will still be spotted here, but so will couples and shop workers grabbing lunch. Unpretentious and reliable.

Gordon's

47 Villiers Street, WC2N 6NE (7930 1408/www.gordonswinebar.com). Embankment tube/Charing Cross tube/rail. **Open** 11am-11pm Mon-Sat; noon-10pm Sun. **Wine bar**. **Map** p115 E4 ⑥

A candelit warren of a wine bar (the oldest in London, established in 1890) where sherry is dispensed from the ageing barrels behind the bar. Atmospheric – and historic: Samuel Pepys lived here in the 1600s, and Rudyard Kipling had a room upstairs.

Great Queen Street

32 Great Queen Street, WC2B 5AA (7242 0622). Covent Garden or Holborn tube. **Open** 6-10.30pm Mon; noon-2.30pm, 6-10.30pm Tue-Sat. **££**. **British**. Map p115 F1 🇬🇧
Sister to the revered Anchor & Hope (p68), Great Queen Street shares the gastropub's buzzy lack of pretension, the pub-style room thrumming with bonhomie. Ranging from snacks to shared mains, the menu is designed to tempt and satisfy rather than educate or impress.

J Sheekey

28-32 St Martin's Court, WC2N 4AL (7240 2565/www.caprice-holdings. co.uk). Leicester Square tube. **Open** noon-3pm, 5.30pm-midnight Mon-Sat; noon-3.30pm, 6pm-midnight Sun. **£££**. **Fish**. Map p115 D3 🇬🇧
Behind mirrored windows, this favoured haunt of the well-known is intimate and as posh as a gentleman's club. The succession of little rooms, including a discreet bar, have black-and-white photos of theatre stars on the walls and are staffed by courteous and immaculately turned-out waiters. The menu offers stupendous fish and seafood platters, and a few meat and vegetarian dishes, all prepared with flair. Booking essential.

Lamb & Flag

33 Rose Street, WC2E 9EB (7497 9504). Covent Garden tube. **Open** 11am-11pm Mon-Sat; noon-10.30pm Sun. **Pub**. Map p115 E3 🇬🇧
A glance up Rose Street from Garrick Street after dark reveals a black street lantern throwing its light on to the frontage of the shamelessly traditional Lamb & Flag, Covent Garden's best pub. This pub wears its history on its sleeve, proudly displaying its classic

boozer credentials of real ale and local memorabilia that adorn the walls. Jazz sessions liven up Sunday evenings.

L'Atelier de Joël Robuchon

13-15 West Street, WC2H 9NE (7010 8600/www.joel-robuchon.com). Leicester Square tube. **Open** *Restaurant* noon-2.30pm, 5.30-10.30pm daily. *Bar* 2pm-2am Mon-Sat; 2-10.30pm Sun. **££££**. **Modern European**. Map p115 D2 🇬🇧
The London branch of French chef Joël Robuchon's international chain of high-concept brasseries is a three-floor extravaganza. Pools of darkness are illuminated by bright spots of colour in the otherwise all-black open kitchen. You can't book after 7pm for the ground level, but you can for the lighter, brighter first floor. The food is terrific – fun and imaginative – but not cheap.

Lowlander

36 Drury Lane, WC2B 5RR (7379 7446/www.lowlander.com). Covent Garden or Holborn tube. **Open** 9.30am-11pm Mon-Fri; 10am-11.30pm Sat; 10am-10.30pm Sun. **££**. **Beer café**. Map p115 E2 🇬🇧
Choose from the finest Dutch and Belgian beers at Lowlander, a treat for hop-lovers. No fewer than 15 tall, gleaming chrome beer taps are lined up on the bar, offering pilsners, blondes, wheat beers, red and dark ales, fruit beers and miscellaneous speciality beers; there are also more than 40 bottled options.

Masala Zone

48-51 Floral Street, WC2E 9DS (7379 0101/www.masalazone.com). Covent Garden tube. **Open** noon-11pm Mon-Sat; noon-10.30pm Sun. **£**. **Indian**. Map p115 E2 🇬🇧
The latest in a rapidly expanding chain. Ceiling-hung Rajasthani puppets shout 'north Indian', but the menu is a round-up of adventurous fast food from every region. The place is hugely popular, with (thankfully fast-moving) queues during busy times. Seating is comfortable, with secluded booths for private conversation.

Oops Restaurante & Vinateria

31 Catherine Street, WC2B 5JS (7836 3609). Covent Garden tube. **Open** noon-11pm Mon-Sat. **££**. **Tapas**. **Map** p115 F3 ⑫

This is a demure little place, with dark wood and tasteful artwork. Most of the dishes are similarly restrained, creating good, old-fashioned tapas with fresh ingredients – but there's an occasional nod to modern Spanish techniques, as with the blue cheese ice-cream.

Princess Louise

NEW *208-209 High Holborn, WC1V 7BW (7405 8816). Holborn tube.* **Open** 11am-11pm Mon-Fri; noon-11pm Sat; noon-10.30pm Sun. **Pub**. **Map** p115 F1 ⑬

In 1997, this grandiose Grade II-listed Victorian gin palace was bought by Yorkshire-based Samuel Smith Brewery, which has now restored it to its gleaming, flamboyant glory. Decorated tiles, stained-glass windows, finely cut mirrors and ornate plasterwork all got a polish, while Victorian partitions were reintroduced to create a dark-wooded warren of snugs and alcoves. The upstairs bar serves unambitious pub grub and the beer is solely from Samuel Smith. The place gets crowded, so avoid peak hours.

Rock & Sole Plaice

47 Endell Street, WC2H 9AJ (7836 3785/www.rockandsoleplaice.com). Covent Garden tube. **Open** 11.30am-11pm Mon-Sat; noon-10pm Sun. **£**. **Fish & chips**. **Map** p115 D1 ⑭

A sociable and busy little chippie in a handy location. The fish and chips are done well and in generous sizes. It's a great spot for alfresco dining in summer, under fairy lights and geraniums.

Scoop

40 Shorts Gardens, WC2H 9AB (7240 7086/www.scoopgelato.com). Covent Garden tube. **Open** 9am-11.30pm daily. **Ice-cream**. **Map** p115 E2 ⑮

We like every flavour at this ice-cream parlour, with the dozen or so options often including something new – fig

and ricotta wowed us recently. Sorbets and dairy-free ices cater to those on special diets, and pastries are sold too.

Wahaca

NEW *66 Chandos Place, WC2N 4HG (7240 1883/www.wahaca.co.uk). Covent Garden or Leicester Square tube.* **Open** noon-11.30pm daily. **£**. **Mexican & Tex-Mex**. **Map** p115 E3 ⑯

With its impressive lime and yellow interior and quirky menu, this Latino venue is keen to show that Mexican cuisine can be cool and stylish. Successes include the 'street food selection', but it's a shame there are no escabeches or stews. Awful acoustics make it noisy; and with no bookings except for groups of eight or more, be prepared to wait.

Shopping

Benjamin Pollock's Toyshop

44 The Market, WC2E 8RF (7379 7866/www.pollocks-coventgarden.co.uk). Covent Garden tube. **Open** 10.30am-6pm Mon-Sat; 11am-4pm Sun. **Map** p115 E3 ⑰

Best known for its toy theatres (from £2.95 for a tiny one in a matchbox), Pollock's is also superb for traditional toys, such as knitted animals, china tea sets, masks, glove puppets, cards, spinning tops and fortune-telling fish.

Cadenhead's Covent Garden Whisky Shop

3 Russell Street, WC2B 5JD (7379 4640/www.coventgardenwhiskyshop. co.uk). Covent Garden tube. **Open** 11am-6.30pm Mon-Sat; noon-4.30pm Sun. **Map** p115 F2 ⑱

Cadenhead's is a survivor of a rare breed: the independent whisky bottler. It selects barrels from distilleries all over Scotland and bottles them without filtration or any other intervention.

Coco de Mer

23 Monmouth Street, WC2H 9DD (7836 8882/www.coco-de-mer.co.uk). Covent Garden tube. **Open** 11am-7pm Mon-Wed, Fri, Sat; 11am-8pm Thur; noon-6pm Sun. **Map** p115 D2 ⑲

London's most glamorous erotic emporium sells books, lingerie and toys such as glass dildos that double as objets d'art. Peepshow-style changing rooms allow your lover to watch you undress from a 'confession box' next door.

Covent Garden Market

Between King Street & Henrietta Street, WC2E 8RF (0870 780 5001/ www.coventgardenmarket.co.uk). Covent Garden, Embankment or Temple tube/Charing Cross tube/rail. **Open** 10am-8pm Mon-Sat; 11am-6pm Sun. **Map** p115 E3 ❸⓪

The lovely colonnaded 19th-century building of the covered market has two halls that connect two piazzas, where buskers continue to steadily draw the crowds, but the place is too commercial and crowded to provide shopping of much character. The individual stalls selling crafts and jewellery in the Apple Market are of more interest.

Koh Samui

65-67 Monmouth Street, WC2H 9DG (7240 4280/www.kohsamui.co.uk). Covent Garden tube. **Open** 10.30am-6.30pm Mon-Wed, Fri, Sat; 10.30am-7pm Thur; noon-5.30pm Sun. **Map** p115 D2 ❽①

Vintage pieces sourced from around the world share rail space with a finely tuned selection of heavyweights at Koh Samui, resulting in a delightfully eclectic mix of stock. Marc by Marc Jacobs, Balenciaga and Dries Van Noten are always well represented, alongside small independent labels. Jewellery is by a global array of independent designers.

Neal's Yard Dairy

17 Shorts Gardens, WC2H 9UP (7240 5700/www.nealsyarddairy.co.uk). Covent Garden tube. **Open** 11am-6.30pm Mon-Thur; 10am-6.30pm Fri, Sat.* **Map** p115 D2 ❽②

Neal's Yard buys from small farms and creameries and matures the cheeses in its own cellars until ready to sell in peak condition. Names such as Stinking Bishop and Lincolnshire Poacher are as evocative as the aromas in the shop. The well-trained staff provide free samples.

Poste Mistress

61-63 Monmouth Street, WC2H 9EP (7379 4040/www.officeholdings.co.uk). Covent Garden tube. **Open** 10am-7pm Mon-Wed, Fri, Sat; 10am-8pm Thur; 11.30am-6pm Sun. **Map** p115 D2 ❻❸

The 1970s boudoir decor at this shop make a suitably glam backdrop for a line-up of high-fashion footwear, plus its own designer-look label. Lulu Guinness bags and other accessories are also sold.

Rokit

42 Shelton Street, WC2 9HZ (7836 6547/www.rokit.co.uk). Covent Garden tube. **Open** 10am-7pm Mon-Sat; 11am-6pm Sun. **Map** p115 D2 ❻❹

With four locations, Rokit has come a long way since its humble Camden beginnings. This flagship has the most comprehensive selection of second-hand items, such as tutus and military wear, cowboy boots and sunglasses. Check out the live DJ sets and window performances. Classic vintage homeware too.

Slam City Skates

16 Neal's Yard, WC2H 9DP (7240 0928/www.slamcity.com). Covent Garden tube. **Open** 10am-6.30pm Mon-Sat; noon-5pm Sun. **Map** p115 D2 ❻❺

Slam City is run by friendly skaters who love their art and know their stuff. The generous range of boards, clothing and accessories includes Vans and Etnies.

Stanfords

12-14 Long Acre, WC2E 9LP (7836 1321/www.stanfords.co.uk). Covent Garden or Leicester Square tube. **Open** 9am-7.30pm Mon, Wed, Fri; 9.30am-7.30pm Tue; 9am-8pm Thur; 10am-7pm Sat; noon-6pm Sun. **Map** p115 D3 ❻❻

Three floors of travel guides, travel literature, maps and language guides. The basement houses British Ordnance Survey maps, and you can plan your next trip over coffee in the new café.

Nightlife

The **Arts Theatre** (p132) programmes lots of comedy, both in the main auditorium and downstairs for Amused Moose.

End & AKA

*18 West Central Street, WC1A 1JJ
(7419 9199/www.endclub.com). Holborn
or Tottenham Court Road tube.* **Open**
10pm-3am Mon, Wed; 10pm-4am Thur;
10pm-5am Fri; 10pm-7am Sat; varies
Tue, Sun. **Map** p115 E1 **⑧**
The End is still mining the rich seams
of electronic music after 13 years.
Recent additions to the roster include
Groove Armada's Lovebox party,
grime and dubstep night FWD, Buzzin'
Fly's slice of deep house and the ace
mash 'n' mosh night Durr. Upstairs, the
bricks and steel AKA bar gets its fair
share of house jamborees.

Island

NEW *Hungerford Lane, WC2N 6NG
(7389 6622/www.theisland-london.
com). Charing Cross tube/rail.* **Open**
10pm-6am Fri, Sat. **Map** p115 E4 **⑧**
Fancy splashing your cash? Gorgeous
to a fault – all bare brick walls, slick
1970s wallpaper and cream sofas – this
new West End grown-ups' playground
is just around the corner from iconic
rave and gay venue Heaven. It's syn-
chronicity at work, with star DJs such
as Danny Rampling and John Digweed
lining up to play Friday nights here.

12 Bar Club

*22-23 Denmark Place, WC2H 8NL
(office 7240 2120/box office 7240
2622/www.12barclub.com). Tottenham
Court Road tube.* **Map** p115 D1 **⑧**
This minuscule and much-cherished
hole-in-the-wall books a real grab-bag
of stuff. Its size (audiences of around
100 people and a stage barely big
enough for three performers) dictates a
predominance of singer-songwriters,
but that doesn't stop the occasional full
band from trying their luck.

Victory

NEW *55 New Oxford Street, WC1A
1BS (7240 0700/www.clubvictory.com).
Tottenham Court Road tube.* **Open**
8pm-4am Fri; 9pm-4am Sat. **Map**
p115 D1 **⑨**
This former underground car park has
been turned into a Victorian high-street
film set. Friday nights see the ultra-

decadent Chopin Scores; there's a dress-
up room for post-work transformations,
a library sitting room, street performers, burlesque girls and lashings of fun.
We're looking forward to the daytime
fashion market for new designers.

Arts & leisure

Arts Theatre

*6 Great Newport Street, WC2H 7JB
(information 7836 2132/www.arts
theatrelondon.com). Leicester Square
tube.* **Map** p115 D3 **⑨**
The Arts stages an adventurous range
of plays, from an Islamic take on *The
Tempest* to *Moths Ate My Doctor
Who Scarf*. In addition to theatre, the
main auditorium hosts one-man comedy shows from the likes of Reginald D
Hunter and Sean Hughes, while downstairs hosts a regular comedy club.

Coliseum

*St Martin's Lane, WC2N 4ES (box
office 0871 911 0200/www.eno.org).
Leicester Square tube/Charing Cross
tube/rail.* **Map** p115 D4 **⑨**
The Coliseum's 2,350-seat auditorium
was restored to its former glory in
2004. Now all the English National
Opera needs is a similarly impressive
programme. Under Edward Gardner,
ex-Glyndebourne, this may happen.
Event highlights 'Riders to the Sea' by
Vaughn Williams, directed by Fiona
Shaw (27-30 Nov 2008).

Donmar Warehouse

*41 Earlham Street, WC2H 9LX (0870
060 6624/www.donmarwarehouse.
com). Covent Garden or Leicester
Square tube.* **Map** p115 E2 **⑨**
The Donmar is less a warehouse than
an intimate chamber. Artistic director
Michael Grandage has kept the venue
on a fresh, intelligent path – helped by
regular celebrity casting scoops – and
will be running a terrific-sounding dual
season at Wyndham's (p135).

Gielgud Theatre

NEW *Shaftesbury Avenue, W1D 6AR
(0870 040 0046). Piccadilly Circus
tube.* **Map** p115 C3 **⑨**

The face behind the label

'I left school at 16 without any GCSEs to pursue the life of a skateboarder.' Meet Toby Shuall (pictured), ex-pro skateboarder and artist, whose clothing label Suburban Bliss has been making waves among skateboarders and hipster bloggers worldwide.

Shuall started the label while working at Slam City Skates (p131), which also sponsored him – until his hobby took its toll. 'I was totally fucked from skating: I had four surgeries and had to accept that I wasn't going to be able to do it every day,' he explains. With no formal training, he borrowed £400 and started printing T-shirts.

Two years on, he gets regular contributions from fellow skating artists and people like Fergadelic, who runs his own T-shirt label, Tonite – also beloved of blogs like www.slamxhype.com and www.hypediss.com. Shuall's own designs range from neon prints of legendary musicians to intricately depicted psychedelic nightmares, inspired by drawings by Ross Noble and comix master Robert Crumb. 'I wanted to put art on to T-shirts. Everything I do I want to look like it could be a screen-printed poster and not just clothing,' he says.

The label is stocked online and in boutiques like Bread & Honey (p166), the Three Threads (p166) and, of course, Slam. But Shuall is keen for it not to be classed as a skating brand and is disdainful of large streetwear labels jumping on the bandwagon: 'They try to use it to market their clothing. I'm from that culture and I've never done a T-shirt with a skateboarder on it', he points out. Next up are all-over-print hooded tops and raglan sweat-shirts. 'I'm a homegrown, small, independent label and I have no backer,' he says. 'There aren't many people in this game who can say that.'

■ www.suburbanbliss.co.uk

Royal Opera House

Yasmina Reza struck box office gold a decade ago with *Art*, which explains the stellar cast (Ken Stott, Janet McTeer, Ralph Fiennes, Tamsin Greig) attracted to her new satire *God of Carnage*. Two couples of bourgeois hypocrites gather for a civilised coffee, but all of them are tiptoeing around the fact that one set's youngster recently broke the other's son's face. The production is a pleasure, the acting superb. Subject to change.

Noël Coward Theatre

St Martin's Lane, WC2N 4BW (0870 850 9175/www.avenueqthemusical. co.uk). Leicester Square tube. **Map** p115 D3 ⑨⑤

The current hit here is Muppet-fest *Avenue Q*, in which the puppet and human residents of a down-at-heel New York street share amusing songs and a cynical sense of humour. Production subject to change.

Novello Theatre

NEW *Aldwych, WC2B 4LD (0870 040 0046). Covent Garden or Holborn tube.* **Map** p115 F3 ⑨⑥

Urban fairytale *Into the Hoods* has already been a hit at the Edinburgh Fringe Festival – and as we went to press was proving so popular that its West End run had been extended. It's a quick-witted, large-spirited treatment of a Sondheim original, presented by a hip hop dance-theatre company.

Royal Opera House

Royal Opera House, WC2E 9DD (7304 4000/www.roh.org.uk). Covent Garden tube. **Map** p115 E2 ⑨⑦

While the ENO has spent the last few years being bashed from pillar to post by critics, staff at the ROH have been keeping their heads down, grateful to be out of the spotlight for a change. The ROH has quietly resumed its position as one of the greatest opera houses in the world. A massive renovation in 2000 gave the largely traditional productions the setting they deserve: the discreetly air-conditioned auditorium and comfortable seating (capacity 2,250) make a night here an appetising prospect, whatever the performance. Book ahead to enjoy one of the behind-the-scenes tours.

Event highlights Bryn Terfel in 'Der Fliegende Holländer' (winter 2008/9); double anniversary of Purcell and Handel (spring 2008/9).

Shaftesbury Theatre

210 Shaftesbury Avenue, WC2H 8DP (0870 040 0046). Tottenham Court Road tube. **Map** p115 D1 ❾❽

Hairspray may be brainless pleasure, but its heart is triumphantly in the right place. Its butt is in the right place too, thanks to glorious choreography. Loveably chubby heroine Tracy Turnblad (victim of her school's anti-fat bimbos) teams up with black kids from Special Ed to overthrow 1960s racial prejudice and fulfil her dreams. Production subject to change.

Wyndham's Theatre

NEW *Charing Cross Road, WC2H 0DA (0870 060 6633). Leicester Square tube.* **Map** p115 D3 ❾❾

From September 2008, Michael Grandage (redoubtable artistic director of the Donmar, p132) takes over Wyndham's for a year. He's hoping to keep quality high and prices relatively low. The 2008-09 season boasts Derek Jacobi as Malvolio in *Twelfth Night,* and *Hamlet*, directed by Kenneth Branagh and starring Jude Law.

Fitzrovia

Fitzrovia, west of Tottenham Court Road, has an enviable reputation as a gathering point for radicals, writers, bohemians and boozers – mostly in reverse order. These days, though, most current residents are wealthy media companies, drawn by some of the capital's hippest restaurants and hotels, especially around strollable Charlotte Street. You'll note that we don't list any of the traditional boozers – the **Green Man** or **Bradley's** will prove more satisfying than the Wheatsheaf or Fitzroy Tavern to all but the most nostalgically bibulous (the truly nostalgic can always dress up for **Bourne & Hollingsworth**) – and

we regret to say that the shops on **Warren Street** have more to say about modern Fitzrovia than a Dylan Thomas biography.

Sights & museums

BBC Broadcasting House

Portland Place, Upper Regent Street, W1A 1AA (0870 603 0304/www.bbc. co.uk/tours). Oxford Circus tube. **Map** p136 A4 ❶

See box p141.

Pollock's Toy Museum

1 Scala Street (entrance on Whitfield Street), W1T 2HL (7636 3452/ www.pollockstoymuseum.com). Goodge Street tube. **Open** 10am-5pm Mon-Sat. **Admission** £3; £1.50-£2 reductions; free under-3s. No credit cards. **Map** p136 C4 ❷

Pollock's is named after Benjamin Pollock, the last of the Victorian toy theatre printers. By turns beguiling and creepy, the museum is a nostalgia-fest of old board games, tin trains and porcelain dolls. It's fascinating for adults but less so for children, for whom the displays may seem a bit static.

Eating & drinking

Bourne & Hollingsworth

NEW *28 Rathbone Place, W1T 1JF (7636 8228/www.bourneand hollingsworth.com). Goodge Street or Tottenham Court Road tube.* **Open** 5pm-midnight Mon-Thur; 5pm-12.30am Fri, Sat. **Bar**. **Map** p136 C4 ❸

Not so much a bar as a reproduction of your granny's sitting room, B&H isn't easy to find (walk down some steps at the junction of Percy and Rathbone Streets), but it's worth the effort. On Tuesdays, bands entertain cool, young boozers; the rest of the week, it's hip pop. The cocktails are good, the prices even better. Friendly atmosphere too.

Bradley's Spanish Bar

42-44 Hanway Street, W1T 1UT (7636 0359). Tottenham Court Road tube. **Open** noon-11pm Mon-Sat; 3-10.30pm Sun. **Pub**. **Map** p136 C4 ❹

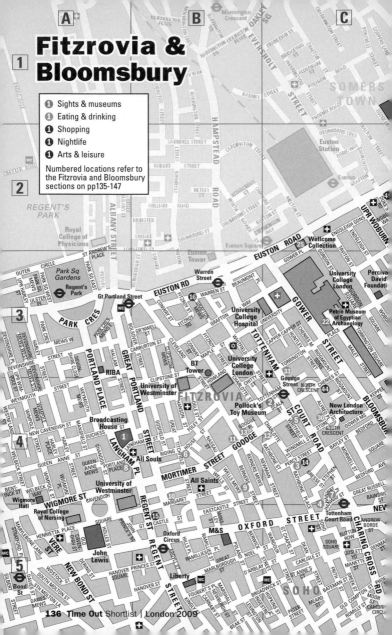

Fitzrovia & Bloomsbury

- ❶ Sights & museums
- ❶ Eating & drinking
- ❶ Shopping
- ❶ Nightlife
- ❶ Arts & leisure

Numbered locations refer to the Fitzrovia and Bloomsbury sections on pp135-147

This much-loved institution remains a fine place in which to spend a gloomy winter afternoon (tucked into a dark corner of the scruffy downstairs bar) or summery evening (when everyone spills out on to the street).

Crazy Bear

26-28 Whitfield Street, W1T 2RG (7631 0088/www.crazybeargroup. co.uk). Goodge Street tube. **Open** noon-10.45pm Mon-Fri; 6-10.45pm Sat. **£££. Cocktail bar/dim sum.** Map p136 C4 ⑤
You may have trouble finding the virtually unmarked building, but you'll have no problem finding the cowhide bar stools, red padded alcoves or low leather armchairs in the downstairs bar. Fine dim sum keep hunger pangs at bay. There's a restaurant upstairs too.

Green Man

NEW *36 Riding House Street, W1W 7ES (7307 9981). Goodge Street or Oxford Circus tube.* **Open** noon-11pm Mon-Sat; noon-10.30pm Sun. **Cider pub.** Map p136 B4 ⑥
This is one pub where modernisation has worked. The Green Man's USP is draught ciders – plus several in bottles, a couple of ales and ice-cold Sierra Nevada on tap. It's all aided by matey staff and a busy yet not noisy vibe.

Hakkasan

8 Hanway Place, W1T 1HD (7907 1888). Tottenham Court Road tube. **Open** noon-12.30am Mon-Wed; noon-1.30am Thur-Sat; noon-midnight Sun. **££££. Chinese.** Map p136 C4 ⑦
Hakkasan whisks customers off a horrible alley into a Narnia of other-worldliness. Suddenly, you find yourself in a moody 1930s Shanghai-style basement dining room, a three-dimensional Chinese woodcut of intimate, interlocking booths, a super setting for sophisticated Chinese-inspired food. Cocktails are the stuff of Asian-influenced fantasy and DJs are on hand from 9pm daily.

Landau

NEW *Langham, Portland Place, W1B 1JA (7965 0165/www.thelandau.com). Oxford Circus tube.* **Open** 7-10.30am, 12.30-2.30pm, 5.30-11pm Mon-Fri; 7-11am, 12.30-2.30pm, 5.30-11pm Sat; 7-11am, 12.30-2.30pm, 5.30-10pm Sun. *Afternoon tea* 3-5.30pm daily. **££££. Modern European.** Map p136 A4 ⑧
Past the greetings man in a bowler hat at the top of the sweeping entrance steps, the Landau's dining room feels exclusive and privileged. A grazing menu allows you to try appetiser-sized portions, a succession of titillating titbits presented in exquisite fashion – perhaps the soft-boiled quail egg with truffle, which is served with a little saucepan of pumpkin soup to pour over it. The à la carte is a lot less busy, but also displays surprising flavours, and the service is delightful.

Long Bar

Sanderson, 50 Berners Street, W1T 3NG (7300 1400/www.sanderson london.com). Oxford Circus or Tottenham Court Road tube. **Open** 11.30am-2am Mon-Wed; 11.30am-3am Fri, Sat; noon-10.30pm Sun. **Cocktail bar.** Map p136 B4 ⑨
The Long Bar's celebrity days have faded, but there's still easy glamour for the taking. The long bar in question is a thin onyx affair, though nabbing one of the eyeball-backed stools is an unlikely prospect. A better bet is the lovely courtyard, where table service, candlelight and watery features make a much nicer setting for cocktails. Bar snacks are priced high.

Match Bar

37-38 Margaret Street, W1G 0JF (7499 3443/www.matchbar.com). Oxford Circus tube. **Open** 11am-midnight Mon-Fri; noon-midnight Sat; 4-10.30pm Sun. **Cocktail bar.** Map p136 B4 ⑩
London's Match cocktail bars celebrate the craft of the bartender with a selection of authentic concoctions, such as juleps and fizzes, made from high-end liquor. DJs spin from 7.30pm Thur-Sat.

Ooze

62 Goodge Street, W1T 4NE (7436 9444/www.ooze.biz). Goodge Street tube. **Open** noon-11pm Mon-Sat. **£. Risotto café.** Map p136 B4 ⑪

Crazy Bear

Ooze's dining room is clean, bright and white, with the odd dash of colour. More colourful still are the dozen or so risotto – comfort food, at comfy prices.

Roka

37 Charlotte Street, W1T 1RR (7580 6464/www.rokarestaurant.com). Goodge Street or Tottenham Court Road tube. **Open** noon-3.30pm, 5.30-11.30pm Mon-Fri; 12.30-3.30pm, 5.30-11.30pm Sat; 5.30-10.30pm Sun. **£££**. **Japanese**. Map p136 C4 ⑫
Everything about Roka, sibling of Zuma (p89), is enticing, not least the aroma of wood burning at the centrepiece grill. The food – a modern take on Japanese cuisine – might rock your budget, but it will rock your taste buds too. The basement Shochu Lounge is half 21st-century style bar, half feudal Japan.

Salt Yard

54 Goode Street, W1T 4NA (7637 0657/www.saltyard.co.uk). Goodge Street tube. **Open** noon-11pm Mon-Fri; 5-11pm Sat. **££**. **Spanish-Italian tapas**. Map p136 B4 ⑬
The Spanish Italian cooking at this classy restaurant is unique in London.

The seasonal menu resembles traditional tapas in spirit, with unfussy recipes allowing the quality of the ingredients to tell; in its detail, the choice is fascinating. Signature dishes include fried courgette flowers stuffed with Spanish cheese, and confit of pork belly with cannellini beans. The only problem? Getting a table.

Shopping

Contemporary Applied Arts

2 Percy Street, W1T 1DD (7436 2344/www.caa.org.uk). Goodge Street or Tottenham Court Road tube. **Open** 10am-5.30pm Mon-Sat. Map p136 C4 ⑭
This airy gallery, run by the charitable arts organisation, represents more than 300 makers. Work embraces the functional – jewellery, tableware, textiles – as well as unique, purely decorative pieces. The ground floor hosts exhibitions by individual artists, or themed by craft, while in the basement shop are pieces for all pockets. Glass is always exceptional here.

LONDON BY AREA

Reiss

172 Regent Street, W1B 4JH (7637 9112/www.reiss.co.uk). Oxford Circus tube. **Open** 10am-7pm Mon-Wed, Fri, Sat; 10am-8pm Thur; noon-6pm Sun. **Map** p136 B5 **⑮**

This chain of stores sits somewhere between high street and high-end, delivering quality mens- and womenswear aimed at the mid-20s to mid-30s market. The womenswear has a designer air, a look that is youthful yet classy. The chic, unfussy dresses are usually key each season, although other strengths include footwear and coats. Menswear covers most basics – from suits to chunky knitwear.

Warren Street

Warren Street tube. **Map** p136 B3 **⑯**

A nondescript little shopping enclave, but with stand-out stores like shoe shop Black Truffle (no.52, 7388 4547, www.blacktruffle.com), which stocks Chie Mihara and Eley Kishimoto, and upbeat Thorsten van Elten (no.22, 7388 8008, www.thorstenvanelten.com), selling clocks and coat hangers from the best young British designers. French's Theatre Bookshop (52 Fitzroy Street, 7255 4300, www.samuelfrench-london.co.uk) provides a little gravitas, and beautiful old royal blue tiles make the former Evans Dairy, on the Conway Street corner, characterful for a snack.

Thorsten Van Elten

Bloomsbury

Bloomsbury's gracious squares can feel a little sterile – not even the area's literary heritage, counting Dickens, Poe, Yeats and the Woolf coterie among its former residents, does much for the district. It does still feel like the academic centre of London, though, with its hospitals, museums (the **British Museum** prime among them) and libraries (the **British Library**). We extend a hearty welcome to **St Pancras International**, albeit one with reservations, and are still loving the **Wellcome Collection**. But

Bloomsbury is still an area that demands an idle browse: perhaps for books on Marchmont Street or Woburn Walk, maybe among the lovely eateries and shops of **Lamb's Conduit Street**.

Sights & museums

British Library

96 Euston Road, NW1 2DB (7412 7332/www.bl.uk). Euston or King's Cross tube/rail. **Open** 9.30am-6pm Mon, Wed-Fri; 9.30am-8pm Tue; 9.30am-5pm Sat; 11am-5pm Sun. **Admission** free. **Map** p137 D2 **⑰**

'One of the ugliest buildings in the world,' opined a Parliamentary committee on the opening of the new British Library in 1997. But don't judge a book by its cover: the interior is a model of cool, spacious functionality, and the reading rooms are a joy to use (although only open to card holders). This is one of the greatest libraries in the world, with holdings of over 150 million items. It receives a copy of every new publication produced in the UK and Ireland, from the daily papers to the most obscure academic treatises. In the John Ritblat Gallery, the library's main treasures are displayed: the Magna Carta, the Lindisfarne Gospels and original manuscripts from Chaucer, as well as Beatles lyrics. The focal point of the building is the King's Library, a six-storey glass-walled tower housing George III's collection. The temporary exhibitions are often superb.

Event highlights 'Taking Liberties: The Struggle for British Freedoms & Rights' (31 Oct 2008-1 Mar 2009); 'Henry VIII' (17 Apr-6 Sept 2009).

British Museum

Great Russell Street, WC1B 3DG (7323 8000/recorded information 7323 8783/ www.thebritishmuseum.ac.uk). Russell Square or Tottenham Court Road tube. **Open** 10am-5.30pm Mon-Wed, Sat, Sun; 10am-8.30pm Thur, Fri. *Great Court* 9am-6pm Mon-Wed, Sun; 9am-11pm Thur-Sat. **Admission** free. *Highlights tours* £8; £5 reductions. *Eye opener tours* free. No credit cards. **Map** p137 D4 🔞

Officially London's most popular tourist attraction, the British Museum is a neoclassical marvel built in 1847 by Robert Smirke, one of the pioneers of the Greek Revival style. As impressive is Lord Norman Foster's glass-roofed Great Court, opened in 2000 and now claimed to be 'the largest covered public square in Europe'. This £100m landmark surrounds the domed Reading Room (used by the British Library until its move to King's Cross), where Marx, Lenin, Dickens, Darwin, Hardy and Yeats once worked. Star exhibits of the museum include ancient Egyptian artefacts – the Rosetta Stone on the ground floor, mummies upstairs – and Greek antiquities including the marble freizes from the Parthenon known as the Elgin Marbles. The Celts gallery has the Lindow Man, killed in 300 BC and preserved in peat. The Wellcome Gallery of Ethnography holds an Easter Island statue and regalia from Captain Cook's travels.

Meet the Beeb

If you want to find someone who still considers the British Broadcasting Corporation to represent all the virtues of public broadcasting, you're best off looking elsewhere than its home country – funding cuts and relentless accusations of 'dumbing down' have left its reputation rather tarnished. But from May 2008, nostalgists and optimists have been able to join a weekly tour round the BBC's headquarters, Britain's first purpose-built broadcast centre (p135), completed in 1932. There are nine tours each Sunday (£6.50; £4.50-£5.50 reductions; £15 family); booking ahead is essential.

The tours highlight such lovely surviving details as the original mosaic floor that is in the main reception area and, on the building's façade, Eric Gill's sculptures of Prospero and Ariel, from Shakespeare's *The Tempest*. Gill used airy sprite Ariel to represent broadcasting, which might leave Ariel's wizard master Prospero, about to 'abjure' his magic, a troubling symbol for the Beeb itself.

Also included in the tour are a look round the newly restored Radio Theatre, home to comedy shows *The Goons* (now defunct) and the indefatigable, 30-year-old *The News Quiz*; the Council Chamber, where BBC Governors' and Board meetings took place; and the new digital radio studios where Radio 3 and Radio 4 are still recorded.

■ www.bbc.co.uk/tours

he King's Library, which opened in 2004, is the finest neoclassical space in London, and home to a permanent exhibition, 'Enlightenment: Discovering the World in the 18th Century', a 5,000-piece collection devoted to the formative period of the museum. The remit covers physics, archaeology and the natural world, with objects such as Indonesian puppets and a beautiful orrery.

You can't see it all in one day, so buy a guide and pick out the showstoppers, or plan several trips. Highlights tours focus on specific aspects of the collection; Eye opener tours offer introductions to world cultures.

Event highlights 'Babylon' (13 Nov 2008-15 May 2009).

Cartoon Museum

35 Little Russell Street, WC1N 2HH (7580 8155/www.cartoonmuseum.org). Tottenham Court Road tube. **Open** 10.30am-5.30pm Tue-Sat; noon-5.30pm Sun. **Admission** £4; free-£3 reductions. No credit cards. **Map** p137 D4 ⑲
The ground floor of this transformed former cartoon dairy displays the best in British cartoon art in chronological order, starting with the early 18th century. From Hogarth it moves through Britain's cartooning 'golden age' (1770-1830) to examples of wartime cartoons, ending up with modern satirists such as Gerald Scarfe and the wonderfully loopy Ralph Steadman. Upstairs is a celebration of UK comic art, with original 1921 Rupert the Bear artwork, Dan Dare, the Bash Street Kids and a painted Asterix cover by that well-known Brit Albert Uderzo.

Charles Dickens Museum

48 Doughty Street, WC1N 2LX (7405 2127/www.dickensmuseum. com). Chancery Lane or Russell Square tube. **Open** 10am-5pm Mon-Sat; 11am-5pm Sun. **Admission** £6; £3-£5 reductions; £14 family. No credit cards. **Map** p137 E3 ⑳
Of the many London homes of the peripatetic Charles Dickens, this is the only one that is still standing. Dickens lived here for three years between 1837 and 1840, during which time he wrote *Nicholas Nickleby* and *Oliver Twist.*

Ring the doorbell to gain access to four floors of Dickensiana, from posters advertising his public speaking to personal letters, manuscripts and his writing desk, exhibited in rooms decorated as they would have been when he lived here. There were minor refurbishments to the museum in spring 2008.

Foundling Museum

40 Brunswick Square, WC1N 1AZ (7841 3600/www.foundlingmuseum. org.uk). Russell Square tube. **Open** 10am-6pm Tue-Sat; noon-6pm Sun. **Admission** £5; free-£4 reductions. **Map** p137 D3 ㉑
This museum recalls the social history of the Foundling Hospital, set up in 1739 by a compassionate shipwright and sailor, Captain Thomas Coram. Returning to England from America in 1720, he was appalled by the number of abandoned children on the streets. Securing royal patronage, he persuaded the artist William Hogarth and the composer GF Handel to become governors; Hogarth decreed the building should

British Museum p141

become the first public art gallery, and artists including Gainsborough and Reynolds donated work. The museum uses pictures, manuscripts and objects to recount the social changes of the period. There are also temporary exhibitions and a monthly programme of classical and early music concerts.

Petrie Museum of Egyptian Archaeology

University College London, Malet Place, WC1E 6BT (7679 2884/www.petrie. ucl.ac.uk). Euston Square, Goodge Street or Warren Street tube. **Open** 1-5pm Tue-Fri; 10am-1pm Sat. **Admission** free. **Map** p136 C3 ②

The museum, set up in 1892, is named after Flinders Petrie, an exhaustive excavator of ancient Egyptian treasures. Where the British Museum's Egyptology collection is strong on the big stuff, the Petrie focuses on the minutiae. Its aged wooden cabinets are full of pottery shards, grooming accessories, jewellery and primitive tools. Highlights include artefacts from the heretic pharaoh Akhenaten's short-lived capital Tell el Amarna. Among the oddities are a 4,000-year-old skeleton of a man who was buried in an earthenware pot. That some corners of this small museum are so gloomy staff offer torches only adds to the fun.

St George's Bloomsbury

Bloomsbury Way (7405 3044/www. stgeorgesbloomsbury.org.uk). Holborn or Tottenham Court Road tube. **Open** 1-2pm Tue-Fri; 11.30am-5pm Sat; 2-5.30pm Sun. **Admission** free. **Map** p137 D4 ㉓

Consecrated in 1730, St George's is a grand and typically disturbing work by Nicholas Hawksmoor, with an offset, stepped spire inspired by the Mausoleum at Halicarnassus. It reopened in October 2006 following major renovations: highlights include the mahogany reredos, and 10ft-high sculptures of lions and unicorns clawing at the base of the steeple. As well as guided tours, there are regular concerts – check the website for details.

LONDON BY AREA

St Pancras International

NEW *Pancras Road, King's Cross, NW1 2QP (7843 4250/www.stpancras. com). King's Cross tube/rail.* **Map** p137 D1 **24**

In November 2007, St Pancras International Station opened after £800 million refurbishment. The most impressive part of the renewed station is the single-span arch of glass and steel, a soaring ethereal structure that was completed by engineer William Barlow… back in 1868. The rest – a giant statue of a kissing couple, another of poet John Betjeman, various eating and drinking options – hardly left us overwhelmed, although the replica station clock is a nice touch. Still, the Champagne Bar (p146) and the Betjeman Arms (see below) make very decent spots to spend some time picturing yourself in a romantic train movie, and there's a Foyles bookshop.

Wellcome Collection

183 Euston Road, NW1 2BE (7611 2222/www.wellcomecollection.org). Euston Square tube/Euston tube/rail. **Open** 10am-6pm Tue, Wed, Fri, Sat; 10am-10pm Thur; 11am-6pm Sun. **Admission** free. **Map** p136 C2 **25**

Sir Henry Wellcome, a pioneering 19th-century pharmacist and entrepreneur, amassed a vast collection of artefacts, implements and curios relating to the medical trade. These fascinating and often grisly items – ranging from delicate ivory carvings of pregnant women to used guillotine blades and Napoleon's toothbrush – form the core exhibits at this new museum, but the curators have been diligently adding serious works of modern art, most of which are on display in a smaller room to one side of the main chamber of curiosities. The temporary exhibitions downstairs are also excellent, exploring connections between medical science and art. There's a great Peyton & Byrne café on the ground floor, and behind-the-scenes tours take place on the first Friday of each month.
Event highlights 'War & Medicine' (20 Nov 2008-15 Feb 2009).

Eating & drinking

Also try the excellent café in the **Wellcome Collection** (see above).

Acorn House

69 Swinton Street, WC1X 9NT (7812 1842/www.acornhouserestaurant.com). King's Cross tube/rail. **Open** 8-11am, noon-3pm, 6-10.30pm Mon-Fri; 10am-3pm, 6-10.30pm Sat. **££**. **Brasserie**. **Map** p137 E2 **26**

'Eco-friendly training restaurant' somehow doesn't convey the charm of Acorn House. Yes, the place is committed to seasonality and environmental responsibility, but visit for flavour-packed food, a great wine list and warm staff.

All Star Lanes

Victoria House, Bloomsbury Place, WC1B 4DA (7025 2676/www.allstar lanes.co.uk). Holborn tube. **Open** 5-11.30pm Mon-Wed; 5pm-midnight Thur; noon-2am Fri, Sat; noon-11pm Sun. **Bar/bowling alley**. **Map** p137 D4 **27**

Part of a mini-chain, All Star Lanes is a well-realised, high-end endeavour, with four bowling lanes and a bar offering good cocktails. It's not a cheap night out – the kitchen serves lobster, for gawd's sake – but rather the gold card brigade's foil to grungier Bloomsbury Bowling (Tavistock Hotel, Bedford Way, WC1H 9EU, 7691 2610, www.bloomsburybowling.com).

Bea's of Bloomsbury

NEW *44 Theobald's Road, WC1X 8NW (7242 8330/www.beasofbloomsbury. com). Chancery Lane or Holborn tube.* **Open** 8am-6pm Mon-Fri; 10.30am-4pm Sat. **£**. **Tearoom**. **Map** p137 E4 **28**

This lovely tearoom will entice you in with its counter of cupcakes, biscuits, muffins and more. Teas are by Jing Tea, coffee is Fairtrade and organic, and savoury treats are also available.

Betjeman Arms

NEW *Unit 53, St Pancras International Station, Pancras Road, NW1 2QP (7923 5440/www.geronimo-inns.co.uk). King's Cross tube/rail.* **Open** 7.30am-11pm daily. **££**. **Gastropub**. **Map** p137 D1 **29**

St Pancras Champagne Bar p146

The Betjeman is cut above most station boozers. The menu is unambitious but well executed, and the wines and real ales well-kept and -chosen. The interior is more handsome than the plentiful garden furniture out front, but then the latter give you a sighter right down the tracks as the Eurostar pulls out.

Busaba Eathai
22 Store Street, WC1E 7DS (7299 7900). Tottenham Court Road tube. **Open** noon-11pm Mon-Thur; noon-11.30pm Fri, Sat; noon-10pm Sun. **££. Thai. Map** p136 C4 ③⓪
Of the current three locations – the others are Wardour Street in Soho, and Bird Street, handy for Selfridges – this is our favourite. The decor at each combines shared tables and bench seating with a touch of oriental mystique (dark wood, incense, low lighting), while the dishes are as interesting as you'd expect of a menu originally developed by David Thompson of Nahm (p95).

Konstam at the Prince Albert
2 Acton Street, WC1X 9NA (7833 5040/www.konstam.co.uk). King's Cross tube/rail. **Open** 12.30-3pm, 6.30-10.30pm Mon-Fri; 6.30-10.30pm Sat. **££. British. Map** p137 E2 ③①
The wild decor – dark green paint and lights made from plug chains – is a nice change from the identikit chains. Chef-owner Oliver Rowe's menu doesn't play safe, either: most ingredients come from within the tube network.

Lamb
94 Lamb's Conduit Street, WC1N 3LZ (7405 0713/www.youngs.co.uk). Holborn or Russell Square tube. **Open** 11am-midnight Mon-Sat; noon-10.30pm Sun. **Pub. Map** p137 E3 ③②
Founded in 1729, this beautifully restored etched-glass and mahogany masterpiece is sheer class. The Pit, a sunken back area, gives access to a summer patio. Most dishes on the pub grub menu cost under a tenner.

Meals
1st floor, Heal's, 196 Tottenham Court Road, W1T 7LQ (7580 2522/www. heals.co.uk). Goodge Street or Warren Street tube. **Open** 10am-6pm Mon-Wed, Fri; 10am-7.30pm Thur; 9.30am-6.30pm Sat; noon-6pm Sun. **£. Café. Map** p136 C3 ③④

LONDON BY AREA

Cross an alpine lodge with a toddler's bedroom, add cut-out cupboards that suggest a fairytale landscape, and marshmallow pink chairs on the ironic side of twee – and you've got the in-store café in Heal's department store. The food doesn't quite taste as well as it reads, but it's enjoyable and cultured.

Museum Tavern

49 Great Russell Street, WC1B 3BA (7242 8987). Holborn or Tottenham Court Road tube. **Open** 11am-11.30pm Mon-Thur; 11am-midnight Fri, Sat; noon-10.30pm Sun. **Pub**. Map p137 D4 ㉞

A rare example of a pub that's as popular with locals as tourists, rejoicing in both a noble history (the splendid interior dates to a mid 19th-century refurb) and an ideal location (opposite the British Museum). Good real ales are also a draw, and there are tables outside.

St Pancras Champagne Bar

NEW *St Pancras International, Pancras Road, NW1 2QP (3006 1550/www.searcystpancras.co.uk). King's Cross tube/rail.* **Open** 8am-11pm daily. **Champagne bar**. Map p137 D1 ㉟

Part of the refurbishment of St Pancras station is the 'longest champagne bar in Europe': 300ft of booth tables and ice buckets, pulled up alongside the Eurostar train tracks. The selection covers both old standards and classics, and although this isn't as romantic as you'd hope, it's pretty fun.

Wagamama

4A Streatham Street, WC1A 1JB (7323 9223/www.wagamama.com). Holborn or Tottenham Court Road tube. **Open** noon-11pm Mon-Sat; noon-10pm Sun. **£**. **Noodle bar**. Map p137 D4 ㊱

The mother of all London noodle bars. Since starting life in this basement in 1992, Wagamama has expanded to more than 80 restaurants around the world (30 in Greater London alone), with its clever concept of no bookings, communal tables, and a menu of Japan-easy noodle soups and dumplings.

Shopping

Tottenham Court Road has the city's main concentration of electronics and computer shops, but for no hard sell and sound advice, we prefer **John Lewis** (p103).

James Smith & Sons

53 New Oxford Street, WC1A 1BL (7836 4731/www.james-smith.co.uk). Holborn or Tottenham Court Road tube. **Open** 9.30am-5.25pm Mon-Fri; 10am-5.25pm Sat. Map p137 D4 ㊲

More than 175 years after it was established, this charming Victorian shop still holds its own, selling lovingly crafted brollies and walking sticks. A repair service is also offered.

Lamb's Conduit Street

Holborn or Russell Square tube. Map p137 E3 ㊳

Tucked away in residential back streets, Lamb's Conduit Street is perfect for browsing, whether you fancy a cool, custom-made suit from Pokit (no.53, 7430 9782, www.pokit.co.uk), cult

Pokit

menswear and cute women's knitwear from Folk (no.49, 7404 6458, www.folk-clothing.com), a photographic book from Matchless Prints (no.36, 7405 8899, www.steidlville.com) or classic vinyl reissues from Synphonic (no.47, 7242 9876). Refuel at the Lamb (p145) or friendly deli-café Kennards (no.57, 7404 4030, www.kennardsgoodfoods.com), then head just off the main drag to peruse the charming accessories at French's Dairy (13 Rugby Street, 7404 7070, www.frenchsdairy.com).

London Review Bookshop

14 Bury Place, WC1A 2JL (7269 9030/www.lrbshop.co.uk). Holborn or Tottenham Court Road tube. **Open** 10am-6.30pm Mon-Sat; noon-6pm Sun. **Map** p137 D4 ⓷⓽
Owned by the eponymous literary-political journal, this bookshop is unrivalled in quality and range, with everything from fiction to film and poetry to politics, plus lighter topics such as food and travel. Staff are passionate, and regular readings and events are also held. The café is lovely too.

Skoob

Unit 66, The Brunswick, WC1N 1AE (7278 8760/www.skoob.com). Russell Square tube. **Open** 10am-8pm Mon-Sat; 10am-6pm Sun. **Map** p137 D3 ④⓪
A back-to-basics basement showcasing about 50,000 second-hand titles on almost every subject, from philosophy and biography to politics and the occult. Haphazard, dusty and brilliant.

Nightlife

Big Chill House

257-259 Pentonville Road, King's Cross, N1 9NL (7427 2540/www.bigchill.net). King's Cross tube/rail. **Open** noon-midnight Mon-Wed, Sun; noon-1am Thur; noon-4am Fri, Sat. **Map** p137 E1 ④①
A festival, a record label, a bar and now also a house, the Big Chill empire rolls on. This three-floor space boasts an enormous sun-catcher of a terrace, while the likes of Sean Rowley and owner Pete Lawrence regularly handle deck duties.

Bloomsbury Ballroom

Victoria House, Bloomsbury Square, WC1B 4DA (7287 3834/box office 0871 220 0260/www.bloomsburyballroom.co.uk). Russell Square tube. **Map** p137 D4 ④②
This smart, well-appointed art deco concert hall has been putting on an excellent and varied bill (King Creosote, Amy Winehouse) since its conversion in 2006 into a multi-purpose music and conference venue. Concerts can include dinner.

Scala

275 Pentonville Road, N1 9NL (7833 2022/www.scala-london.co.uk). King's Cross tube/rail. **Map** p137 E1 ④③
Built as a cinema after World War I, this large building now stages a broad range of ultra-cool indie, electronica, avant hip hop and weird folk. Sound quality is decent and the staff are friendly.

Arts & leisure

Drill Hall

16 Chenies Street, WC1E 7EX (7307 5060/www.drillhall.co.uk). Goodge Street tube. **Map** p136 C4 ④④
Polyfunctional (it's a theatre, cabaret, gig venue and photo studio) and polysexual, Drill Hall is London's biggest gay and lesbian theatre.

Place

17 Duke's Road, WC1H 9PY (7121 1000/www.theplace.org.uk). Euston tube/rail. **Map** p136 C2 ④⑤
The Place has plenty to offer, as both a site for professional dance training and a home for visiting acts. It hosts an annual season of short, live dance works by emerging choreographers, and is an intimate venue for shows.

Renoir

Brunswick Square, WC1N 1AW (7837 8402). Russell Square tube. **Map** p137 D3 ④⑥
A comfy little underground arthouse cinema in the refurbished Brunswick centre. You'll get to see a fine programme of foreign rarities and various obscurities – and there's an underpowered bar to discuss them in afterwards.

LONDON BY AREA

Tower of London p162

The City

Holborn

At first sight, Holborn doesn't seem to be the nicest part of London – or even the City, for that matter. But forget the hectic crossroads dominated by chain stores and faceless office blocks by Holborn tube, and head towards the river. Among the legal profession's ancient **Inns of Court**, you'll find a couple of top museums (**Hunterian Museum**; **Sir John Soane's Museum**). Right in the backstreets, **Ye Old Mitre** is one of our favourite traditional pubs, while beside the Thames, the magnificent fountain courtyard of **Somerset House** is sweetly complemented by the wonderful eccentricity of the Courtauld Institute, one of its three fine constituent museums.

Sights & museums

Hunterian Museum

Royal College of Surgeons, 35-43 Lincoln's Inn Fields, WC2A 3PE (7869 6560/www.rcseng.ac.uk/museums). Holborn tube. **Open** 10am-5pm Tue-Sat. **Admission** free. **Map** p150 A4 ❶
John Hunter (1728-93) was a pioneering surgeon and anatomist who amassed a huge collection of medical specimens: check out the brain of 19th-century mathematician Charles Babbage and Winston Churchill's dentures. A gallery displays painting and sculpture by Stubbs and Shipley, among others.

Royal Courts of Justice

Strand, WC2A 2LL (7947 6000/ www.courtservice.gov.uk). Temple tube. **Open** 9am-5pm Mon-Fri. **Admission** free. **Map** p150 A4 ❷
The magnificent Royal Courts preside over the most serious civil cases in British law. Members of the public are

allowed to attend these trials (although exceptions are made for sensitive cases), so if you want to see the justice system in action, step inside. Few trials are held during the months of August and September. Note that cameras and children under 14 are not permitted.

Sir John Soane's Museum

13 Lincoln's Inn Fields, WC2A 3BP (7405 2107/www.soane.org). Holborn tube. **Open** 10am-5pm Tue-Sat; 10am-5pm, 6-9pm 1st Tue of mth. **Admission** free. *Tours £5; free reductions.* **Map** p150 A3 ❸

An obsessive collector of art, furniture and architectural ornamentation, architect Sir John Soane turned his house into a museum before his death in 1837. The smallish rooms were modified by Soane with devices to channel and direct natural daylight and to expand available space, including walls that open out like cabinets to display some of his many paintings (including works by Canaletto and Turner, as well as two series by Hogarth). The Breakfast Room has a beautiful domed ceiling inset with convex mirrors, but the real wow is the Monument Court, a multi-storey affair filled with sculpted stone detailing removed from ancient buildings and a sarcophagus carved for the pharaoh Seti I (1291-78 BC).

Somerset House

Strand, WC2R 1LA (7845 4600/ www.somersethouse.org.uk). Temple or Embankment tube/Charing Cross tube/rail. **Open** 10am-6pm daily. **Admission** *Courtyard & terrace free. 1 museum £5; £4 reductions. 2 museums £8; £7 reductions. 3 museums £12; £11 reductions.* No credit cards. **Map** p150 A5 ❹

The original Somerset House was a Tudor palace commissioned by the Duke of Somerset in 1547, but it was demolished in 1775 to make way for an entirely new building. The architect Sir William Chambers spent the last 20 years of his life working on the vast neoclassical mansion that now overlooks the Thames. It accommodated learned societies such as the Royal Academy and government offices, including the Inland Revenue. The taxmen are still here, but the rest of the building is open to the public, and houses three formidable art and museum collections, the beautiful fountain court (given over to an immensely popular ice rink each winter), a little café and a classy restaurant.

Courtauld Institute of Art Gallery

7848 2526/www.courtauld.ac.uk/gallery. The Courtauld has one of Britain's greatest collections of paintings, and it contains several works of world importance. Although there are some outstanding works from earlier periods (don't miss Lucas Cranach's *Adam & Eve*), the collection's strongest suit is Impressionist and post-Impressionist paintings. There are some popular masterpieces: Manet's *A Bar at the Folies-Bergère* is undoubtedly the centrepiece, alongside Monets, Cézannes, Gauguins, Van Goghs and Seurats. The top floor is devoted to the 20th century, with Fauvist works, a room of Kandinskys and plenty more. The café, hidden away downstairs, is a joy.

Gilbert Collection

7420 9400/www.gilbert-collection.org.uk. In 1949, Sir Arthur Gilbert uprooted to California, where he made millions in real estate. He developed a predilection for silver, gold and all sorts of gemmed, gilded and shiny objects. In 1996, Britain became the beneficiary of this opulence when he donated his entire collection, saying 'I felt it should return to the country of my birth'. The two floors are dazzling, bedecked with candelabras, mosaics, vases, urns, plates, mosaics and snuff boxes. Themed exhibitions are held throughout the year.

Hermitage Rooms

7845 4630/www.hermitagerooms.co.uk. The Hermitage Rooms host rotating exhibitions of items belonging to the Winter Palace in St Petersburg; the rooms even recreate in miniature the decor of their Russian twin. New shows arrive twice a year and can include anything from paintings and drawings to decorative art and fine jewellery.

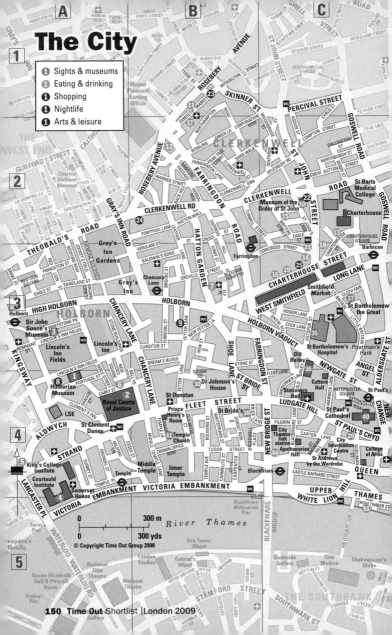

The City

- ❶ Sights & museums
- ❶ Eating & drinking
- ❶ Shopping
- ❶ Nightlife
- ❶ Arts & leisure

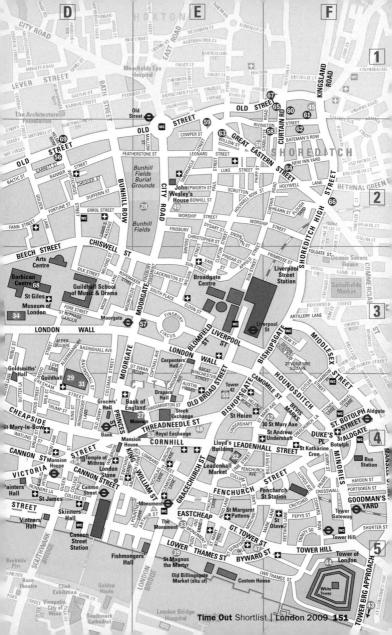

Eating & drinking

Lobby Bar

*One Aldwych, the Strand, WC2B 4RH
(7300 1070/www.onealdwych.com).
Covent Garden or Temple tube.* **Open**
8am-11.30pm Mon-Sat; 8am-10.30pm
Sun. **Cocktail bar.** Map p150 A4 ⑤
The lobby bar of the One Aldwych
hotel innovates as much as it sparkles.
The cocktail menu offers an improba-
ble 30 kinds of martini, proceedings are
overseen by impeccable staff and the
setting is grand. Pure class.

Seven Stars

*53 Carey Street, WC2A 2JB (7242
8521). Chancery Lane or Holborn
tube.* **Open** 11am-11pm Mon-Fri;
noon-11pm Sat; noon-10.30pm Sun.
££. Gastropub. Map p150 A4 ⑥
By the Royal Courts of Justice, Roxy
Beaujolais's little pub-cum-bar-cum-
eaterie is magic. Posters for courtroom
dramas overlook the legal fraternity
tucking into well-chosen (and well-
priced) merlots, malbecs and house
dulucs. Craftily conceived daily dishes
chalked up by the bar (such as Napoli
sausages and mash, or dill-cured her-
ring) are devoured in a side room.

Ye Old Mitre

*1 Ely Court, Ely Place, at the side of
8 Hatton Gardens, EC1N 6SJ (7405
4751). Chancery Lane tube/Farringdon
tube/rail.* **Open** 11am-11pm Mon-Fri.
Pub. Map p150 B3 ⑦
This old pub (established 1546) is only
accessible through a narrow passage –
incongruously described as 25m long.
Still, the Mitre needs no yard conversion or 'ye olde' embellishment to prove
its worth. Walk into its venerable,
cramped three-room space, see what's
on as the guest ale, then settle down
amid the portraits of Henry VIII and
sundry beruffed luminaries.

Shopping

Old Curiosity Shop

*13-14 Portsmouth Street, WC2A 2ES
(7405 9891). Holborn tube.* **Open**
noon-7pm Mon-Sat. Map p150 A4 ⑧

This location is said to be both the oldest shop in London and the inspiration
for the Dickens novel. Regardless, the
shop has a wonderful, off-kilter charm.
The stock is by Japanese designer Daiko
Kimura, whose avant-garde unisex
styles are mostly made by hand in the
workshop downstairs. George Cox also
sells retro Brit classics on the premises.

Nightlife

Volupté

*7-9 Norwich Street, EC4A 1EJ (7831
1622/www.volupte-lounge.com).
Chancery Lane tube.* **Open** noon-
late Tue-Sat. Map p150 B3 ⑨
Volupté is one of the pioneers of
London's new breed of supper clubs.
The ground-floor bar might be part
of a 1980s office block, but it still thinks
it's a swish NYC cocktail bar. Down the
opulent stairwell is a Moulin Rouge-
style basement; ivy leaves hang from
the ceiling and candlelit tables are
gathered around a piano. DJ El Nino
runs dressed-up vintage nights here,
and there are cabaret shows too (Wed-
Sat). The top price (£55) includes a
meal, while entrance to the bar is free.

Clerkenwell to Smithfield Market

Clerkenwell's left-leaning,
tracksuit-wearing yuppies and the
meat-hauling Smithfield
butchers seem an unlikely pairing,
but they are joined at places like
St John, birthplace of modern
British cooking. At one time a
devoutly religious area, home to
monastic orders and nunneries,
at another a fiercely revolutionary
one (as a centre of dissent down the
centuries), Clerkenwell is today a
foodie heartland – it was here that
the **Eagle** pioneered the wild idea
of serving restaurant-quality food
in a boozer. Don't come for the
sights, but do come to eat – and,
on **Exmouth Market**, to shop.

Magnificent mystery tour

Meet the Americans who are about to unleash a new kind of tour on the unsuspecting City.

Guided walking tours can be enriching experiences, but even the best of them conjure images of bookish types, lavish trivia and a mildly embarrassing flag. This year, however, Londoners are in for a treat – the Accomplice tours are coming to town.

The brainchild of brother and sister Tom and Betsy Salamon, the three-hour tours are unlike any other. Accomplice: New York and its 'sequel' Accomplice: West Village are defiantly non-educational: there are no historical anecdotes and no guides. Instead, participants are swept up in a crime drama, a mission that feels close enough to a real adventure to thrill the most jaded tourist.

Completing the tours is no mean feat. At some point, in between being shepherded to the back of an Italian restaurant by a 'mobster' or rescuing a femme fatale with amnesia, it becomes difficult to differentiate between genuine locals and the Accomplice cast. Participants are given a mobile phone number in case they get lost or make a mistake, which happens with some regularity.

So what can you expect from Accomplice: London? A unique experience, tailored to the capital, as offbeat and individual as the bespoke tours the Salamons created in 2008 for Hollywood and San Francisco.

'Knowing what I know about London, it's one I'm really excited about,' Tom told Shortlist. 'One of the things that makes it easier is to have a lot of interesting things within a small area, which London has. Right there it solves half of the problems, as there are always different things within half a block of each other.'

Tom has a producer for London, and an early 2009 launch date, but the exact location might only be revealed as it is in Accomplice: New York – via a frantic phone call from your 'criminal contact', only hours before the adventure begins.

Visit www.accompliceny.com to find out how to catch Accomplice: London. And leave the guidebook (yes, even this one) at home.

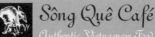

Sights & museums

Museum & Library of the Order of St John

St John's Gate, St John's Lane, EC1M 4DA (7324 4005/www.sja.org.uk/ museum). Farringdon tube/rail. **Open** 10am-5pm Mon-Fri; 10am-4pm Sat. **Admission** free. **Map** p150 C2 ⑩

Today, the Order of St John is best known in London for its provision of ambulance services, but its roots lie in Christian medical practices during the Crusades of the 11th, 12th and 13th centuries. This fascinating collection of objects and artworks charts the evolution of the medieval Order of Hospitaller Knights through Jerusalem, Malta, the Ottoman Empire and beyond.

Eating & drinking

Ambassador

55 Exmouth Market, EC1R 4QL (7837 0009/www.theambassadorcafe.co.uk). Farringdon tube/rail/19, 38, 341 bus. **Open** 8.30am-10.15pm Mon-Sat. **££**. **Modern European**. **Map** p150 B1 ⑪

A day-long café-style operation that aims to please all the people all the time – and it succeeds. The various menus include breakfast waffles and pastries, a weekend brunch, dinner, and small sharing dishes for those wanting to enjoy the beautifully crafted wine list.

Eagle

159 Farringdon Road, EC1R 3AL (7837 1353). Farringdon tube/rail. **Open** noon-11pm Mon-Sat; noon-5pm Sun. **££**. **Gastropub**. **Map** p150 B2 ⑫

The Eagle's renown as birthplace of London's gastropub movement means that, 15 years in, it's still pretty much impossible to get a seat here. To have a hope, come early: once people get settled, they shift for no one, tucking into steak sandwiches, tapas and heartier Med-influenced meat and fish dishes. Drinkers are well taken care of too.

Fox & Anchor

NEW *115 Charterhouse Street, EC1M 6AA (7250 1300/www.foxandanchor. com). Barbican or Farringdon tube.*

Open 7am-11pm Mon-Fri; noon-11pm Sat, Sun. *Food served* 8-11am Mon-Fri; noon-10pm Mon-Sat; noon-5pm Sun. **££**. **Gastropub**. **Map** p150 C2 ⑬

After 108 years, this cherished boozer closed in 2006. Thanks to Malmaison, then, for reopening it and restoring its beautiful interior. The long bar remains in place, as do the wood fixtures, snugs and the 7am opening. With an array of rarely seen bottled beers and six cask ales, the Fox is a beer-drinker's paradise (the brews are served in traditional glass-bottomed, pewter tankards), but the British cooking is also a cut above. There are fine rooms to stay in too (p208).

Hix Oyster & Chop House

NEW *35-37 Greenhill Rents, off Cowcross Street, EC1M 6BN (7017 1930/www.restaurantsetcltd.co.uk). Farringdon tube/rail.* **Open** noon-3pm, 6-11pm Mon-Fri; 6-11pm Sat; noon-3pm Sun. **£££**. **British**. **Map** p150 C3 ⑭

Comfortable and unpretentious, Hix subscribes to the fashion for austerity, utility and nostalgia: tap water is served in retro whisky jugs. Mark Hix has been a pioneer of the reinvention of British dishes and, from a high-priced starter of elvers (£35) to affordable dishes like deep-fried skate knobs or the extraordinarily good mutton chop curry, the food here is all excellent.

Jerusalem Tavern

55 Britton Street, EC1M 5UQ (7490 4281/www.stpetersbrewery.co.uk). Farringdon tube/rail. **Open** 11am-11pm Mon-Fri. **Pub**. **Map** p150 C2 ⑮

With its wooden interior painted green and its clutter of tables tucked into nooks and crannies, the Jerusalem could be from Tolkien's Shire. Run by the estimable St Peter's Brewery, it's justly popular with punters of all ages and occupations.

Le Comptoir Gascon

61-63 Charterhouse Street, EC1M 6HJ (7608 0851/www.comptoirgascon.com). Farringdon tube/rail. **Open** noon-2pm, 7-11pm Tue-Fri; 10.30am-2pm, 7-11pm Sat. **££**. **French**. **Map** p150 C3 ⑯

Le Comptoir Gascon p155

This cosy corner of Smithfield is a temple to culinary south-west France, and its devotees are an unashamedly carnivorous bunch. The blackboard proffers the likes of veal kidneys and suckling pig, and a whole section of the menu is devoted to duck derivations, foie gras included. The warm atmosphere and the quality and price of the food ensure it's always busy. The two sister organisations on West Smithfield, bijou restaurant Club Gascon (no.57, 7796 0600, www.clubgascon.com) and superb wine bar Cellar Gascon (no.59, 7600 7561, www.cellargascon.com), are also well worth checking out.

Moro

34-36 Exmouth Market, EC1R 4QE (7833 8336/www.moro.co.uk). Farringdon tube/rail/19, 38 bus. **Open** 12.30-11.45pm Mon-Sat (last entry 10.30pm). **£££. Spanish.** **Map** p150 B2 ⑰

The superb Moro has an unrivalled setting, coming into its own in summer when tables are set outside. The softly lit open-plan dining room is no less pleasant – restrained, yet cosily romantic – but the food is the main draw, with a daily changing modern Mediterranean ensemble featuring Spanish and North African accents. Book ahead.

St John

26 St John Street, EC1M 4AY (7251 0848/4998/www.stjohnrestaurant. com). Barbican tube/Farringdon tube/ rail. **Open** noon-3pm, 6-11pm Mon-Fri; 6-11pm Sat. **££. British.** **Map** p150 C3 ⑱

Fergus Henderson's St John has become a world-famous pioneer of British food (including the forgotten wonders of offal), while managing to remain an extremely congenial restaurant where you can still get a table. It looks the same as ever: a beautifully white airy dining room with a semi-open kitchen, reached through a spacious bar with an even loftier ceiling. The menu changes daily, but there are recurring treats – roast bone marrow and parsley salad being the most renowned. Down in the bar, welsh rarebit is enough to answer most hunger pangs and the wines are brilliant. In short, an inspirational, admirable restaurant.

Smiths of Smithfield

67-77 Charterhouse Street, EC1M 6HJ (7251 7950/www.smithsofsmithfield. co.uk). Barbican tube/Farringdon tube/ rail. **Open** *Bar* 11am-11pm Mon-Sat; noon-10.30pm Sun. *Café* 7am-4.30pm Mon-Fri; 9.30am-5.30pm Sat, Sun. *Dining Room* noon-2.45pm, 6-10.45pm

Mon-Fri; 6-10.45pm Sat. **£** Café. **£££**
Restaurant. **Modern European**.
Map p150 C3 ⑲
The popularity of John Torode's industrial chic, four-floor brick warehouse is
testament to its reliability. No matter
how busy it gets, standards remain
constant. The ground-floor café-bar is
packed with a mix of City workers and
night owls, but the hub of the operation
is the second-floor Dining Room, its
menu confidently focused on meat.

Three Kings of Clerkenwell

*7 Clerkenwell Close, EC1R 0DY (7253
0483). Farringdon tube/rail.* **Open**
noon-11pm Mon-Fri; 5.30-11pm Sat.
No credit cards. **Pub**. **Map** p150 B2 ⑳
It's a relief to find a boozer with such
brazen personality. From the bonkers
figurines standing guard over the
entrance to the triumphant collection
of tat cluttering every available surface
inside (Egyptian cat statues, snow-
globes, a fake rhino's head above the
fireplace), the Three Kings is a true
original. The pub takes one thing seriously: its music. But it also makes room
for three real ales and board games.

Vinoteca

*7 St John Street, EC1M 4AA (7253
8786/www.vinoteca.co.uk). Farringdon
tube/rail.* **Open** 11am-11pm Mon-Sat.
Wine bar. **Map** p150 C3 ㉑
This bar's main room has the feel of
a packed tapas bar in Spain, with a
young crowd enjoying British and
European food along with one of the
best wine lists in London (25 by the
glass, and wonderfully low mark-ups).

Shopping

Craft Central

*33-35 St John's Square, EC1M 4DS
(7251 0276/www.craftcentral.org.uk).
Farringdon tube/rail.* **Open** 5-8pm
Thur; noon-6pm Fri-Sun. **Admission**
free-£2.50. **Map** p150 C2 ㉒
Each item for sale – be it jewellery,
fashion and textiles, homeware or a traditional craft product such as a bound
book or letterpress print – is a one-off
produced right here in Clerkenwell.

Exmouth Market

Farringdon tube/rail. **Map** p150 B1 ㉓
Despite the closure of the superb
Metropolitan Books in early 2008, this
nondescript street still has a slew of
great independent shops: ec one (no.41,
7713 6185, www.econe.co.uk) has jewellery from more than 50 small designers, while little CD shop-cum-café
Brill (no.27, 7833 9757) turns its size to
advantage with its selective approach
– if it's stocked here, it's going to be
good. And, for the makings of a gourmet
Med-style picnic, don't miss the brilliant Spanish deli Brindisa (no.32, 7713
1666, www.brindisa.com).

Magma

*117-119 Clerkenwell Road, EC1R 5BY
(7242 9503/www.magmabooks.com).
Chancery Lane tube/Farringdon
tube/rail.* **Open** 10am-7pm Mon-Sat.
Map p150 B2 ㉔
If you can visualise it, this art and
design specialist probably has a book
on it. Magazines, DVDs, trendy toys,
T-shirts and limited-edition posters
and cards are also sold.

Nightlife

Fabric

*77A Charterhouse Street, EC1M 3HN
(7336 8898/advance tickets 0870
902 0001/www.fabriclondon.com).
Farringdon tube/rail.* **Open** 9.30pm-
5am Fri; 10pm Sat-7am Sun. **Map**
p150 C3 ㉕
A decade after opening, Fabric is now
one of the world's most important
clubs, needing no introduction to music
fans. Its three rooms still get superstar
DJs and regularly introduce new talent.
Too crowded and sweaty for some;
heaven on a stick for others. Watch out
for the new Fabric inside O2 (p188).

The City

This area was the original
Londinium, and as such is full of
history and heraldry, institutions
and monuments – not least the
deliciously spruced-up **St Paul's**

LONDON BY AREA

Cathedral. The City of London, the self-governing 'square mile' that is still England's financial heart, has pretty much the same boundaries the Romans gave it. It also has the tall buildings to glorify and expensive restaurants to feed the incumbent financial establishment. Enjoy wandering the maze of streets whose ancient geography and names may not even the Great Fire of London could eradicate. The City is most itself at either end of the business day, when commuters plunge through the tube stations, but it's often more enjoyable to explore it at weekends and in the later evening, when the streets are eerily quiet. Many businesses are closed at the weekend, although the handsome pedestrian bridge across the river between St Paul's and Tate Modern means things are getting busier.

For nightlife, head north-east of the City, where the pleasure zones of Shoreditch soak up bankers' loose change – this area's edginess and artiness has begun to follow cheaper rents further out of town, but the bars and clubs are still lively (indeed, Friday and Saturday nights can be unpleasantly hectic).

City of London Information Centre

St Paul's Churchyard, EC4M 8BX (7332 1456/www.cityoflondon.gov.uk). St Paul's tube. **Open** 9.30am-5.30pm Mon-Fri. **Map** p150 C4 **26**
Run by the City of London, this office has information and brochures on sights, events and walks in the area.

Sights & museums

The **Barbican** frequently hosts free live music, and its geometric duck ponds, brutalist architecture and art gallery appeal to aesthetes. The area's other landmarks are 'the Gherkin' (**30 St Mary Axe**), the **Monument** and Tower 42,

which provides magnificent views to the champagne-bibbers in lofty bar **Vertigo 42**.

Bank of England Museum

Entrance on Bartholomew Lane, EC2R 8AH (7601 5545/www.bankofengland. co.uk/museum). Bank tube/DLR. **Open** 10am-5pm Mon-Fri. **Admission** free. **Map** p151 E4 **27**
Housed inside the former Stock Offices of the Bank of England, this engaging museum explores the history of the national bank. As well as ancient coins and original artwork for British bank-notes, the museum offers a rare chance to manhandle a real 13kg gold bar. Child-friendly temporary exhibitions take place in the museum lobby.

Bunhill Fields

Old Street tube/rail. **Admission** free. **Map** p151 E2 **28**
This was an important non-conformist burial ground until the 19th century, and it contains memorials to John Bunyan, Daniel Defoe and William Blake. Opposite, the home and chapel of John Wesley is now a museum of Methodism (49 City Road, 7253 2262, www.wesleyschapel.org.uk); downstairs are some of London's finest public loos, with original Victorian fittings by Thomas Crapper.

Clockmakers' Museum

Guildhall Library, Aldermanbury, EC2V 7HH (Guildhall Library 7332 1868/ www.clockmakers.org). Mansion House or St Paul's tube/Bank tube/DLR/ Moorgate tube/rail. **Open** 9.30am-4.45pm Mon-Sat. **Admission** free. **Map** p151 D4 **29**
Hundreds of ticking, chiming clocks and watches are displayed here, from egg-sized Elizabethan pocket watches to John Harrison's famous Marine Chronometer H5, built in 1772 to solve the problem of longitude.

Dr Johnson's House

17 Gough Square, off Fleet Street, EC4A 3DE (7353 3745/www.dr johnsonshouse.org). Chancery Lane or Temple tube/Blackfriars tube/rail. **Open** May-Sept 11am-5.30pm Mon-Sat. *Oct-*

Clockmakers' Museum

Apr 11am-5pm Mon-Sat. **Admission** £4.50; free-£3.50 reductions. No credit cards. **Map** p150 B4 ③⓪

Author of the enormously significant *Dictionary of the English Language*, Dr Samuel Johnson (1709-84) also wrote poems, a novel and one of the earliest travelogues, an acerbic account of a tour of the Western Isles with James Boswell. You can visit his stately Georgian townhouse, where he came up with his inspired definitions – 'to make dictionaries is dull work,' was his definition of the word 'dull'.

Guildhall Art Gallery

Guildhall Yard, off Gresham Street, EC2P 2EJ (7332 3700/www.guildhall-art-gallery.org.uk). Mansion House or St Paul's tube/Bank tube/DLR/Moorgate tube/rail. **Open** 10am-5pm Mon-Sat; noon-4pm Sun. **Admission** £2.50; free-£1 reductions. No credit cards. **Map** p151 D4 ③①

The City of London's gallery is most famous for the *Siege of Gibraltar* by John Copley, which is thought to be the largest painting in Britain, but it's also home to some surprises, including works by Constable and Reynolds and some charming paintings by the Pre-Raphaelites. A sub-basement contains the scant remains of London's Roman amphitheatre, dating from AD 70.

Lloyd's of London

1 Lime Street, EC3M 7HA (www.lloyds.com). Monument tube. **Map** p151 E4 ③②

Lord Rogers' high-tech Lloyd's of London building has all its mechanical services (ducts, stairwells, lift shafts and even loos) on the outside, making it look like a disassembled washing machine. The original Lloyd's Register of Shipping, decorated with bas-reliefs of sea monsters and nautical scenes, is around the corner on Fenchurch Street.

Monument

Monument Street, EC3R 8AH (7626 2717/www.towerbridge.org.uk). Monument tube. **Open** 9.30am-5pm daily. **Admission** £2; free-£1 reductions. No credit cards. **Map** p151 E5 ③③

The Monument is the world's largest free-standing Doric column. It was designed by Sir Christopher Wren and Robert Hooke as a memorial to the Great Fire of London, its 202 feet in height matching the distance to Farriner's bakery in Pudding Lane, where the fire

LONDON BY AREA

began. Inside, a spiral staircase winds up 311 steps to a narrow gallery with fantastic views. It is currently undergoing extensive renovations, due for completion in early 2009.

Museum of London

150 London Wall, EC2Y 5HN (0870 444 3851/www.museumoflondon. org.uk). Barbican or St Paul's tube. **Open** 10am-5.50pm Mon-Sat; noon-5.50pm Sun. **Admission** free; suggested donation £2. No credit cards. **Map** p151 D3 ㉞

This expansive museum, set in the middle of an unpromising roundabout on London Wall, shares the job of recreating London's history with the Museum in Docklands (p178). The chronological displays begin with 'London Before London': flint axes from 300,000 BC and suchlike, while 'Roman London' includes an impressive reconstructed dining room complete with mosaic floor. Windows overlook a sizeable fragment of the City wall, whose Roman foundations have clearly been built upon many times over the centuries. Sound effects and audio-visual displays illustrate the medieval city, with clothes, shoes and armour on display. From Elizabethan and Jacobean London comes the Cheapside Hoard, an astonishing cache of jewellery unearthed in 1912. The downstairs galleries (Victorian London, 'World City' and Lord Mayor's coach) are closed for major remodelling until 2010. The website has details of temporary exhibitions and activities for children.

Museum of St Bartholomew's Hospital

West Smithfield, EC1A 7BE (7601 8152). Barbican or Farringdon tube/ rail. **Open** 10am-4pm Tue-Fri. **Admission** free. **Map** p150 C3 ㉟

Many of the displays in this small museum inside St Bart's Hospital relate to the days before anaesthetics, when surgery and carpentry were kindred occupations. Every Friday at 2pm visitors can take a guided tour (£5, book ahead on 7837 0546), which takes in the Hogarth paintings in the Great Hall, the little church of St Bartholomew-the-Less, neighbouring St Bartholomew-the-Great and Smithfield.

Tower Bridge p162

Old Bailey (Central Criminal Court)

Corner of Newgate Street & Old Bailey, EC4M 7EH (7248 3277). St Paul's tube. **Open** Public gallery 10am-1pm, 2-4.30pm Mon-Fri. **Admission** free. No under-14s; 14-16s only if accompanied by adults. **Map** p150 C3 ③⑥

A gilded statue of blind (meaning impartial) justice stands atop London's most famous criminal court, which has hosted some of the most controversial trials in British history, including those of Oscar Wilde, the Kray brothers and IRA bombers. The public is welcome to attend trials, but note that bags, cameras, dictaphones, mobile phones and food are prohibited (and no storage facilities are provided).

St Bartholomew-the-Great

West Smithfield, EC1A 9DS (7606 5171/www.greatstbarts.com). Barbican tube/Farringdon tube/rail. **Open** 8.30am-5pm Mon-Fri (until 4pm Nov-Feb); 10.30am-4pm Sat; 2.30-6.30pm Sun. **Admission** £4; £3 reductions. **Map** p150 C3 ③⑦

This wonderfully atmospheric medieval church was built over the remains of the 12th-century priory hospital of St Bartholomew, founded by Prior Rahere, a former courtier of Henry I. The church was chopped about during Henry VIII's reign and the interior is now firmly Elizabethan. You might recognise the main hall from the movies *Shakespeare in Love* and *Four Weddings and a Funeral*. Benjamin Franklin trained here as a printer in 1724 before launching his political career in America.

St Bride's Church

Fleet Street, EC4Y 8AU (7427 0133/ www.stbrides.com). Temple tube/ Blackfriars tube/rail. **Open** 8am-6pm Mon-Fri; 11am-3pm Sat; 10am-1pm, 5-7.30pm Sun. Times vary Mon-Sat; phone ahead to check. **Admission** free. **Map** p150 B4 ③⑧

Hidden down an alley south of Fleet Street, St Bride's is still popularly known as the journalists' church. In the north aisle is a shrine that is dedicated to journalists killed in action. Down in the crypt, a fine museum displays fragments of the churches that have existed on this site since the sixth century. The Wren-designed spire is said to have been the inspiration behind the traditional tiered wedding cake.

St Magnus the Martyr

Lower Thames Street, EC3R 6DN (7626 4481/www.stmagnusmartyr. org.uk). Monument tube. **Open** 10am-4pm Tue-Fri; 10am-1pm Sun. **Admission** free. **Map** p151 E5 ③⑨

Downhill from the Monument, this looming Wren church marked the entrance to the original London Bridge, which was sold brick and mortar in 1971 to an Arizona millionaire who, so the story goes, believed he was buying Tower Bridge. A cute scale model of the old bridge is displayed inside the church (the Museum in Docklands, p178, has an even better one), along with a statue of axe-wielding St Magnus, the 12th-century Earl of Orkney. The church is mentioned in TS Eliot's *The Wasteland*.

St Paul's Cathedral

Ludgate Hill, EC4M 8AD (7236 4128/ www.stpauls.co.uk). St Paul's tube. **Open** 8.30am-4pm Mon-Sat. *Galleries, crypt & ambulatory* 9.30am-4pm Mon-Sat. **Admission** *Cathedral, crypt & gallery* £9.50; free-£8.50 reductions. *Tours* £3; £1-£2.50 reductions. No credit cards. **Map** p150 C4 ④⓪

The passing of three centuries has done nothing to diminish the magnificence of London's most famous cathedral. In the last decade, restoration has stripped most of the Victorian grime from the walls and the extravagant main façade looks as brilliant today as it must have when first unveiled in 1708. Sir Christopher Wren had to fight to get his plans for this epic cathedral past the authorities – many politicians thought it too large and expensive. His first two designs were rejected and he was forced to keep the construction of his third design a secret in order to create the massive dome for which St Paul's is now famous. In fact, there are three domes – the inner and outer domes are separated by a hidden brick dome that supports the entire structure (believed to weigh 64,000 tons).

Most visitors walk around in awe at the vast open spaces and grandiose memorials to national heroes such as Nelson, Wellington and Lawrence of Arabia. You can also look down on it all from the Whispering Gallery inside the dome, reached by 259 steps from the main hall (the acoustics here are so good that a whisper can be bounced clearly to the other side of the dome). Steps continue to the outdoor Golden Gallery (530 steps), which offers giddying views over London.

Before leaving St Paul's, head down to the crypt, which contains the small, plain tombstone of Wren, inscribed with the epitaph, 'Reader, if you seek a monument, look around you'. As well as tours of the main cathedral and self-guided audio tours (£3.50, £3 reductions), you can join special tours of the Triforium – visiting the library and Wren's 'Great Model' (pre-book on 7246 8357, £14.50 including admission).

Temple Church & the Inns of Court

King's Bench Walk, EC4Y 7BB (7353 8559/www.templechurch.com). Temple tube. **Open** 2-4pm Wed; 11am-12.30pm, 1-4pm Thur, Fri; times vary weekends. **Admission** free. **Map** p150 B4 ㊶

Inspired in its style by Jerusalem's Church of the Holy Sepulchre and consecrated in 1185, the Temple Church was the private chapel of the mystical Knights Templar – and hence gained sudden fame as 'The Da Vinci Code church'. It's the only round church in London and contains the worn gravestones of several Crusader knights, but you might have more fun exploring the Inns of Court. Middle Temple (7427 4800, www.middletemple.org.uk) and Inner Temple (7797 8183, www.innertemple.org.uk) aren't open to the public, but you can still potter through the courtyards; Inner Temple has fine buildings and lovely lawns for a peaceful picnic. North of the Royal Courts, Lincoln's Inn (7405 1393, www.lincolns

inn.org.uk) is a catalogue of architectural styles surrounding London's largest public square, while the gardens of the serene Gray's Inn (7458 7800, www.graysinn.org.uk) are open to the public on weekday mornings.

30 St Mary Axe

(www.30stmaryaxe.com). Liverpool Street tube/rail. **Map** p151 F4 ㊷
Completed only in 2004, Lord Foster's skyscraper has already become a cherished icon of modern London. The appropriateness of its 'Erotic Gherkin' nickname is immediately apparent; the sophistication of the technology within much less so – it cools and heats itself with maximum efficiency, as well as reducing fuel wastage by making the most of any available natural light.

Tower Bridge

Tower Bridge, SE1 2UP (7403 3761/ www.towerbridge.org.uk). Tower Hill tube/Tower Gateway DLR. **Open** *Apr-Sept* 10am-6.30pm daily. *Oct-Mar* 9.30am-6pm daily. **Admission** £6; free-£4.50 reductions. **Map** p151 F5 ㊸
Dating from 1894, this is the 'London bridge' that wasn't sold to America. Originally powered by steam, the drawbridge is now opened by electric rams when big ships need to venture this far upstream. An entertaining exhibition on the history of the bridge is displayed in the old steamrooms and the west walkway, which provides a crow's-nest view along the Thames.

Tower of London

Tower Hill, EC3N 4AB (0870 950 4466/www.hrp.org.uk). Tower Hill tube/Tower Gateway DLR/Fenchurch Street rail. **Open** *Mar-Oct* 10am-6pm Mon, Sun; 9am-6pm Tue-Sat. *Nov-Feb* 10am-5pm Mon, Sun; 9am-5pm Tue-Sat. **Admission** £16; free-£13 reductions. **Map** p151 F5 ㊹
Despite the exhausting crowds and long climbs up narrow stairways, this is one of Britain's finest historical attractions. Who wouldn't be fascinated by a close-up look at the crown of Queen Victoria or the armour (and prodigious codpiece) of King Henry VIII? The

Brill, Exmouth Market p157

buildings of the Tower span 900 years of history and the bastions and battlements house a series of interactive displays on the lives of British monarchs – and excruciatingly painful deaths of traitors. The highlight has to be the Crown Jewels, viewed from a slow-moving travelator at a steady glide, but the other big draw is the Royal Armoury in the White Tower, four floors of swords, armour, poleaxes, halberds and other gruesome tools for separating human beings from their body parts. Executions of noble prisoners were carried out on the green in front of the Tower – the site is marked by a glass pillow, sculpted by poet and artist Brian Catling in 2006.

Tickets are sold in the kiosk just to the west of the palace and visitors enter through the Middle Tower, but there's also a free audio-visual display in the Welcome Centre outside the walls. There's plenty here to fill a whole day, but you can skip to the highlights using the audio tour, or by joining one of the highly recommended and entertaining free tours led by the Yeoman Warders (Beefeaters), who also care for the Tower's ravens.

Event highlights 'Dressed to Kill', a display of arms and armour to celebrate Henry VIII's accession (Apr-Sept 2009).

Eating & drinking

Bar Kick

127 Shoreditch High Street, E1 6JE (7739 8700/www.cafekick.co.uk). Liverpool Street or Old Street tube/ rail. **Open** noon-11pm Mon-Wed, Sun; noon-midnight Thur-Sat. **Table football bar**. Map p151 F1 ⑮

A big square room with a bar, open kitchen, flags of all nations tacked to the ceiling and foosball tables under TVs that silently screen international football. Cool and excellently boisterous, Kick takes enough of a hint from European cafés (quality food, a curated selection of drinks) to draw in nearly as many women as men. The busy staff remain calm and friendly under the onslaught of twirl-crazed party groups.

Black Friar

174 Queen Victoria Street, EC4V 4EG (7236 5474). Blackfriars tube/rail. **Open** 11am-11pm Mon-Wed, Sat; 11am-11.30pm Thur, Fri; noon-10.30pm Sun. **Pub**. Map p150 C4 ⑯

LONDON BY AREA

Sir John Betjeman justifiably and successfully led the campaign to save this remarkable venue. Built in the 1880s on the site of a medieval Dominican friary, the Black Friar had its interior completely remodelled by H Fuller Clark and Henry Poole of the Arts and Crafts movement. Bright panes, intricate friezes and carved slogans ('Industry is Ale', 'Haste is Slow') make a work of art out of the main saloon.

Bodean's

NEW *16 Byward Street, EC3R 5BA (www.bodeansbbq.com). Tower Hill tube.* **Open** noon-11pm Mon-Fri; noon-10.30pm Sat. **££. Barbecue.** **Map** p151 E5 ④

Not a place for vegetarians, the new branch of Bodean's (which was due to open shortly after we went to press) should nonetheless be a hit, pleasing everyone else with spare, baby-back and beef ribs, big grilled steaks, pulled pork, chicken and brisket, served in huge, perfectly grilled portions. As at the original Soho location, there will be a small, informal upstairs, and a bigger downstairs with TVs for sport.

Bonds Bar & Restaurant

Threadneedle Hotel, 5 Threadneedle Street, EC4R 8AY (7657 8088/www. theetongroup.com). Monument tube/ Bank tube/DLR. **Open** 11am-11pm Mon-Fri; 3-11pm Sat; 3-10.30pm Sun. **Bar. Map** p151 E4 ④

The best bar in the City? All is as it should be: the attentive, black-shirted staff; the padded swivel bar-chairs; the reading lights over the bar; and, above all, the superb wines and cocktails, the latter covering more than 60 varieties.

East Room

NEW *2A Tabernacle Street, EC2A 4LU (7374 9570/0700 847 876/www. thstrm.com). Moorgate or Old Street tube/rail.* **Open** 11am-1am Mon-Wed; 11am-3am Thur, Fri; 7pm-3am Sat. **Cocktail bar. Map** p151 E2 ④

Private clubs seem to have had their day, but East Room won't have any difficulty in getting members to cough up £350 per year: it's a very good-looking

Bonds Bar & Restaurant

space, but, more importantly, it's a first-rate bar. Non-members have to book in advance for admission before 11pm, after that it's members-only. There are automatic drinks dispensers in the corridor, while the main lounge bar has comfy sofas and chairs around dining tables. The food is excellent, Matt Skinner is director of wine, and Gilles Peterson is director of music. We like.

Great Eastern Dining Room

54-56 Great Eastern Street, EC2A 3QR (7613 4545/www.greateasterndining. co.uk). Old Street tube/rail/55 bus. **Open** *Bar* noon-midnight Mon-Fri; 6pm-midnight Sat. *Restaurant* 12.30-3pm, 6.30-10.45pm Mon-Fri; 6.30-10.45pm Sat. **£££. Oriental bar-restaurant**. Map p151 E2 ⑩

GEDR is relaxed, good-looking and people-friendly, with squishy banquettes, paper-over-cloth tables, dark wooden floors and a chandelier conspiring to create a space you camp in as much as eat in. The menu pushes all the right buttons too, with its tour of South-east Asia, from dim sum to curries, although Thai food is the forte.

Northbank

NEW *One Paul's Walk, EC4V 3QH (7329 9299/www.northbankrestaurant. com). Blackfriars tube/rail or St Paul's tube.* **£££. British. Open** noon-midnight Mon-Sat; noon-5pm Sun. **Map** p150 C5 ㉛

Adjacent to Lord Foster's infamous wobbly bridge, Northbank specialises in food that comes from the south-west of England, one of the nation's best larders. The views are impressive, as is the menu, featuring the likes of Falmouth crab tart with clotted cream, and apple and blackberry crumble. The raised terrace has heated parasols for cooler evenings.

1 Lombard Street

1 Lombard Street, EC3V 9AA (7929 6611/www.1lombardstreet.com). Bank tube/DLR. **Open** *Bar* 11am-11pm Mon-Fri. **££** Brasserie **£££** Restaurant. **French**. Map p151 E4 ㉜

If you're going to dine in the City, you may as well go the whole hog and dine in a bank. This temple of Mammon is a Grade II-listed building, made bright and welcoming by big windows and neoclassical domed skylights. The food has won a Michelin star, merited both in the swish brasserie section and haute cuisine restaurant.

Sauterelle

Royal Exchange, EC3V 3LR (7618 2483/www.danddlondon.com). Bank tube/DLR. **Open** noon-2.30pm, 6-10pm Mon-Fri. **££. French**. Map p151 E4 ㉝

With its stunning location around the gallery of the lovely Royal Exchange, Sauterelle doesn't have to worry much about how it produces the wow factor. Instead it focuses all of its energy on food and service. The former is at the intersection between French and modern European (not too haute or pricey); the latter enjoyably mixes sycophancy and professionalism.

Sweetings

39 Queen Victoria Street, EC4N 4SA (7248 3062). Mansion House tube. **Open** 11.30am-3pm Mon-Fri. **£££. Fish**. Map p151 D4 ㉞

Small and spartan (except for a lovely mosaic-tiled floor), this century-old City institution remains determinedly old-fashioned – in a good way. Simple fish dishes are served at linen-covered counters, followed by classic schoolyard fantasies such as fruit crumble and spotted dick.

Vertigo 42

Tower 42, 25 Old Broad Street, EC2N 1HQ (7877 7842/www.vertigo42.co.uk). Bank tube/DLR/Liverpool Street tube/rail. **Open** noon-3pm, 5-11pm Mon-Fri. **Bar**. Map p151 E4 ㉟

Situated on the 42nd floor of the tallest edifice in the City, Vertigo 42 enjoys a stunning London panorama. Visitors have to earn their vista: the check-in process, including X-ray machines and guest passes, is reminiscent of an airport. Champers is surely the only appropriate order, so a night here isn't cheap – but it's a genuine London must-do.

Shopping

Bread & Honey

*205 Whitecross Street, EC1Y 8QP
(7253 4455/www.breadnhoney.com).
Barbican tube/Old Street tube/rail.* **Open**
10am-6.30pm Mon-Wed, Fri; 10am-7pm
Thur; 11am-5pm Sat. **Map** p151 D2 ❺❻
Owned by streetwear expert Laurent
Roure and club promoter Laurent
Chaumer, this boutique sells upscale
sports and casualwear. Check out, in
particular, the Baracuta G9 Harrington
jacket, as worn by Steve McQueen, and
military-inspired bags from QWST.

Flittner

*86 Moorgate, EC2M 6SE (7606 4750/
www.fflittner.com). Moorgate tube/rail.*
Open 8am-6pm Mon-Wed, Fri; 8am-
6.30pm Thur. **Map** p151 E3 ❺❼
In business since 1904, Flittner seems
unaware the 21st century has begun.
Hidden behind beautifully frosted doors
is a simple, handsome room, done out
with classic barber's furniture. Within
these hushed yet welcoming confines,
straightforward haircuts and shaves
are delivered with skill and dignity.

Three Threads

*47-49 Charlotte Road, EC2A 3QT
(7749 0503/www.thethreethreads.com).
Old Street tube/rail.* **Open** 11am-7pm
Mon-Sat; 2-5pm Sun. **Map** p151 F2 ❺❽
Unintimidating, laid-back, unique and
super-stylish, this Shoreditch menswear
shop serves free beer, has a free juke-
box full of dad rock, and has bar stools
conveniently placed at the till. Expect
cult labels such as Japan's Tenderloin
or Sweden's Fjall Raven.

Nightlife

Aquarium

*256 & 260 Old Street, EC1V 9DD
(7251 6136/www.clubaquarium.co.uk).
Old Street tube/rail.* **Open** 10pm Fri-
11am Sat; 10pm Sat-11am Sun; 10pm
Sun-4am Mon. **Map** p151 E2 ❺❾
This club opened in 1995, adding a
healthy dash of knowing cheesiness to
trendy Old Street. It's famous for its
bubble-icious jacuzzi (take swimming

togs) and long-running cheese 'n' funk
fest, Carwash. Hedonistic electro and
deep house after-parties like Insomnia
and Red Light kick off in the wee
hours, and the large tiered roof terrace
is the place for summer all-dayers.

Bar Music Hall

*134-146 Curtain Road, EC2A 3AR
(7729 7216/www.barmusichall.com).
Old Street tube/rail.* **Open** 11am-
midnight Mon-Thur, Sun; 11am-
2am Fri, Sat. **Map** p151 F1 ❻⓿
Not much to look at, it's true, but this
club was home to the notorious polysexual debauchery that was AntiSocial.
Nowadays, there are queues on
Saturday nights as Shoreditch's edgier
club kids wait for the door whore to
wave them into electro party Foreign.

Cargo

*83 Rivington Street, EC2A 3AY (7749
7840/www.cargo-london.com). Old
Street tube/rail.* **Open** noon-1am
Mon-Thur; noon-3am Fri, Sat; 1pm-
midnight Sun. **Map** p151 F2 ❻❶
While much of Shoreditch concerns
itself with how you look, Cargo's only
concern is what you're dancing to: if it's
good, it can call this converted railway
arch home for as long as it likes. There's
a small restaurant serving tapas, and
the first arch has a large, raised seating area. Summer gets the cool urban
garden smoking with barbecues.

Comedy Café

*66-68 Rivington Street, EC2A 3AY
(7739 5706/www.comedycafe.co.uk).
Liverpool Street or Old Street tube/rail.*
Map p151 F2 ❻❷
This purpose-built Shoreditch venue
usually plays host to three to four stand-
up comedians – most of them decent,
and one of which is usually a big name.
Wednesday is open mic night.

East Village

🆕 *89 Great Eastern Street, EC2A
3HX (7739 5173/www.eastvillageclub.
com). Old Street tube/rail.* **Open** 5pm-
1am Mon, Tue; 5pm-3am Wed-Sun.
Map p151 E2 ❻❸
Small club, big line-ups, they say – and
we wholeheartedly agree. Since East

The rebirth of City clubbing

Turnmills, London's key 1990s superclub, is dead – what's the future for City clubbing?

Turnmills, the karaoke wine bar that opened in Clerkenwell in 1985, became the first UK venue to get a 24-hour music and dance licence in 1990. Two 'absolutely mental' decades later, the music finally stopped with a 72-hour Easter extravaganza. 'Getting asked to DJ there was even more exciting than having a number one record,' says Sister Bliss of Faithless, one of the DJs on the closing weekend; the experiences of another, Norman Cook (aka Fatboy Slim), are probably closer to the norm: 'That club means a lot to Zoë and me. We did a lot of copping off there.'

So where do the party-crazed kids go now when there's DJing and copping off to be enjoyed? Bizarrely, the paucity of residents in the Square Mile – you know, the financial heartland of Britain – and consequent lack of licensing hassles have made the area attractive to promoters. Right opposite Lloyd's of London (p159), for example, Sintillate plays funky house and electro to dressed-up twenty- and thirtysomethings in the swanky and spacious former bank **Revolution Leadenhall** (140-144 Leadenhall Street, EC3V 4QT, 7929 4233, www.revolutionin thecity.com). Compared to the West End, promoter Gary Sewell points out, 'it's cheaper. Nicer. Safer. Much easier to park.' The Vault's £500 minimum-spend tables give a sense of the anticipated clientele.

For something more in the sweatily exuberant mood of Turnmills, there's neighbouring Shoreditch. Old raveheads moan that London's clubbing district now just feels like an adjunct of the City – and head further and further east to get their unhinged, arty, all-night kicks. But gems are still opening: **East Village** (opposite; pictured) has beautiful sound, a handsome venue, top–class music – and a central enough location that you don't need a major crash course in nightbus and taxi lore to get back to your hotel.

Village opened in February 2008, with a classy facelift and killer sound system, savvy promoters have been lining up to put on nights here. Although the interior is quite swanky, it's all about what happens on the basement dancefloor. Stuart Patterson rolls in the Faith house party one Friday a month, and Justin Robertson's Black Rabbit electro party is just as jammed. Plans for a kitchen were going ahead as we went to press.

Old Blue Last

38 Great Eastern Street, EC2A 3ES (7739 7033/www.theoldbluelast.com). Old Street tube/rail. **Map** p151 F2 **64**
This friendly, frenetic, scuzzy pub venue is of the type usually associated with Camden. The punters – most of them youthful and sporting Shoreditch uniform trilby-with-skinny jeans, but enlivened by the occasional grizzled bohemian – booze or nod along to the likes of prog-punk and indie synth-pop.

Plastic People

147-149 Curtain Road, EC2A 3QE (7739 6471/www.plasticpeople.co.uk). Liverpool Street or Old Street tube/rail. **Open** 10pm-2am Thur; 10pm-4am Fri, Sat; 8-11.30pm Sun. **Map** p151 F1 **65**

Dark basement? Check. A swung cat would brush its ears on all four walls? Check. A sound system that has had songs written about it? Check – and how! FWD has long called this tiny space home, and is now in residence every Saturday with its heavyweight dubstep and grime beats; CDR (second Thursday of the month) lets bedroom producers play their music-in-progress.

T Bar

Tea Building, 56 Shoreditch High Street, E1 6JJ (7729 2973/www.tbar london.com). Liverpool Street tube/rail. **Map** p151 F2 **66**
When T Bar opened in the over-saturated Shoreditch market, it changed the face of London's nightlife. A bunker-like place, it manages to book DJ stars such as Ivan Smagghe and Damian Lazarus – for no money whatsoever. Which means it's best to get down here early if you want to get in.

333

333 Old Street, EC1V 9LE (7739 5949/www.333mother.com). Old Street tube/rail. **Open** 10pm-2.30am Fri; 10pm-5am Sat. *Bar* 8pm-2.30am daily. **Map** p151 F1 **67**

Barbican Centre

A haven for Shoreditch's cutting-edge for more than a decade, this three-floored, no-frills party space has found its feet again thanks to quality house nights like Reverb, strange gay mash-ups at the midweek Dirty Fairy, and the filthy minimal antics of Zombies Ate My Brain.

Arts & leisure

Barbican Centre
Silk Street, EC2Y 8DS (7638 4141/ box office 7638 8891/www.barbican. org.uk). Barbican tube or Moorgate tube/rail. **Map** p151 D3 ⑱
The Barbican recently spent millions on a refurbishment aimed at making its labyrinthine array of public spaces more welcoming. It hasn't really helped, although the reworking of the acoustics in the arts centre's main concert hall is appreciated. At the core of the music roster, performing 90 concerts a year, is the London Symphony Orchestra (LSO). Other highlights include the annual BITE season, which cherry-picks exciting and eclectic theatre companies from around the globe, while the tiny Pit theatre hosts chic and atmos-pheric shorts. There's a good pro-gramme of world and independent cin-ema shown on the Barbican's three screens, as well as occasional excellent live accompaniments to silent films in the main auditorium. The Barbican Art Gallery (£8; free-£6 reductions) has exhibitions on art, design, architecture and pop culture that are pretty divert-ing, while the free Curve hosts crazy and interesting installations.

LSO St Luke's
161 Old Street, EC1V 9NG (information 7490 3939/box office 7638 8891/ www.lso.co.uk/lsostlukes). Old Street tube/rail. **Map** p151 D2 ⑲
Although it was designed by Nicholas Hawksmoor in the early 1700s, the Grade I-listed St Luke's church was left to decay during the 20th century. Its recent renovation and conversion by the London Symphony Orchestra into a rehearsal room, music education centre and a 370-seat concert hall cost around £20m, but it was worth every penny. The programme takes in lunchtime recitals (some of them free), evening chamber concerts, and even some jazz and rock shows.

Big Chill Bar p182

Neighbourhood London

Like many a modern metropolis, London is really two different cities. The centre is for work, play and lucky tourists, with most locals living where the rent is cheaper. This means restaurants and bars are often more vital – and exciting scenes more apt to develop – on the city's periphery. In **Greenwich**, the **Royal Botanic Gardens** at Kew and **Hampton Court**, however, neighbourhood London has tourist attractions that could easily fill a sightseeing day each on their own.

North London

The key destinations in north London are Islington and Camden. The gentrification of **Islington**'s Georgian squares and Victorian terraces have attracted boutiques and cafés, with arterial Upper Street drawing a steady stream of visitors. **Camden** – famous for its market (still one of London's biggest tourist draws) and situated beside London Zoo – is one of London's liveliest nightlife areas. Under the impetus of significant redevelopment just to the south in **King's Cross** (and contrary to its scuzzy reputation), it is also beginning to attract classy eateries and bars. West of Camden, snooty **St John's Wood** is the spiritual home of cricket, while further to the north, **Hampstead** and **Highgate** are prettily leafy, well-off villages either side of the lovely heath.

Sights & museums

Hampstead Heath

Hampstead Heath or Gospel Oak rail.
The heath's charming contours and woodlands make it feel far larger and more rural than it is. Views from the top of Parliament Hill are wonderful and on a hot day the bathing ponds are a godsend. The heath is popular for flying kites and sailing model boats, and there are bandstand concerts on Sunday afternoons in summer. At the northern end of the park is Kenwood House (see below).

Highgate Cemetery

Swains Lane, Highgate, N6 6PJ (8340 1834/www.highgate-cemetery.org). Highgate tube. **Open** *East Cemetery* Apr-Oct 10am-4.30pm Mon-Fri; 11am-4.30pm Sat, Sun. Nov-Mar 10am-3.30pm Mon-Fri; 11am-3.30pm Sat, Sun. *West Cemetery* tours only. *Tours* Dec-Feb 11am, noon, 1pm, 2pm, 3pm, 4pm Sat, Sun. Mar-Nov 2pm Mon-Fri. **Admission** £3. *Tours* £5. No credit cards.
With its dramatic tombs topped by towering angels, shrouded urns and broken columns, Highgate exudes a romantic atmosphere of ivy-covered neglect. The original 1839 West Cemetery (by tour only, book ahead) – is breathtaking; the less atmospheric East Cemetery has memorials to Karl Marx and George Eliot. The cemetery closes during burials, so call ahead.

Kenwood House

Hampstead Lane, Hampstead, NW3 7JR (8348 1286/www.english-heritage. org.uk). Hampstead tube/Golders Green tube then 210 bus. **Open** *Apr-Oct* 11am-5pm daily. *Nov-Mar* 11am-4pm daily. **Admission** free. *Tours* £5.
Built in 1616, Kenwood House was bought by brewing magnate Edward Guinness in 1925, who filled it with his art collection – a Vermeer and a Rembrandt are among the treasures. Outside, the 18th-century landscaped gardens are mostly unchanged, with a terrace giving lovely views of the lakes. The charming café is always busy.

London Zoo

Regent's Park, NW1 4RY (7722 3333/ www.zsl.org/london-zoo). Baker Street or Camden Town tube then 274, C2 bus. **Open** *Late Oct-mid Mar* 10am-4pm daily. *Mid Mar-late Oct* 10am-5.30pm daily. **Admission** £14.50; free-£12.70 reductions.
Opened in 1828, this was the world's first scientific zoo. The zoo's habitats keep pace with the times – the elephants have been given room to roam at the Whipsnade sister-site out in Bedfordshire, and the penguins have been moved from Lubetkin's famous modernist pool to a more suitable space by the main entrance. The 16,000sq ft walk-through squirrel monkey enclosure allows you to get close to the animals in an open environment, while Gorilla Kingdom, a forest walk among the big apes, has been a huge success. The newest draw is the Blackburn Pavilion's tropical bird habitat – again a walk-through space, this time with exotic hummingbirds – while in spring 2009 a dedicated Children's Zoo will open, featuring lots of new animals including red pandas. Check the daily programme for feeding times.

Lord's & MCC Museum

St John's Wood Road, St John's Wood, NW8 8QN (7616 8595/www.lords.org). St John's Wood tube. **Tours** *Nov-Mar* noon, 2pm daily. *Apr-Oct* 10am, noon, 2pm daily. **Admission** £10; free-£6 reductions.
The wearers of the famous egg-and-bacon striped tie have come to love the NatWest Media Centre, the funky raised pod that dominates the self-proclaimed home of cricket. The centre is included in the guided tour (book ahead), as are WG Grace ephemera, and, of course, the Ashes urn.

Eating & drinking

Charles Lamb

16 Elia Street, Islington, N1 8DE (7837 5040/www.thecharleslambpub. com). Angel tube. **Open** 4-11pm Mon, Tue; noon-11pm Wed-Sat; noon-10.30pm Sun. **££. Gastropub.**

A gem of a pub consisting of two small rooms decorated in a down-home fashion, with fairy lights around the fireplace and a notice saying 'Don't feed Mascha' (the dog). Food is no-nonsense, with bar snacks and hearty dishes.

Crown & Goose

100 Arlington Road, Camden, NW1 7HP (7485 8008). Camden Town tube. **Open** 11am-1am Mon-Thur, Sun; 11am-2am Fri, Sat. **Pub**.

Off Camden High Street, this lovely little pub feels deliciously out of the way. With dark green-painted panelling, glimmering candlelight and an open fire on chilly nights, it's delightfully old-fashioned and romantic. It also does simple but seriously good food.

Gilgamesh

Stables Market, Chalk Farm Road, Camden, NW1 8AH (7482 5757/ www.gilgameshbar.com). **Open** 6pm-2.30am Mon-Thur; noon-2.30am Fri-Sun. **£££. Asian bar/restaurant**.

This bar is a theatrical temple to excess. The scale is breathtaking, from the lapis lazuli bar to huge sphinxes that survey intricate hand-carved wall panels, pillars inset with polished stones, and an immense carved tree. Grab a table by the floor-to-ceiling windows to enjoy cocktails or pan-Asian food.

Osteria Stecca

NEW *1 Blenheim Terrace, St John's Wood, NW8 0EH (7328 5014/www. osteriastecca.com). St John's Wood tube.* **Open** 6.30-10.30pm Mon; noon-2.30pm, 6.30-10.30pm Tue-Fri; noon-3pm, 6.30-10.30pm Sat; noon-3.30pm, 6-9.30pm Sun. **£££. Italian**.

Chef-proprietor Stefano Stecca covers classic dishes from north and south Italy, often with a modern interpretation. Service is hospitable if somewhat disorganised, and the vibe is lively and laid-back. Great wine list too.

Ottolenghi

287 Upper Street, Islington, N1 2TZ (7288 1454/www.ottolenghi.co.uk). Angel tube/Highbury & Islington tube/rail. **Open** 8am-10.30pm Mon-Sat; 9am-7pm Sun. **££. Mediterranean**.

Ottolenghi is a treat, with food to die for. Nothing feels laboured, from the cool white furniture to the stylish but friendly staff. After your main, go and swoon over cakes and tarts at the front.

S&M Café

4-6 Essex Road, Islington, N1 8LN (7359 5361/www.sandmcafe.co.uk). Angel tube. **Open** 7.30am-11pm Mon-Fri; 8.30am-11pm Sat; 8.30am-10.30pm Sun. **£. Café**.

A good balance between caff and trendy diner, S&M (that's sausage and mash) serves everyone from celebs to bricklayers. You can 'mix & mash' from ten sausages, four types of mash and three of gravy. This branch of the mini chain has preserved features of the original Alfredo's café.

Warrington

NEW *93 Warrington Crescent, Maida Vale, W9 1EH (7592 7960/www. gordonramsay.com). Maida Vale or Warwick Avenue tube.* **Open** noon-11pm daily. **££. Gastropub**.

The Warrington is a grand gesture of a pub, lavishly decorated around 1900 in an idiosyncratic version of art nouveau. Up the sweeping staircase is Gordon Ramsay's dining room – dull in decor, but with excellent food and a month-long waiting list. Best to snack elsewhere and enjoy a beer downstairs.

Shopping

Camden Market

Camden Canal Market *off Chalk Farm Road, south of junction with Castlehaven Road (7485 8355/www.camdenlock.net).* **Open** 10am-6pm daily.

Camden Lock *Camden Lock Place, off Chalk Farm Road, NW1 8AF (7485 7963/www.camdenlockmarket.com).* **Open** 10am-6pm Mon-Wed, Fri-Sun; 10am-7pm Thur.

Camden Market *Camden High Street, junction with Buck Street, NW1 (7351 5353/www.camdenmarkets.org).* **Open** 9.30am-5.30pm daily.

Stables *off Chalk Farm Road, opposite junction with Hartland Road, NW1 8AH (7485 5511/www.stables*

Gilgamesh

market.com). **Open** 10am-6pm daily.
All *Camden Town or Chalk Farm tube.*
Camden Market, just next to the tube,
flogs cheap sunglasses and cut-price
interpretations of current fashions.
Camden Lock is much better, with an
attractive courtyard setting beside the
canal. There are pleasant cafés, some
good bars and shops selling things you
might actually buy. Crafty stalls sell
mostly decorative items from funky
lighting to ethnic art. North of the
courtyard is the Stables area, with vintage clothing and clubwear, while
antiques and contemporary designer
furniture are sold at the Horse Hospital.
It's all changing now, however, due to
a huge fire in spring 2008 and long-
term plans for massive redevelopment.

Camden Passage
Angel tube.
Once famous for antiques, this little
Islington street now offers pretty jew-
ellery at Kirt Holmes (no.16, 7226 1080)
and wonderful vintage clothes at
Annie's (no.12, 7359 0796).

Sefton
*196 Upper Street, Islington, N1 1RQ
(7226 7076/www.seftonfashion.com).*

Highbury & Islington tube. **Open** 10am-
6.30pm Mon-Wed, Sat; 10am-7pm Thur,
Fri; noon-6pm Sun.
This menswear boutique is strong on
Costume National, Miu Miu, McQueen
and Comme des Garçons, while Junk de
Luxe and Yohji Yamamoto will please
those with quieter tastes. Acessories
including Tom Ford sunnies complete
the stock. Womenswear is at no.271.

Nightlife

The nearby **Big Chill House**
(p147) is also superb.

Barfly
*49 Chalk Farm Road, Camden, NW1
8AN (7424 0800/www.barflyclub.com).
Camden Town or Chalk Farm tube.*
Open 7.30pm-midnight Mon-Wed, Sun;
7.30pm-2am Thur; 7.30pm-3am Fri;
1pm-3am Sat. No credit cards.
The Barfly chain does a fine job of sup-
porting up-and-coming musical talent.
This pokey upstairs venue is perfect
for indie guitar-meets-electro parties.
Kill Em All (fortnightly Saturdays) and
Adventures Close to Home (second
Fridays) are guaranteed to get the
enthusiastic crowd on the dancefloor.

EGG

*200 York Way, King's Cross, N7
9AP (7609 8364/www.egglondon.net).
King's Cross tube/rail then free shuttle
bus from York Way.* **Open** 10pm-6am
Fri; 10pm Sat-2pm Sun. No credit cards.
This gorgeous, three-floored party
palace is big enough to lose yourself in,
yet still manages to be cosy. You get
comfy red leather banquettes and wait-
ress service in the loft; a middle floor
with pole-dancing columns that seem
to belong in a warehouse dance studio;
and a ground floor that leads to the
spacious, AstroTurf-clad garden.

Jazz Café

*5 Parkway, Camden, NW1 7PG
(information 7534 6955/box office
7485 6834/0870 060 3777/www.jazz
cafe.co.uk). Camden Town tube.*
There is some jazz on the schedule
here, but this club deals more in soul,
R&B and hip hop these days, and has
become the first port of call for soon-to-
be-huge US acts. Note: tickets can cost
a lot more on the door than in advance.

KOKO

*1A Camden High Street, Camden,
NW1 7JE (7388 3222/www.koko.uk.
com). Mornington Crescent tube.* **Open**
9.30pm-4am Fri; 10pm-4am Sat; phone
to check other times. No credit cards.
Opened in 1900 as a music hall, this
venue got a major scrub-up in 2004 and
has since built a fine roster of events.
The large auditorium stages club
nights (including indie-focused Fridays
and the occasional Saturday Guilty
Pleasures cheese-fest) alongside an
indie-heavy gig programme.

Lock Tavern

*35 Chalk Farm Road, Chalk Farm,
NW1 8AJ (7482 7163). Chalk Farm
tube.* **Open** noon-midnight Mon-Thur;
noon-1am Fri, Sat; noon-11pm Sun.
Excellent bar-pub with DJs most
nights of the week, although Sundays
are the musical staple, attracting off-
duty DJs from elsewhere. Young indie
bands jostle for space with DJs from
regular nights such as Asbo. Plenty of
outdoor areas for sunny days.

Luminaire

*307-311 Kilburn High Road, Kilburn,
NW6 7JR (7372 8668/www.the
luminaire.co.uk). Kilburn tube/
Brondesbury rail.* No credit cards.
The booking policy here is excellently
broad, running from alt-rock legend
Mark Eitzel to hip electro-poppers
Junior Boys. The sound is well up to
scratch and the decor stylish. Drinks are
fairly priced. Even staff are friendly. If
only all venues were like this.

Proud

NEW *Horse Hospital, Stables Market,
Chalk Farm Road, Camden, NW1 8AH
(7482 3867/www.atproud.net). Camden
Town or Chalk Farm tube.*
After summarily closing down in 2007,
north London's premier lounge-about
hip spot returns in a cacophony of
superstar bands and celebrity DJs. Will
this new location reel the 'cool' brigade
back in? Opening events mixed up the
Enemy, Lethal Bizzle and Jodie Harsh
DJing – so the answer is probably yes.

Roundhouse

*Chalk Farm Road, Camden, NW1 8EH
(information 7424 9991/box office
0870 389 1846/www.roundhouse.
org.uk). Chalk Farm tube.*
A one-time railway turntable shed and
gin warehouse, the Roundhouse was
used for hippie happenings in the
1960s, then became a legendary rock
venue. Businessman Torquil Norman
reopened it in 2006 after a £30m refurbishment. The programme mixes arty
rock gigs with dance, theatre and
multimedia events. The acoustics are
good, and the bars and cafés excellent.

Arts & leisure

King's Place (see box p177)
should be a key addition to
local arts venues.

Almeida

*Almeida Street, Islington, N1 1TA
(7359 4404/www.almeida.co.uk).
Angel tube.*
Well groomed and with a funky bar,
the Almeida turns out well-crafted

theatre for grown-ups. Under artistic director Michael Attenborough it has drawn world premières and top directors, among them Richard Eyre.

Emirates Stadium

Ashburton Grove, Highbury, N7 7AF (7704 4040/www.arsenal.com). Arsenal tube.

Although Arsenal's challenge for the Premiership faltered badly at the latter end of the 2007/08 season, the team's attractive passing football and exciting young players had many neutrals (and even some rivals) purring. The team's grand new stadium is one of the most attractive in the country, and you can check out the club's illustrious history at the museum (£6, £3 reductions; incl stadium tour £12, £6 reductions).

Open Air Theatre

Regent's Park, Camden, NW1 4NR (7935 5756/box office 0870 060 1811/www.openairtheatre.org). Baker Street tube.

The verdant setting of this alfresco theatre lends itself perfectly to summery Shakespeare romps in a season that runs June to September, and standards are far above village green dramatics. Book well ahead and take an extra layer to fight chills during Act Three.

Project Space 176

NEW *176 Prince of Wales Road, Chalk Farm, NW5 3PT (7491 5720/www. projectspace176.com). Chalk Farm tube/Kentish Town West rail. No credit cards.*

This former Methodist chapel holds three shows a year, enabling artists to create experimental new work and curators to build exhibitions around the Zabludowicz Collection of emerging art in all media.

Sadler's Wells

Rosebery Avenue, Islington, EC1R 4TN (box office 0870 737 7737/www.sadlers wells.com). Angel tube.

World-famous Sadler's Wells remains the epicentre of London dance, with a terrific roster of visitors, ranging from Alvin Ailey's American Dance Theater

Roundhouse

to Spain's Paco Peña. The complex also provides a home for Matthew Bourne's New Adventures and Wayne McGregor's Random Dance.

Tricycle

269 Kilburn High Road, Kilburn, NW6 7JR (7328 1000/www.tricycle. co.uk). Kilburn tube.

Passionate and political, this theatre consistently finds original ways into difficult subjects such as Guantánamo Bay. There's also a buzzy bar.

Wembley Stadium

Stadium Way, Wembley, Middx HA9 0WS (8795 9000/www.wembley stadium.com). Wembley Park tube/ Wembley Stadium rail.

Britain's most famous sporting venue finally reopened in early 2007, more than three years behind schedule. Now it's complete, the new 90,000-seat Wembley, designed by Sir Norman Foster, is some sight, its futuristic steel arch an imposing feature of the skyline. All England football internationals and

SAGAR

BEST VEGETARIAN RESTAURANT

www.gosagar.com

'One of the Best South Indian Vegetarian Restaurants in London'
-Time Out

Time Out's Top 50 places you must eat before you leave London.
-January 2008

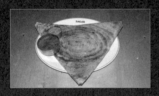

domestic cup finals are played here, as are rugby league finals and other sporting events, plus regular pop concerts.

East London

Right on the doorstep of the City, **Spitalfields** is known for its redeveloped Victorian covered market, around which spread gourmet food shops, restaurants and bars. To the east, **Brick Lane** may be world-famous for its curries, but the rise in reputation has been mirrored by a decline in quality. It is increasingly home to hip bars and new boutiques. Just north, **Hoxton** begins where the City overspill into Shoreditch comes to an end: the hip arts are moving east, but this is still your best bet for late drinking and clubbing. East of Shoreditch, **Bethnal Green** would be of scant interest to time-poor visitors were it not for the excellent Museum of Childhood, while unheralded **Dalston** has suddenly developed a cluster of very interesting music and arts venues – a beneficiary of the movement east from Shoreditch triangle. For a taste of a different kind of modern London – an area of high-finance that is getting cocky enough to take on the bankers and lawyers of the City itself – head to **Docklands**.

Sights & museums

Although work started on the new **Olympic Stadium** in May 2008, there's still little of interest around the 2012 site.

Dennis Severs' House

18 Folgate Street, Spitalfields, E1 6BX (7247 4013/www.dennissevershouse. co.uk). Liverpool Street tube/rail. **Open** noon-4pm 1st & 3rd Sun of mth; noon-2pm Mon following 1st & 3rd Sun of mth; times vary Mon evenings. **Admission** £5-£12.

Culture fit for a King's Place

Due to open for autumn 2008 just off York Way, **King's Place** is a symbol of the thoroughgoing transformation of King's Cross. Just a decade ago, suited gentlemen wandering the night streets would as likely have been after prostitutes as their last train, and crack cocaine was prime local merchandise. But the spiffy refurbishment of St Pancras (p144) has brought shiny new restaurants, as well as steadily gentrifying nightclubs (watch out for Pacha King's Cross on Caledonian Road).

King's Place, though, is something new. Look past the corporate tenants – albeit the *Guardian* newspaper's move here after having spent three decades in Farringdon raised some eyebrows – and you'll see a rather enticing mix of creative possibilities. The 420-seat King's Hall, for example, plays host to a pair of very different resident orchestras: not just the Orchestra of the Age of Enlightenment (www.oae.co.uk), baroque specialists, but also the London Sinfonietta, which is best known for superlative interpretations of contemporary classical music.

In addition to the music, there's to be a resident sculpture gallery – with an Eduardo Paolozzi permanently on display. The bar-brasserie, overlooking the canal basin, should be pretty cool too.
■ www.kingsplace.co.uk

London Zoo p171

This Huguenot house recreates, down to the tiniest detail, snapshots of life in Spitalfields between 1724 and 1914, a tour through a compelling 'still-life drama', as American creator Dennis Severs described it. With hearth and candles burning, smells lingering and objects scattered haphazardly, it's as if the inhabitants left just moments before.

Geffrye Museum

Kingsland Road, Hoxton, E2 8EA (7739 9893/recorded information 7739 8543/www.geffrye-museum.org.uk). Liverpool Street tube/rail then 149, 242 bus/Old Street tube/rail then 243 bus. **Open** 10am-5pm Tue-Sat; noon-5pm Sun. **Admission** free. No credit cards.
The Geffrye Museum is a marvellous physical history of English interiors, housed in converted almshouses. It recreates typical English living rooms in sequence from the 17th century to the present day, and has a series of lovely gardens designed on similar chronological lines. There's an airy restaurant and special exhibitions are held throughout the year.

Museum in Docklands

No.1 Warehouse, West India Quay, Hertsmere Road, Docklands, E14 4AL (recorded information 0870 444 3856/box office 0870 444 3857/ www.museumindocklands.org.uk). West India Quay DLR/Canary Wharf tube/DLR. **Open** 10am-6pm daily. **Admission** £5; free-£3 reductions.
This huge museum explores the complex history of London's docklands over the course of two millennia. Many exhibits are narrated by people who saw the changes for themselves; the Docklands at War section is very moving. There are also full-scale mock-ups of a quayside and a dingy riverfront alley. A brand new permanent gallery explores the links between the slave trade and sugar imports.
Event highlights 'Jack the Ripper and the East End' (until 2 Nov 2008).

V&A Museum of Childhood

Cambridge Heath Road, Bethnal Green, E2 9PA (8983 5200/recorded information 8980 2415/www.museum ofchildhood.org.uk). Bethnal Green tube/rail/Cambridge Heath rail. **Open** 10am-5.45pm daily. **Admission** free.
The Museum of Childhood has had a refurb and emerged sparkling, with a new entrance and a variety of fresh exhibits and play areas spread over its two floors. The huge collection of toys,

doll's houses, games and costumes has been steadily amassed since 1872, and is continuing to grow. The museum presents plenty of hands-on activities for kids, including dressing-up boxes. **Event highlights** 'Top to Toe' – exploring of changes in children's fashion (4 Oct 2008-19 Apr 2009).

Whitechapel Art Gallery

NEW *80-82 Whitechapel High Street, Whitechapel, E1 7QX (7522 7888/ www.whitechapel.org). Aldgate East tube.* **Open** *Whitechapel Laboratory* 11am-6pm Wed-Sun. **Admission** free.
Whitechapel's architecturally impressive art gallery has presented contemporary, forward-thinking exhibitions for more than a century. The gallery is undergoing a complete overhaul as it takes over the historic former library next door, with the hugely expanded premises due to reopen in 2009. Until then, Whitechapel Laboratory runs a doughty programme of events.

White Cube

48 Hoxton Square, Hoxton, N1 6PB (7930 5373/www.whitecube.com). Old Street tube/rail. **Open** 10am-6pm Tue-Sat. **Admission** free.
White Cube is still pretty much the only East End gallery that can attract paparazzi, here to snap the A-list celebs who turn up in black cabs for openings. The reason? A-list Young British Artists, among them Tracey Emin, Damien Hirst, Jake and Dinos Chapman and Sam Taylor-Wood. The gallery has also reasserted its West End presence by opening White Cube Mason's Yard (nos.25-26, 7930 5373).

Eating & drinking

Brick Lane Beigel Bake

159 Brick Lane, E1 6SB (7729 0616). Liverpool Street tube/rail/8 bus. **Open** 24hrs daily. **£.** No credit cards.
Bakery.
This charismatic East End institution rolls out perfect bagels both plain and filled, superb bread and moreish cakes. No wonder the queue trails out the door when the local bars and clubs close.

Carluccio's Caffè

Reuters Plaza, Docklands, E14 5AJ (7719 1749/www.carluccios.com). Canary Wharf tube/DLR. **Open** 7am-11pm Mon-Fri; 9am-11pm Sat; 10am-10.30pm Sun. **££. Italian**.
Antonio Carluccio's idea of providing traditional Italian food in unassuming café surroundings informs his successful chain. The utilitarian deli-cum-cafés are blessed with generously long opening hours, making them as perfect for breakfast as for a late dinner. They can be super-busy and noisy at lunchtime, but staff accommodate.

dreambagsjaguarshoes

34-36 Kingsland Road, Hoxton, E2 8DA (7729 5830/www.dreambags jaguarshoes.com). Old Street tube/rail. **Open** 5pm-midnight Mon; 5pm-1am Tue-Sat; 5pm-12.30am Sun. **Bar**.
The ultimate Shoreditch poster-bar: thoughtfully shambolic, with floor-to-ceiling windows, a grungey cellar and an experimental music policy (DJs Wed-Sat from 8pm, Sun from 4pm).

E Pellicci

332 Bethnal Green Road, Bethnal Green, E2 0AG (7739 4873). Bethnal Green tube/rail/8, 253 bus. **Open** 6.15am-5pm Mon-Sat. **£.** No credit cards. **Café**.
This much-loved caff has played an integral role in the social history of the East End as a home-from-home for gangsters, cabbies, local workers and families. Eat fry-ups, sarnies and old-fashioned Italian food amid maquetry panelling and yellow Vitrolite.

Gun

27 Coldharbour, Docklands, E14 9NS (7515 5222/www.thegundocklands. com). Canary Wharf tube/DLR/South Quay DLR. **Open** 11am-midnight Mon-Fri; 11.30am-midnight Sat; 11.30am-11pm Sun. **££. Gastropub**.
Although this place qualifies as a gastropub, it's effectively a smartish British restaurant attached to a local boozer (Thames-side terrace, roaring fire) with a more informal menu (roast beef sandwiches, chips and the like).

Hey big spender

Bucking the trend towards smaller-scale, individualistic and diversified shopping, west London is about to welcome the largest urban shopping centre in Europe. **Westfield London** should open for Christmas 2008. The 37-acre site will contain five major department stores, another 265 boutiques and a 14-screen multiplex. The Village, a high-end shopping area to the south-east of the complex, will have 40 cafés, bars and restaurants to fuel shoppers through two levels of luxury brands. There will be a gym and spa, personal shoppers, valet parking – even 'handsfree shopping'.

The infrastructure gives a sense of scale – 4,500 new parking spaces, a new tube stop (Wood Lane), a new overland station (Shepherd's Bush) and two bus terminals – and the cost is impressive: £1.6b will have been spent, £170m on transport.

Aware of the contradictions involved in opening a supersize mall in the current climate, Westfield stresses the cultural aspects of the development – music, fashion and art shows will be hosted in the massive indoor Pavilion – and such eco-friendly initiatives as rainwater harvesting, dedicated cycle and pedestrian routes, and a nature reserve. But they aren't shy of mentioning an estimated £5b annual spend in the centre's catchment area.

■ http://uk.westfield.com

Loungelover

1 Whitby Street, off Brick Lane, E1 6JU (7012 1234/www.loungelover. co.uk). Liverpool Street tube/rail. **Open** 6pm-midnight Mon-Thur, Sun; 6pm-1am Fri; 7pm-1am Sat. **Bar**.
Shoreditch loves this bar for its OTT approach to glamorous bonhomie. The deep red, luxe junkshop decor does much to impress, and the cocktails are utterly fabulous. Tables need to be booked in advance.

Plateau

4th floor, Canada Place, Canada Square, Docklands, E14 5ER (7715 7100/www.danddlondon.com). Canary Wharf tube/DLR. **Open** *Bar & grill* noon-11pm Mon-Sat; noon-4pm Sun. *Restaurant* noon-3pm, 6-10.30pm Mon-Fri; 6-10.30pm Sat. **£££**. **Modern European**.
Plateau absorbs the length of Canada Place's fourth floor, huge windows affording views of the area's dazzling modernity. It's a vast place, stretching from buzzing bar (with its own menu) to private dining rooms. The restaurant is sleek, if a bit monochrome, but the food comes with more colour.

Song Que

134 Kingsland Road, Hoxton, E2 8DY (7613 3222). Old Street tube/rail. **Open** noon-3pm, 5.30-11pm Mon-Sat; noon-11pm Sun. **£**. **Vietnamese**.
Song Que is still the culinary king of Little Vietnam. Despite its spartan decor and brusque waiters, hungry Hoxtonites flock here for wonderful northern and southern Vietnamese specialities. Avoid the Chinese items.

Tea Smith

6 Lamb Street, Spitalfields, E1 6EA (7247 1333/www.teasmith.co.uk). Liverpool Street tube/rail. **Open** 11am-6pm daily. **£**. **Tearoom**.
For tea-drinkers after something special, this little shop and tearoom is a godsend. The interior has a recognisably Japanese aesthetic with simple, clean lines. Teas are sourced directly from the Far East – their quality is matched by the accompanying nibbles.

Kew Gardens p185

Water House

NEW *10 Orsman Road, Dalston, N1 5QJ (7033 0123). Bus 242, 243.* **Open** 8am-10pm Mon-Fri; 10am-10pm Sat; 10am-4pm Sun. **£££. International.**
This is the second eco-restaurant from the people behind Acorn House (p144). In deepest, darkest Dalston, the location isn't exactly promising, but they've made the most of a modern building. It's the menu that really stands out, though. Wines are organic or biodynamic, and the food is low on carbon usage and highly seasonal. And, of course, all the fish comes from sustainable stocks.

Shopping

A Butcher of Distinction

11 Dray Walk, Old Truman Brewery, off Brick Lane, E1 6QL (7770 6111). Liverpool Street tube/rail. **Open** 10am-7pm daily.
This is a haven of impeccable fashion, with the butcher theme (meat hooks, framed joint charts, porcelain tiles) off-setting the clothes to perfection. The labels are a successful mix of old and new: Haversack, Nom de Guerre, MHL and Brit classic Steven Alan.

A Gold

42 Brushfield Street, Spitalfields, E1 6AG (7247 2487/www.agold.co.uk). Liverpool Street tube/rail. **Open** 11am-8pm Mon-Fri; 10am-6pm Sat; 11am-6pm Sun.
A Gold resembles a village shop from a bygone era. The Eccles cakes, English mead, marmalades, chutneys, amazing cheese straws, teas and traditional sweets are all great purchases.

Beyond Retro

112 Cheshire Street, Spitalfields, E2 6EJ (7613 3636/www.beyond retro.com). Liverpool Street tube/rail. **Open** 10am-6pm Mon-Wed, Fri-Sun; 10am-8pm Thur.
This huge bastion of second-hand clothing and accessories is the starting point for stylists, thrifters and designers on the hunt for bargains and inspiration. Many items are under £20.

Columbia Road Market

Columbia Road, Bethnal Green, E2. Liverpool Street tube/rail, then 26, 48 bus/Old Street tube/rail then 55, 243 bus. **Open** 8am-2pm Sun.
On Sunday mornings, this unassuming East End street is transformed into a

green swath of fabulous plant life and the air is fragrant with blooms. But it's not just about flora: alongside the flower market is a growing number of shops selling everything from pottery, groovy furniture and Mexican glassware to cupcakes and perfume. Refuel at Jones Dairy (23 Ezra Street, E2 7RH, 7739 5372, www.jonesdairy.co.uk).

Labour & Wait

18 Cheshire Street, off Brick Lane, E2 6EH (7729 6253/www.labourandwait. co.uk). Aldgate East tube/Liverpool Street tube/rail. **Open** 1-5pm Sat; 10am-5pm Sun.

Labour & Wait pays homage to timeless, unfaddy domestic goods that combine beauty with utility. The quintessentially British homewares include feather dusters, simple enamelware and sturdy canvas bags. There's a concession at Dover Street Market (p109).

Old Spitalfields Market

Commercial Street, between Lamb Street & Brushfield Street, E1 (7247 8556/www.visitspitalfields. com). Liverpool Street tube/rail. **Open** *General* 10am-4pm Mon-Fri; 9am-5pm Sun. *Antiques* 9am-4pm Thur. *Food* 10am-5pm Wed, Fri, Sun. *Fashion* 10am-4pm Fri. *Records & books* 10am-4pm 1st & 3rd Wed of the mth.

Spitalfields now consists of the refurbished 1887 covered market and an adjacent modern shopping precinct. Around the edge of Old Spitalfields Market, stands sell grub from around the world. The busiest day is Sunday, when the nearby Brick Lane Market and the Sunday (Up)Market in the Old Truman Brewery (strong on edgy designer and vintage; www.sundayupmarket.co.uk) create an *iD* photoshoot-meets-Bangladeshi bazaar vibe.

Rough Trade

NEW *Dray Walk, Old Truman Brewery, 91 Brick Lane, E1 6QL (7392 7788).* **Open** 8am-10pm Mon-Thur; 8am-8pm Fri, Sat; 11am-7pm Sun.

Despite the fading fortunes of many record shops, the people behind Rough Trade's Notting Hill outpost – revered

as a temple to all things alternative – recently opened this warehouse-style, 5,000sq ft store, café and gig space.

Nightlife

It will surprise no one that Hoxton is at the forefront of the latest nightlife trend (see box p191).

Bethnal Green Working Men's Club

42 Pollards Row, Bethnal Green, E2 6NB (7739 2727/www.workers playtime.net). Bethnal Green tube/rail/ 8, 55 bus. **Open** 8pm-2am Thur-Sat; 10.30am-2am Sun.

One of London's coolest clubs. The sticky red carpet and broken lampshades perfectly suit its quirky lounge, retro rock 'n' roll and fancy-dress burlesque parties, among them Mexican wrestling-cum-darkside cabaret Lucha Britannia and Grind a Go Go, burlesque with a hip 1960s dancefloor.

Big Chill Bar

Old Truman Brewery, off Brick Lane, E1 6QL (7392 9180/www.bigchill.net). Aldgate East tube/Liverpool Street tube/rail. **Open** noon-midnight Mon-Thur; noon-1am Fri, Sat; 11am-midnight Sun.

The Big Chill's original outlet (the other is in Bloomsbury, p147) is a hit with easy-going punters. Nightly changing DJs spin an enticing medley of laid-back tunes, and there's plenty of room to kick back while sipping a freshly mixed mojito in the loungey front area.

Bardens Boudoir

38-44 Stoke Newington Road, Dalston, N16 7XJ (7249 9557/www.bardensbar. co.uk). Dalston Kingsland rail/67, 76, 149, 243 bus. **Open** 8pm-2am Tue-Sat (days vary; check website for details). No credit cards.

This terrific basement club is tiny but has somehow put Stoke Newington High Street on the clubbing map. Mismatched wallpaper, battered sofas and scuffed wood floors give it cosy, worn-in vibe, while upcoming indie bands and edgy DJs keep it supercool.

Bistrotheque

23-27 Wadeson Street, Bethnal Green, E2 9DR (8983 7900/www.bistrotheque. com). Bethnal Green tube/Cambridge Heath rail/55 bus. **Open** *Shows* 9.30pm Fri, Sat (check website for details).

Bistrotheque's small cabaret room was launched as an addendum to the restaurant and bar, but is now internationally famous among alternative performance types. Jonny Woo's collective of alternative drag stars works from here, and the Underconstruction series gives performers a chance to try out works in progress.

Cafe Oto

NEW *18-22 Ashwin Street, Dalston, E8 3DL (info@cafeoto.co.uk). Dalston Kingsland rail.*

An interesting little space, hosting a great programme of wide-ranging music, from 1960s folk rediscoveries and post-rock outfits. The venue has whitewashed walls, jumbled chairs and tables, huge picture windows and a very informal bar.

On the Rocks p184

Hoxton Square Bar & Kitchen

2-4 Hoxton Square, Hoxton, N1 6NU (7613 0709/www.hoxtonsquare bar.com). Old Street tube/rail. **Open** 11am-1am Mon-Thur, Sun; 11am-2am Fri, Sat.

A long, industrial bunker of a bar with a big square back room that's perfect for gigs and post-work drinkies. It's all change on a Sunday, however, when fashionistas, freaks and wannabes descend for Boombox: a riot of extreme outfits and great mash-up DJs (dress like a civilian and you might not get in).

93 Feet East

150 Brick Lane, E1 6QN (7247 3293/ www.93feeteast.com). Aldgate East tube/Liverpool Street tube/rail. **Open** 5-11pm Mon-Thur; 5pm-1am Fri, Sat; noon-10.30pm Sun. No credit cards.

With its three rooms, a balcony and a wrap-around courtyard for barbecues, 93 Feet East offers plenty of good nights: 90 Free Fridays showcase up-and-coming and established bands for

Hampton Court Palace

(you guessed) free, while the winter season of Rock 'n' Roll Cinema is a great mix of short films and local ska and rockabilly bands.

On the Rocks

25 Kingsland Road, Hoxton, E2 8AA (no phone). Old Street tube/rail. **Open** 10.30pm-late Fri; 9pm-2am Sat.

There are run-down, after-the-after-party clubs… and then there's On the Rocks. Dark, small and full of UV lights, it's a haven for Shoreditch's dedicated party people. Hannah Holland is a cracking local DJ whose star is on the up and up; her dressed-up, mainly gay and thoroughly twisted electro Trailer Trash party is here every Friday.

Unit 7

NEW *Cable Studios, 566 Cable Street, Limehouse, E1W 3HB (no phone/ www.unitseven.co.uk). Limehouse rail/DLR.* No credit cards.

Unit 7 is part of a huge warehouse full of small artists' and music studios and creative start-ups. The promoters are open-minded types, so you're as likely to see a polysexual masked ball as a thumping great, all-night electro rave.

Vortex Jazz Club

Dalston Culture House, 11 Gillet Street, Dalston, N16 8JN (7254 4097/www.vortexjazz.co.uk). Dalston Kingsland rail.

A fixture on Stoke Newington Church Street for many years, the Vortex reopened in 2005 in a handsome new building. The upstairs space (all blond wood and chrome) sometimes feels a little sterile, but the line-ups are as good as ever, packed with left-field talent from Britain, Europe and the US.

South London

South London's attractions are manifold, although not always immediately obvious. Heading due south brings you to residential districts such as boisterous **Brixton**, with its lively nightlife and market, and **Clapham** and **Battersea**, both with an excellent range of bars and restaurants. To the east is **Greenwich**, laden with centuries of royal and maritime heritage. Here, in May 2007, a fire devastated the historic *Cutty Sark* tea clipper, which was already in the process of being restored; for information, see www.cuttysark.org.uk. Further to the west, you'll find **Kew** and **Hampton Court Palace**.

Sights & museums

Hampton Court Palace

East Molesey, Surrey KT8 9AU (0870 751 5175/0870 752 7777/0870 753 7777/24hr information 0844 482 7777/www.hrp.org.uk). Hampton Court rail/riverboat from Westminster or Richmond to Hampton Court Pier (Apr-Oct). **Open** *Palace* Apr-Oct 10am-6pm daily. Nov-Mar 10am-4.30pm daily. *Park* dawn-dusk daily. **Admission** £13; free-£10.50 reductions. *Maze only* £3.50; £2 reductions. *Gardens only* Apr-Oct £4, £2.50-£3 reductions; Nov-Feb free.

This spectacular palace was built in 1514 by Cardinal Wolsey, but Henry VIII liked it so much he seized it for himself in 1528. For the next couple of centuries it became one of the focal points of English history: Elizabeth I was imprisoned in a tower by her elder sister Mary I, and Shakespeare gave his first performance to James I in 1604. The palace's vast size can be daunting, so take advantage of the guided tours. King Henry VIII's State Apartments include the Great Hall, noted for its splendid hammer-beam roof; in the Haunted Gallery, the ghost of Catherine Howard – Henry's fifth wife – can reputedly be heard shrieking. Outside, the exquisitely landscaped gardens include peaceful Thames views and the famous maze.

Event highlights 'Young Henry VIII', a new permanent exhibition.

National Maritime Museum

Romney Road, Greenwich, SE10 9NF (8858 4422/information 8312 6565/ tours 8312 6608/www.nmm.ac.uk). Cutty Sark DLR/Greenwich DLR/rail. **Open** *July, Aug* 10am-6pm daily. *Sept-June* 10am-5pm daily. *Tours* phone for details. **Admission** free. No credit cards.

Opened in 1937, the museum's massive holdings include the world's largest collections of maritime art, cartography, ship's models, flags, instruments and costumes. Nelson's Navy exhibits more than 250 objects, including the undress coat worn by Nelson at the Battle of Trafalgar, weaponry, arte-facts and art. Elsewhere, Explorers includes a small, chilling *Titanic* exhibition, Seapower covers naval battles from Gallipoli to the Falklands, and the Art of the Sea is the world's largest maritime art collection. A colonnaded walkway takes you to the Queen's House (8312 6565), designed by Inigo Jones and holding art by the likes of Hogarth and Gainsborough. The Observatory and Planetarium (see p186), up the hill, are another part of the same museum.

Event highlights Sculptures by Simon Patterson, using old charts, ancient myth and memories of Jacques Cousteau (until 26 Oct 2008).

Royal Botanic Gardens (Kew Gardens)

Kew, Richmond, Surrey TW9 3AB (8332 5655/information 8940 1171/ www.kew.org). Kew Gardens tube/rail/ Kew Bridge rail/riverboat to Kew Pier. **Open** *Apr-Aug* 9.30am-6.30pm Mon-Fri; 9.30am-7.30pm Sat, Sun. *Sept-late Oct* 9.30am-6pm daily. *Late Oct-early Feb* 9.30am-4.15pm daily. *Early Feb-Mar* 9.30am-5.30pm daily. **Admission** £12.25; free-£10.25 reductions.

From the early 1700s until 1840, when the gardens were given to the nation, these were the grounds for two royal residences. The 18th-century inhabitants George II and Queen Caroline were enthusiastic gardeners. In the mid 1700s, Lancelot 'Capability' Brown began designing an organised layout for the property, using the plants Caroline had collected from voyaging botanists. This was the start of today's beautiful collection, now covering around half a square mile. Check out the two huge greenhouses and, for an interesting perspective on the 17th-century, Kew Palace. Queen Charlotte's

Cottage has a dazzling springtime blue-bell garden, while the Rose Garden and Woodland Garden are the stuff of fairy-tales. The new 60ft high walkway gives a new perspective on Kew's trees. **Event highlights** Kew's 250th anniversary, celebrated through 2009 with a new garden by Diarmuid Gavin.

Royal Observatory & Planetarium

Greenwich Park, SE10 9NF (8312 6565/www.rog.nmm.ac.uk). Cutty Sark DLR/Greenwich DLR/rail. **Open** 10am-5pm daily. **Admission** free. *Planetarium* £6; £4 reductions; £16 family.

A £15m refurbishment has added a new planetarium alongside the Observatory originally built for Charles II. As well as four galleries charting the development of timekeeping since the 14th century, the observatory has a dome housing the largest refracting telescope in the country. In the courtyard is the Prime Meridian Line – star of a billion snaps of grinning tourists with a foot in each hemisphere. The planetarium's architecture cleverly reflects its astrological position: the semi-submerged cone tilts at 51.5 degrees, the latitude of Greenwich, pointing to the north star, and its reflective disc is aligned with the celestial equator. The Starlife show describes the birth and death of stars.

Wimbledon Lawn Tennis Museum

Centre Court, All England Lawn Tennis Club, Church Road, SW19 5AE (8946 6131/www.wimbledon.org/museum). Southfields tube/39, 493 bus. **Open** 10.30am-5pm daily; ticket holders only during championships. **Admission** (incl tour) £15.50; free-£13.25 reductions.

Highlights here include a 200° cinema screen that allows you to find out what it's like to play on Centre Court. There are behind-the-scenes tours, except during the famous tournament; to watch a match, queue from stupidly early in the morning for one of the 6,000 tickets released daily.

World Rugby Museum/ Twickenham Stadium

Twickenham Rugby Stadium, Rugby Road, Twickenham, Middx TW1 1DZ (8892 8877/www.rfu.com). Hounslow East tube then 281 bus/Twickenham rail. **Open** *Museum* 10am-5pm Tue-Sat; 11am-5pm Sun. *Tours* 10.30am, noon, 1.30pm, 3pm Tue-Sat; 1pm, 3pm Sun. **Admission** £10; £7 reductions.

The impressive Twickenham Stadium is the home of English rugby union. Tickets for international matches are extremely hard to come by, but the World Rugby Museum, whose memorabilia charts the history of the game, offers some compensation. Tours take in the England dressing room, the players' tunnel and the Royal Box.

Eating & drinking

Botanist on the Green

3-5 Kew Green, Kew, Surrey TW9 3AA (8948 4838/www.thebotaniston thegreen.com). Kew Gardens tube/rail/65, 391 bus. **Open** noon-11pm Mon-Wed; noon-midnight Thur-Sat; noon-10.30pm Sun. **££**. **Gastropub**.

This is the perfect place for a pint after a visit to neighbouring Kew Gardens. The decor mixes exposed brick walls and trad china plates, retro light fittings and Anaglypta walls, while the outdoor space is as twinkly as a fairy grotto. There's a great selection of wine and draught beer, as well as coffee and leaf teas, and the food is impressive.

Dusk

339 Battersea Park Road, Battersea, SW11 4LF (7622 2112/www.duskbar.co.uk). Battersea Park rail. **Open** 6pm-12.30am Tue, Wed; 6pm-1.30am Thur; 6pm-2am Fri, Sat. **Cocktail bar**.

The absurdly friendly waiting staff clearly love working at this refurbished cocktail bar – and we love drinking here. The Mr Scruff soundtrack sums up the place perfectly: fun, clever and not prepared to take itself seriously.

Gipsy Moth

60 Greenwich Church Street, Greenwich, SE10 9BL (8858 0786). Cutty Sark

Hereford Road p190

DLR. **Open** noon-11pm Mon-Thur;
noon-midnight Fri, Sat; noon-10.30pm
Sun. **Pub**.
This formerly staid tourist pub has
been transformed into a bright and
busy bar, thanks to a bohemian refurb
(loungey furniture, funky wallpaper,
braided curtains, retro lamps, open
kitchen). There's also a huge garden.

Glasshouse

*14 Station Parade, Kew, Surrey
TW9 3PZ (8940 6777/www.glasshouse
restaurant.co.uk). Kew Gardens tube/
rail*. **Open** noon-2.30pm, 7-10.30pm
Mon-Sat; 12.30-2.45pm, 7.30-10pm Sun.
£££. **Modern European**.
Kew's connection with perennials bred
from fine root-stock extends to this
lovely restaurant. The glass-fronted
room has a subtle, classy comfort and
the pace is perfect. As good for a long
lunch as an unrushed evening meal.

Nightlife

Amersham Arms

NEW *388 New Cross Road, New
Cross, SE14 6TY (8469 1499/www.
amersham-arms.co.uk). New Cross tube*.
Open noon-midnight Wed, Sun; noon-
2am Thur; 10am-3.30am Fri, Sat.
Until recently, this was just another
boozer with a backroom. Now it puts

together the character (and prices) of
a trad pub with a souped-up soundsystem and 3am licence, an arts space
upstairs and a walled garden where
smokers can puff in peace. Expect rock
and rave, live gigs and clubby knees-
ups – as well as a fine carvery roast.

Babalou

*Crypt, St Matthew's Church, Brixton
Hill, Brixton, SW2 1JF (7738 3366/
www.babalou.net). Brixton tube/rail*.
Open 7pm-3am Mon-Thur, Sun;
7pm-5am Fri, Sat.
It's hard to imagine these church
crypts as anything but a gorgeous club
and bar. The prevailing Moroccan
theme – flickering lamps, wooden panels and decadent, red velvet booths –
makes the low-ceilinged space seem
positively cosy; the large dancefloor
fills up on Fridays and Saturdays with
a house crowd; comedy nights, potent
cocktails and salsa sessions keep the
midweek crowd happy.

Carling Academy Brixton

*211 Stockwell Road, Brixton, SW9
9SL (information 7771 3000/box
office 0870 771 2000/www.brixton-
academy.co.uk). Brixton tube/rail*.
Looking a little shabby, the Brixton
Academy nonetheless remains the

The Walmer Castle

Ledbury Road p192

city's most credible major rock venue. Despite being echo-ey when shows are half full, the 5,000-capacity space is popular because of its sloping surface, which allows pretty good sight lines from quite far back. Pop acts like Mika play here, but the programming leans more to metal, indie and alt-rock.

Dex Club

NEW *467 Brixton Road, Brixton, SW9 8HH (7326 4455/www.dexclub.co.uk). Brixton tube/rail.*
A seriously classy art deco club, that includes a mini-boutique hotel and two huge terraces (with hot tub). A great place for parties three seasons of the year, bringing urban sounds to nights like Southern Hospitality.

Dogstar

389 Coldharbour Lane, Brixton, SW9 8LQ (7733 7515/www.thedogstar. co.uk). Brixton tube/rail. **Open** 4pm-2am Mon-Thur; noon-4am Fri, Sat; noon-2am Sun.
A Brixton institution, the Dogstar is a big street-corner pub exuding that urban authenticity that's so loved by clubbers. The vibe can be intense, but the nightly changing music is always

highest quality. It's a training ground for the superstar DJs of tomorrow.

O2 Arena

Millennium Way, North Greenwich, SE10 0BB (8463 2000/box office 0871 984 0002/www.theo2.co.uk). North Greenwich tube.
The Millennium Dome has been converted into a state-of-the-art 23,000-capacity enormodome, with good sight lines and acoustics. Since opening in July 2007, it's hosted heavy-hitters such as the Rolling Stones, as well as a sporting events. Next door to the Arena but also inside the Dome is IndigO2 (0844 844 0002, www.theindigo2.co. uk), which holds 3,000 to 4,000 people. The complex also contains a Vue multiplex and the Bubble exhibition space. Exciting news for late 2008 is the arrival of a 2,700-capacity new gig and club venue from the people behind Fabric (p157). Public transport links are excellent, especially the Thames Clipper boat service.

Vauxhall Village

Vauxhall tube/rail.
London's centre for night-and-day gay hedonism, the 'Vauxhall Village' is a

compact cluster of clubs with some frighteningly extended opening times. Many of the clubs are tucked into industrial spaces under the railway arches, among them Area (67-68 Albert Embankment, 7091 0080, www.area-club.info), popular on Fridays and Saturdays, and Bar Code Vauxhall (69 Goding Street, 7582 4180, www.bar-code.co.uk), which – despite its shiny surfaces – draws a bloke-ish crowd every night. South Lambeth Road has two standout venues: Fire (7820 0550, www.fireclub.co.uk) is the primary port of call for serious clubbers, with three rooms of DJs catering for most tastes (but big on tech house) from Friday to Sunday, while the men-only Hoist (no.47B&C, 7735 9972, www.the hoist.co.uk) is one of two genuine leather bars in London. Kennington Lane is home to the irrepressible Royal Vauxhall Tavern (no.372, 7737 4043, www.theroyalvauxhalltavern.co.uk). This pub-turned-legendary-gay venue operates a booking policy of anything goes and a 'no attitude' dress code. The most famous night is queer perfor- mance night Duckie on a Saturday, but Sunday's Dame Edna Experience is also essential. At no.349, South Central (7793 0903, www.southcentrallondon. co.uk) is a multi-purpose drinking hole that draws together bears and fashion- istas for Sunday night's deliciously random music mix at Horse Meat Disco – expect a mash-up of disco, soul, new wave and punk.

Arts & leisure

BAC (Battersea Arts Centre)
Lavender Hill, Battersea, SW11 5TN (7223 2223/www.bac.org.uk). Clapham Common tube/Clapham Junction rail/77, 77A, 345 bus.
The forward-thinking BAC, which inhabits the old Battersea Town Hall, plays alma mater to new writers and theatre companies. Artistic director David Jubb started the famous Scratch programme, which shows a work in progress to larger and larger audiences

until it's polished. Over the next five years he aims to transform BAC into a radical promenade performance space.

West London

The triangle between **Notting Hill Gate**, **Ladbroke Grove** and **Westbourne Park** tube stations contains some lovely squares, grand houses and fine gardens, along with the shops, bars and restaurants that serve the kind of bohemian who can afford to live here. Turning north from Notting Hill Gate takes you towards the boutique-heavy streets of **Westbourne Grove** and **Ledbury Road**. To get a feel for lived-in west London, seek out **Shepherd's Bush** to the west and riverside **Hammersmith**.

Sights & museums

Museum of Brands, Packaging & Advertising
Colville Mews, Lonsdale Road, Notting Hill, W11 2AR (7908 0880/www. museumofbrands.com). Notting Hill Gate tube. **Open** 10am-6pm Tue-Sat; 11am-5pm Sun. **Admission** £5.80; free-£3.50 reductions.
Started when he was 16, Robert Opie's collection has grown to include every- thing from milk bottles to cereal pack- ets. The emphasis is on British consumerism: watch as your favourite brands transmogrify over the years.

Eating & drinking

Assaggi
1st floor, 39 Chepstow Place, Bayswater, W2 4TS (7792 5501). Bayswater, Queensway or Notting Hill Gate tube. **Open** 12.30-2.30pm, 7.30- 11pm Mon-Sat. **£££. Italian**.
Although Assaggi is renowned for celebrity custom and premium prices, it's also suprisingly informal. Upstairs from a pub, it's decorated in simple, bright colours and the brief menu is purist, but the cooking is superb.

Café García

246 Portobello Road, Ladbroke Grove, W11 1LL (7221 6119/www.cafegarcia. co.uk). Ladbroke Grove tube. **Open** 9am-5pm daily. **£**. **Spanish**.
The café arm of this Spanish groceries importer is hard to beat for tapas, a pastry or a quick coffee. The bright, modern eaterie is often peaceful, even when the market is bustling – surprising, given the high standard of food.

Clarke's

124 Kensington Church Street, Kensington, W8 4BH (7221 9225/www.sallyclarke.com). Notting Hill Gate tube. **Open** 12.30-2pm Mon; 12.30-2pm, 7-10pm Tue-Fri; 11am-2pm, 7-10pm Sat. **£££**. **Modern European**.
Having brought Cal-Ital cooking to the UK in the 1980s, Sally Clarke's approach to food remains uncompromising: impeccable sourcing, deceptively simple preparation, perfect tastes.

Cow

89 Westbourne Park Road, Westbourne Grove, W2 5QH (7221 0021/www. thecowlondon.co.uk). Royal Oak or Westbourne Park tube. **Open** noon-11pm Mon-Thur; noon-midnight Fri, Sat; noon-10.30pm Sun. **£££**.
Gastropub.
Gastrobar guru Tom Conran runs this two-storey operation: an Irish pub downstairs and renowned restaurant upstairs, with another dining area at the back. Plates of rock oysters sit atop the bar counter, invariably accompanied by a decent pint of Guinness.

Hereford Road

NEW *3 Hereford Road, Bayswater, W2 4AB (7727 1144/www.herefordroad. org). Bayswater or Royal Oak tube.* **Open** noon-3pm, 6-10.30pm Mon-Sat; noon-3pm, 6-10pm Sun. **British**. **£££**.
Hereford Road is sparsely but comfortably furnished, with leather banquettes in the lower dining area and an open kitchen to watch upstairs. Chef Tom Pemberton was previously at St John (p156), and it shows: this is British food at its boldest, with seasonal ingredients used imaginatively.

Kiasu

NEW *48 Queensway, Bayswater, W2 3RY (7727 8810). Bayswater or Queensway tube.* **Open** 11pm daily. **£**. **Singaporean**.
Winner of *Time Out*'s Best Cheap Eats award in 2007, Kiasu offers exceptional Singaporean cooking at decent prices. The Hainanese chicken rice and laksa are as good as any we've ever had, and the atmosphere is informal.

Urban Turban

NEW *98 Westbourne Grove, W2 5RU (7243 4200). Bayswater, Notting Hill Gate or Queensway tube.* **Open** 5-11pm Mon-Fri; noon-11pm Sat, Sun. **££**.
Indian & Pakistani.
Despite decor and a soundtrack that screams 'trendy lounge bar', Urban Turban is all about the food. At the helm is Indian chef Vineet Bhatia, famed for his innovation in the kitchens of upscale Asian restaurants; here, he has returned to his roots, offering simpler dishes that are all the better for it. Don't miss the proper birianis.

Westbourne House

NEW *65 Westbourne Grove, W2 4UJ (7229 2233). Royal Oak or Bayswater tube.* **Open** noon-11.30pm Mon-Thur; noon-midnight Fri; 11am-midnight Sat; 11am-11.30pm Sun. **Cocktail bar**.
A great new bar, just when we were starting to wonder if Notting Hill's cocktail bar scene was moribund. Transformed with gilded mirrors and faux-French furniture, this big, handsome pub now has a cocktail list that focuses on the classics. Spirits are premium and the delivery is pristine; admirable wine list too. The bijou list of antipasti, meze, bruschetta, plus a few daily specials, comes second place to the drink, but is no afterthought.

Shopping

The massive **Westfield London** mall (see box p180) opens in 2008.

Alice & Astrid

30 Artesian Road, Notting Hill, W2 5DD (7985 0888/www.aliceandastrid.

Crawling with mad music

If three's a trend, then four's a craze on a par with doin' the mashed potato. And just such a concatenation of events is taking place in the brave new world of the urban festival-cum-pub crawl.

It all started with the **Camden Crawl** (p41), back in the mists of time, but this year everything really kicked off. **Concrete & Glass** (2-3 October) will be the fourth Crawl-style event of 2008, following the original in April and two newcomers: **Stag & Dagger** and the calamitously named **Hox to Dot**, both in May 2008.

So what's the big idea? You buy a wristband, which grants you access to a number of small venues within walking distance of each other (inevitably in Camden or Hoxton). At the venues, a mishmash of under-the-radar and just plain peculiar bands (as well as occasional well-known surprise guests) play over the course of an evening or a weekend.

You simply chart a route between your favourite acts in some kind of vomit-flecked pub crawl – or, most likely, entirely miss everything you thought you wanted to see and instead stumble across all sorts of great new acts. By encouraging you outside between bands, this approach provides a service to music fans with short attention spans and nicotine addictions, as well to gig-goers whose knees seize up after being stood still for ten minutes at a time.

The line-ups capture London's hyperactive listening habits perfectly, veering from maniacal electro-pop to maudlin Americana, via melon-twisting hip hop and things born of an unholy union between the Buggles and Van Halen. You have been warned.

- www.concreteandglass.co.uk
- www.dottodotfestival.co.uk
- www.staganddagger.com
- www.thecamdencrawl.com

com). *Notting Hill Gate tube.* **Open**
10am-6pm Mon-Fri; 11am-6pm Sat, Sun.
The lingerie and loungewear displayed
in this sweet little shop is feminine and
flirtatious. Items for sale here include
bloomers and pretty camisoles in taste-
fully pale colours.

Ledbury Road
*Westbourne Park or Notting
Hill Gate tube.*
Just off Westbourne Grove is this
enclave of chic boutiques. Matches
(nos.60-64, 7221 0255, www.matches
fashion.com) has a well-selected range
of pricey gear , while Caramel (no.77,
7727 0906, www.caramel-shop.co.uk) is
a charming children's clothes shop.
Paul and Joe (nos.39-41, 7243 5510,
www.paulandjoe.com) is wonderful for
accessories. More specialist shops
include Brora (nos.66-68, 7229 1515,
www.brora.co.uk), stocking Scottish
cashmere knits, and Bodas (no.38B,
7229 4464, www.bodas.co.uk), selling
simply designed but practical lingerie.
Foodies are well catered for as well:
Melt (no.59, 7727 2348, www.melt
chocolates.com) is home to Keith
Hurdman's scrumptious choccies, and
there's a branch of posh deli-café
Ottolenghi (p172) at no.63 (7727 1121,
www.ottolenghi.co.uk).

Oxfam Boutique
NEW 245 Westbourne Grove, W11
2SE (7229 5000/www.oxfam.org.uk).
Notting Hill Gate tube. **Open** phone
or check the website for details.
An Oxfam shop, but not as we know it
– after all, former Topshop director
Jane Shepherdson is behind it. Due to
open in May 2008, this will be the first
of the charity's new 'sustainable fashion' boutiques, selling chic one-offs,
quality secondhand, reworked pieces
and a range of Fair Trade clothes.

Portobello Road Market
*Portobello Road, Notting Hill, W10
& W11 (7229 8354/www.portobello
road.co.uk). Ladbroke Grove or Notting
Hill Gate tube.* **Open** 8am-6.30pm Mon-
Wed, Fri, Sat; 8am-1pm Thur. *Antiques*
4am-4pm Sat.

Best known for its antiques and col-
lectibles, this is several markets rolled
into one: antiques start at the Notting
Hill end; further along are food stalls;
under the Westway up to Ladbroke
Grove are emerging designer and vintage clothes on Fridays and (crazily
busy) Saturdays.

Rellik
*8 Golborne Road, Ladbroke Grove,
W10 5NW (8962 0089/www.rellik
london.co.uk). Westbourne Park tube.*
Open 10am-6pm Tue-Sat.
This celeb fave was set up in 2000 by
three Portobello market stallholders.
Expect a mix of pieces by the likes of
Westwood, Dior and Ossie Clark.

Nightlife

Notting Hill Arts Club
*21 Notting Hill Gate, W11 3JQ (7460
4459/www.nottinghillartsclub.com).
Notting Hill Gate tube.* **Open** 6pm-1am
Mon; 6pm-2am Tue-Fri; 4pm-2am Sat;
4pm-1am Sun. No credit cards.
This small basement club may not be
much to look at, but it does host influential nights like Thursday's YoYo,
playing everything from funk to 1980s
boogie, and Wednesday's Death Disco,
featuring bands and indie DJs.

Shepherd's Bush Empire
*Shepherd's Bush Green, W12 8TT
(8354 3300/box office 0870 771 2000/
www.shepherds-bush-empire.co.uk).
Shepherd's Bush tube.*
This former variety hall and BBC the-
atre is London's best mid-sized venue.
The sound is decent and the staff are
friendly. Bookings take in anyone from
Amy Winehouse to Athlete.

Arts & leisure

Lyric Hammersmith
*King Street, Hammersmith, W6 0QL
(0870 050 0511/www.lyric.co.uk).
Hammersmith tube.*
The Lyric has a knack for vibrant, offbeat scheduling. It also offers good
kids' theatre. Look out for site-specific
shows on the terrace.

Essentials

Hoxton Hotel p208

Hotels

When visitors to London moan about the prices, the case is at its strongest when it comes to hotels. The average room rate is now around £120 a night – hence, **£** in the listings below represents a rack rate of £100 or less a night. There are encouraging signs, however. Both at the absolute budget end – hostels like the **Clink** and **Meininger** – and in the increasingly competitive moderate sector – the **Hoxton**, **B&B Belgravia**, **Twenty Nevern Square**, the **Mayflower** – quality is rising. In the latter category, formerly luxury touches (fluffy robes, wireless internet, bespoke interiors) are becoming standard.

We're largely convinced by the emerging 'micro-boutique' concept: booking by the hour for a sleep in a tiny, fun, purpose-built, all mod cons room. The only problem is that **Yotel** (www.yotel.com) has opened its first two pod hotels in Gatwick's South Terminal and Heathrow Terminal 4 – great if you're heading that way, perfect for an unfriendly check-in or arrival time, useless otherwise. Keep an eye on the rival **nitenite** chain (www.nitenite.com), which has acquired a Waterloo site that may be up and running in 2009.

Other trends we're intrigued by include luxury chains creating boutiquey sub-brands – such as Hilton's **Trafalgar** and Hyatt's **Andaz Liverpool Street** – and the rebirth of B&Bs (see box p203).

Even classy old-stagers are having to work hard to justify their top rates: the **Connaught** reopened after major refurbishments this year, and the **Savoy** is due to follow in 2009 (see box p208).

Money matters

Hotels are constantly offering special deals, particularly at weekends; check websites or ask when you book. Also check discount hotel websites – such as www.alpharooms.com or www.london-discount-hotel.com.

Many high-end hotels quote prices exclusive of VAT, so check before booking.

South Bank

LSE Bankside House

24 Sumner Street, South Bank, SE1 9JA (7107 5773/www.lsevacations. co.uk). London Bridge tube. **£**.
During the university vacations (July-Sept), much of London's dedicated student accommodation is opened up to visitors, providing a source of cheap digs. The London School of Economics must have the best located: Bankside House is tucked behind Tate Modern.

Premier Inn London County Hall

County Hall, Belvedere Road, SE1 7PB (0870 238 3300/www.premiertravelinn. com). Waterloo tube/rail. **££**.
With Premier Inn-branded purple walls, bedspreads and headboards, this hotel is institutional in feel but has the USP of rooms for £99 just inland of the impressive London Eye. There are no riverside windows, but the first-floor restaurant looks out at the Southbank Centre. The neat rooms are spacious, with a kettle and good wardrobe space.

Southwark Rose

47 Southwark Bridge Road, SE1 9HH (7015 1480/www.southwarkrosehotel. co.uk). London Bridge tube/rail. **££**.
Well sited for Tate Modern, Borough Market and the Globe, the hotel and its rooms are purpose-built and budget-conscious, all sleek, dark wood, crisp white linen and mosaic-tiled bathrooms. Suites are equipped with kitchenettes and an extra sofabed, and guests can use the gym at the Novotel next door.

S H O R T L I S T

Best new
- Andaz Liverpool Street (p207)
- Connaught (p202)
- Fox & Anchor (p208)

Most exciting prospects
- Boundary (p208)
- Soho House Bed & Brasserie (see box p203)
- Savoy (p207)

All-round winners
- Haymarket Hotel (p205)
- One Aldwych (p205)
- Rookery (p209)
- Trafalgar (p197)

Glossy mag faves
- Brown's (p202)
- Rockwell (p201)
- Sanderson (p207)
- Soho Hotel (p207)

Best hotel bars
- Brumus at the Haymarket Hotel (p205)
- Coburg at the Connaught (p202)
- Library at the Lanesborough (p194)
- Lobby Bar at One Aldwych (p205)

Great bargains
- City Inn Westminster (p197)
- Clink Hostel (p202)
- Hoxton Hotel (p208)

Budget style
- B&B Belgravia (p197)
- Hoxton Hotel (p208)
- Montagu Place (p205)

Best hostels
- Clink Hostel (p202)
- Holland Park Youth Hostel (p199)
- Meininger (p199)

Money the only object
- easyHotel (p197)

Before you book your **London hotel** check the **London hotel map** on LondonTown.com

London's hotels all on one map

Visually compare best hotel rates and availability

Hotel Price Guarantee: "Find it cheaper, get £100"

View entertainment, including ticket prices and availability

See real customer feedback on all hotels

full screen, fully interactive
The new ∧ hotel map on LondonTown.com
www.londontown.com/hotelmap

LONDONTOWN.com
Your Best Friend in London

Westminster & St James's

B&B Belgravia

64-66 Ebury Street, SW1W 9QD (7823 4928/www.bb-belgravia.com). Victoria tube/rail. **££**.

One of the most attractive B&Bs we've seen. The black and white lounge could be straight out of *Elle Decoration*. But the place isn't precious: you'll find a laptop with free internet connection, plus DVDs to watch on the flatscreen TV. The bedrooms are chic and contemporary (each also has a flatscreen TV) and the bathrooms are very sleek.

City Inn Westminster

30 John Islip Street, SW1P 4DD (7630 1000/www.cityinn.com). Pimlico tube. **££**.

Aside from some modern art in the airy lobby, there's nothing particularly flash about this new-build hotel, but it is superbly located for Tate Britain. The rooms are excellently thought-out, with CD and DVD players, free broadband and flatscreen TVs. River-facing suites on the 12th and 13th floors have superb night views – you can sometimes get bargain rates at weekends.

easyHotel

36-40 Belgrave Road, SW1V 1RG (www.easyhotel.com). Pimlico tube/ Victoria tube/rail. **£**.

Airline entrepreneur Stelios Haji-Ioannou's no-frills approach is here applied to compact hotels for compact wallets, this being the most central of three London locations. Rooms come in three sizes – small, really small and tiny – the last of which is the width of the bed. There's no wardrobe, hairdryer, lift or breakfast, you pay extra for a window, and check-out is at 10am.

Trafalgar

2 Spring Gardens, off Trafalgar Square, SW1A 2TS (7870 2900/ www.thetrafalgar.com). Charing Cross tube/rail. **£££**.

The Trafalgar is a Hilton – but you'd hardly notice. The good-sized rooms have a masculine feel, with minimalist walnut furniture, and the bathtubs are made for sharing. Yet the central location is the real draw – corner suites look directly into the square and even guests without a room view can enjoy themselves at the small rooftop champagne bar. The ground-floor Rockwell Bar has DJs and fine bourbon whiskey.

Windermere Hotel

142-144 Warwick Way, SW1V 4JE (7834 5163/www.windermere-hotel. co.uk). Victoria tube/rail. **££**.

Minutes from Victoria Station, Warwick Way is lined with small hotels and B&Bs. The Windermere edges ahead of the competition with good facilities (satellite TV, free internet, power showers), smart rooms, a hospitable atmosphere and terrific levels of service – a dozen staff for just 20 rooms. The excellent breakfasts are included in the price.

South Kensington & Chelsea

Aster House

3 Sumner Place, SW7 3EE (7581 5888/www.asterhouse.com). South Kensington tube. **££**.

The Aster attempts to live up to its upmarket address with a lush garden (leading off the slightly kitsch lobby) with duckpond, and a palm-filled conservatory. Bedrooms are comfortable, with trad floral upholstery, air-con and smart marble bathrooms (ask for one with a power shower). The museums and big-name shops are all nearby.

Baglioni

60 Hyde Park Gate, SW7 5BB (7368 5700/www.baglionihotellondon.com). High Street Kensington or Gloucester Road tube. **££££**.

The upscale Baglioni and its exciting designer style can't fail to impress. Despite occupying a Victorian mansion opposite Kensington Palace, the hotel has none of the snooty formality of some of its counterparts. The Italian restaurant-bar is part baroque, part Donatella Versace, but the chic

ESSENTIALS

B&B Belgravia p197

bedrooms are more subdued: black
floorboards, taupe and gold-leaf walls,
dark wood furniture enlivened by jewel-
coloured cushions and throws.

Base2Stay

*25 Courtfield Gardens, SW5 0PG
(0845 262 8000/www.base2stay.com).
Earl's Court tube.* **££**.
A cross between a hotel and serviced
apartments, Base2Stay looks good in
modernist limestone and taupe tones.
If you don't mind having to do everything yourself (the 'kitchenette' is little
larger than a cupboard), the prices are
certainly agreeable, and it's less than
ten minutes from the station.

Bentley Kempinski

*Harrington Gardens, SW7 4JX (7244
5555/www.thebentley-hotel.com).
Gloucester Road tube.* **££££**.
Although it isn't large, the Bentley's
look is on a grand scale: Louis XV-style
furniture, gilt mirrors, gleaming marble and a sweeping circular staircase.
Bedrooms feature chandeliers, plush

carpets, satin bedspreads and marble
bathrooms. The restaurant is glitzy and
the Malachite Bar is a decadent hide-
away, but the real showpiece is the spa,
with a full-size Turkish hammam.

Blakes

*33 Roland Gardens, SW7 3PF (7370
6701/www.blakeshotels.com). South
Kensington tube.* **££££**.
Still enticing a celebrity clientele with
its discreet, residential location, Blakes
remains as original as when Anouska
Hempel opened it in 1983. Each room
adopts a different style of maximalism;
exotic antiques – carved beds, Chinese
birdcages – are complemented with
sweeping drapery and plump cushions.
Downstairs, there's an Eastern-influ-
enced restaurant and a gym.

Gore

*189 Queen's Gate, SW7 5EX (7584
6601/www.gorehotel.com). South
Kensington tube.* **£££**.
Despite its recent refurbishment, this
fin-de-siècle period place retains a

special atmosphere. The lobby and staircase are hung with old paintings, and the rooms have 19th-century oak beds, sumptuous drapes and shelves of old books. The suites are spectacular: tragedy queens should plump for the Venus room and Judy Garland's old bed (complete with ruby slippers). The wood-panelled 190 bar is charming.

Halkin
Halkin Street, SW1X 7DJ (7333 1000/ www.halkin.como.bz). Hyde Park Corner tube. **£££.**
When it opened in 1991, the first hotel of fashion magnate Christina Ong was ahead of the East-meets-West design trend – and it still looks more current than hotels half its age. The rooms combine stylish classical sofas with black lacquer tables and Southeast Asian artefacts, and each floor is themed by element. Gracious and discreet behind a Georgian-style façade, the Halkin is renowned for its Michelin-starred Thai restaurant, Nahm.

Holland Park Youth Hostel
Holland Walk, W8 7QU (0870 770 5866/www.yha.org.uk). High Street Kensington tube. **£.**
In these days of super-chic hostelling, this place is no slouch. It actually is where it says it is – right in Holland Park, one of west London's loveliest green spaces – and one wing is a 17th-century mansion. A shared dorm costs non-members just over £20 a night, including breakfast.

Lanesborough
1 Lanesborough Place, Hyde Park Corner, SW1X 7TA (7259 5599/ www.lanesborough.com). Hyde Park Corner tube. **££££.**
In an 1820s Greek Revival building by National Gallery designer William Wilkins, the Lanesborough's luxurious rooms are traditionally decorated with antique furniture and lavish marble bathrooms. Electronic keypads control everything from the air-conditioning to the 24hr room service, and other nice touches include complimentary high-speed internet, personalised business cards and free movies. The Library Bar and, for afternoon tea, Conservatory maintain the high standards.

Meininger
Baden-Powell House, 65-67 Queen's Gate, SW7 5JS (7590 6910/www. meininger-hostels.com). Gloucester Road or South Kensington tube. **£.**
This classy German hostel chain's first London operation is set in the modern, six-storey Scouts' Association centre. The three main floors offer airy dormitory, twin and single accommodation, all bedrooms en suite with TV, wireless access and air-conditioning, as well as bedside tables and lamps. More basic dorms are on the top floor. There is 24-hour tea and coffee provision for both communal and single or twin rooms.

Milestone Hotel & Apartments
1 Kensington Court, W8 5DL (7917 1000/www.milestonehotel.com). High Street Kensington tube. **£££.**
American visitors make annual pilgrimages here, their arrival greeted by the gravel tones of their regular concierge. Yet amid old-school luxury thrives inventive modernity. Rooms overlooking Kensington Gardens have inspired decor: the spectacular Tudor Suite has an elaborate inglenook fireplace and a minstrels' gallery. For relaxation there's a pool and spa.

myhotel chelsea
35 Ixworth Place, SW3 3QX (7225 7500/www.myhotels.com). South Kensington tube. **£££.**
The Chelsea myhotel has a softer, more feminine feel than its sleekly modern Bloomsbury sister (11-13 Bayley Street, WC1B 3HD, 7667 6000). Pink walls, a floral sofa and a plate of scones in the lobby offer a posh English foil to feng shui touches such as the aquarium and candles. The feminine mood continues in the rooms with dusky pink wallpaper, white wicker headboards and velvet cushions, but it feels fresh and modern rather than chintzy. If you overdo things in the bar-dining room, the Jinja area offers treatments.

ESSENTIALS

1000 *Time Out*
things to do in London

1000 *Time Out*
things to do in Britain

Number Sixteen

16 Sumner Place, SW7 3EG (7589 5232/www.firmdale.com). South Kensington tube. **£££**.
This may be Kit Kemp's most affordable hotel, but there's no slacking in style or comforts. Bedrooms are generously sized, bright and individually decorated with tasteful floral patterns, stripes and muted creams, greens and mauves. The whole place has an appealing freshness, not least the drawing room with its fresh flowers and modern art. Breakfast is served in the cheery conservatory or the lovely garden. It's all utterly relaxing and feels like a real retreat from the city.

Rockwell

181 Cromwell Road, Earl's Court, SW5 0SF (7244 2000/www.therockwellhotel. com). Earl's Court tube. **££**.
Rockwell isn't your average London four-star: you'll find no identikit furniture, rather rooms thoughtfully kitted out with funky wallpaper and Egyptian cotton. Thanks to triple glazing, you'd never know busy Cromwell Road is just outside. The reception area has jazz on the stereo, while the One-Eight-One restaurant, bar and outside walled garden are destinations in their own right. Corridors are a bit dingy, and some bathrooms are on the poky side – but at these prices, we're not complaining.

Twenty Nevern Square

20 Nevern Square, Earl's Court, SW5 9PD (7565 9555/www.twentynevern square.co.uk). Earl's Court tube. **££**.
The less-than-posh location of this immaculate boutique hotel keeps rates reasonable. Tucked away in a secluded (private) garden square, Twenty Nevern's modern-colonial style was created by its well-travelled owner, who sourced many of the exotic furnishings. The beds are real stars, from elaborate four-posters to Egyptian sleigh styles.

Vicarage Hotel

10 Vicarage Gate, W8 4AG (7229 4030/www.londonvicaragehotel.com). High Street Kensington or Notting Hill Gate tube. **£**.
The off-High Street Ken location makes this hotel understandably popular. A Victorian townhouse on a quiet dogleg of Vicarage Gate, across from Kensington Gardens, the Vicarage has a glitzy lobby, with ornate mirrors and a chandelier, and rooms in traditional B&B pastel, furnished with faux antiques and floral fabrics. Nine of them have bathrooms.

West End

Academy Hotel

21 Gower Street, WC1E 6HG (7631 4115/www.theetoncollection.com). Goodge Street tube. **££**.
Comprising five Georgian townhouses, the Academy has a restrained country-house style – decor in most rooms is soft, summery florals and checks, although eight suites have more sophisticated colour schemes. Guests are cocooned from busy Bloomsbury and those in the split-level doubles get plenty of breathing space at decent rates. The library and conservatory open on to fragrant walled gardens.

Arosfa

83 Gower Street, WC1E 6HJ (7636 2115/www.arosfalondon.com). Goodge Street tube. **£**.
Arosfa means 'place to stay' in Welsh, but we reckon that description sells this townhouse B&B short. Yes, the accommodation is fairly spartan, but it is also spotless, and all the rooms have en suite shower/WC (albeit tiny). Arosfa also has a great location – in the heart of Bloomsbury, just opposite a huge Waterstone's – and a pleasing walled garden. Internet is available on a shared terminal in the lounge.

Ashlee House

261-265 Gray's Inn Road, WC1X 8QT (7833 9400/www.ashleehouse.co.uk). King's Cross tube/rail. **£**.
The more established of a pair of classy hostels, Ashlee House is a short walk from its sister, the Clink (p202). Features standard to the Clink will soon be added here: coded card keys,

trendy bed steps and so on. But the Ashlee already has plenty of panache, its funky lobby decorated with sheep-skin-covered sofas and wallpaper digitally printed with London scenes. The rooms are basic: each contains between two and 16 beds, and a sink. Breakfast is served in a large communal kitchen, and a £5 deposit gets you the tools for self-catering. There's a TV room with nightly film screenings and an Xbox, internet, luggage storage and laundry.

Brown's

Albemarle Street, W1S 4BP (7493 6020/www.roccofortecollection.com). Green Park tube. £££££.
Brown's was opened in 1837 by Lord Byron's butler, James Brown, and became the quintessential Mayfair hotel. In 2003 the Rocco Forte Collection acquired the place and gave it a top-to-toe refurbishment. The public spaces remain gloriously old English (particularly the Tea Room) and the Donovan Bar is sheer class. All bedrooms, super-large and extremely comfortable, remain in character.

Charlotte Street Hotel

15-17 Charlotte Street, W1T 1RJ (7806 2000/www.firmdale.com). Goodge Street or Tottenham Court Road tube. £££.
This gorgeous hotel is a fine exponent of Kit Kemp's trademark style, fusing trad English furnishings with avant-garde art. Bedrooms mix English understatement with bold flourishes: soft beiges and greys spiced up with plaid/floral combinations. The huge beds and trademark polished granite and oak bathrooms are wonderfully indulgent. On Sunday nights you can combine a three-course set meal with a screening of a classic film in the mini-cinema (booking advisable).

Claridge's

55 Brook Street, W1K 4HR (7629 8860/www.claridges.co.uk). Bond Street tube. £££££.
Claridge's is synonymous with history and class, its decorative character linked to its 1898 reopening and signa-ture art deco redesign. While remaining traditional, its bars and restaurant (Gordon Ramsay) are actively fashionable. The rooms divide equally between deco and Victorian, with period touches such as deco toilet flushes in the swanky marble bathrooms. Bedside panels control the mod con facilities at the touch of a button.

Clink Hostel

78 King's Cross Road, WC1X 9QG (7183 9400/www.clinkhostel.com). King's Cross tube/rail. £.
The Clink is well ahead of the field for style, comfort, facilities and setting – as well as being located near the new St Pancras International station. A 300-year-old courthouse where Dickens once scribbled, the Clink was taken over by the management of Ashlee House (p201) and converted into a contemporary lodging for up to 500 backpackers. The beds, like Japanese pods, are sectioned off for privacy, with a reading light and little safety box above each.

Connaught

NEW *16 Carlos Place, W1K 2AL (7499 7070/www.the-connaught.co.uk). Bond Street tube. £££££.*
Reopened in early 2008, the 100-year-old Connaught's revamp is of the kind that demands adjectives like 'discreet' and 'refined'. The place has been gently modernised without damage to its traditional appeal. Expect a personal butler (one per floor) to cater for needs sartorial and technical (they're all IT trained), while Alain Ducasse alumnus Hélène Darroze replaces Angela Hartnett in charge of the food. The Coburg bar is mighty impressive too.

Covent Garden Hotel

10 Monmouth Street, WC2H 9LF (7806 1000/www.firmdale.com). Covent Garden or Leicester Square tube. £££.
A perennial favourite among Kit Kemp's hotels, the Covent Garden is snug and stylish, with its excellent location ensuring a steady stream of starry customers. In the guest rooms Kemp's distinctive modern English style mixes traditional touches – pinstriped wall-

Small is beautiful

London's hip new take on the B&B.

Last year's hotel sensation was Kit Kemp's magnificent 50-room Haymarket Hotel (p205), but for the coming year the buzzword is likely to be bijou.

Due to open just as this guide hits the shelves in autumn 2008 is the **Boundary Project** (p208). Set in a Victorian warehouse just off Shoreditch High Street and near the surprisingly secluded Arnold Circus, Terence and Vicki Conran's newest venture will combine just 17 bedrooms (including a suite and four loft rooms) with a rooftop bar and grill. The Albion (www.albioncaff.co.uk) downstairs, a mixture of all-day café and a takeaway deli-bakery, will specialise in British food.

The next opening to excite the cognoscenti is **Soho House B&B** – that's 'Bed & Brasserie', by the way. Due to open in early 2009, this 24-room venue will open in a pair of 18th-century townhouses on Soho's Dean Street (they're being coy about the specific address), just round the corner from parent establishment, the exclusive private members' club Soho House. Again all-day food will be served from the ground floor, this time a brasserie run by one of the owners of the noted French restaurant Racine (p89). Being a Soho House off-shoot, you can expect the place to be stylish (much care is being lavished on restoring Georgian interiors destroyed by previous tenants), but it will also be affordable... and open to non-members.

Finally, Malmaison has opened a new venture beside Smithfield Market: half a dozen handsome little rooms above the **Fox & Anchor** (p208, see also p155; pictured). The decor makes much of the historic market location with archive photos and free-standing baths, but each room features little modern luxuries like plasma screens and drench showers, as well as wireless internet access.

■ www.theboundary.co.uk
■ www.sohohouse.com
■ www.foxandanchor.com

ESSENTIALS

paper, pristine white quilts, floral upholstery – with bold, contemporary elements. The ground-floor Brasserie Max buzzes like Paris in the 1920s, and there's a tucked-away screening room.

Cumberland

Great Cumberland Place, off Oxford Street, W1H 7DL (0870 333 9280/ www.guoman.com). Marble Arch tube. **£££**.

With 900 rooms, plus another 119 in an annexe down the road, the Cumberland is a monster – but it's also well run. Decor is minimalist, with acid-etched headboards, neatly modern bathrooms and plasma TVs in each room – nicely designed, but a bit small. The hotel's dining room is the excellent Rhodes W1, there's impressive modern art in the vast lobby, and there's a boisterous late-night Shoreditch-industrial DJ bar.

Dorchester

53 Park Lane, W1K 1QA (7629 8888/ www.thedorchester.com). Hyde Park Corner tube. **££££**.

A glitzy Park Lane fixture since 1931, the Dorchester is enjoying its first major upgrade since 2002. The Alain Ducasse team of Nicola Canuti and Bruno Riou

launched a restaurant here in 2007, just after Alexandra Champalimaud's redesigned trio of rooftop suites reopened. Of the 49 other suites, General Eisenhower planned the D-Day landings in one and Prince Philip held his stag-do in another. This opulence is reflected in the grandest lobby in town, complete with Liberace's piano.

Harlingford Hotel

61-63 Cartwright Gardens, WC1H 9EL (7387 1551/www.harlingford hotel.com). Russell Square tube/ Euston tube/rail. **£**.

On the corner of a sweeping Georgian crescent lined with hotels, the Harlingford is a stylish trailblazer. Enter, and you'll hear a gentle fountain from a garden behind the receptionist. There's also a tasteful guests' lounge with trendy light fittings and modern prints. The staff are eager to please, and an adjacent square has a pretty garden and tennis court for guests. You'll almost forget you're in a budget hotel.

Hazlitt's

6 Frith Street, W1D 3JA (7434 1771/ www.hazlittshotel.com). Tottenham Court Road tube. **£££**.

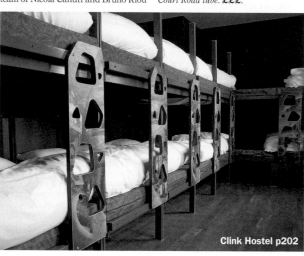

Clink Hostel p202

This charming place, named after essayist William Hazlitt (he died here in 1830), provides an upmarket version of the Soho accommodation of his time. All rooms are individual, named after various great writers, with fireplaces, superb carved wooden four-posters and half-testers, free-standing bathtubs and handsome cast-iron toilet cisterns. But don't worry: 21st-century comforts such as air-con come as standard.

Haymarket Hotel

1 Suffolk Place, off Piccadilly Circus, SW1Y 4BP (7470 4000/www.firmdale. com). Piccadilly Circus tube. **£££**.
The latest offering from Kit Kemp was designated the best hotel in London by journalists before it even opened in 2007, and it is probably her most luxurious: rooms are generously sized, individually decorated and discreetly stuffed with facilities, and there is plenty of personal attention from switched-on staff. The building was designed by John Nash, the architect of Regency London, and it's a pleasure simply to inhabit a space he created, one that Kemp's decor enhances. The central location and basement swimming pool and bar are further draws.

Metropolitan

19 Old Park Lane, W1K 1LB (7447 1000/www.metropolitan.como.bz). Hyde Park Corner tube. **££££**.
Christina Ong's chic, contemporary Metropolitan remains a cut above London's other modern urban retreats. Look no further than the destination dining spot Nobu to appreciate its credentials. Ong's background in retail and interior design stands out in spacious soundproofed rooms, which come with Shambhala smellies in the marble bathrooms. The gym has recently been refitted; personal trainers and massages are also available.

Montagu Place

2 Montagu Place, W1H 2ER (7467 2777/www.montagu-place.co.uk). Baker Street tube. **££**.
A stylish, small hotel in a pair of Grade II-listed Georgian townhouses. Catering primarily for the business traveller, the Montagu's 16 rooms are divided into Comfy, Fancy and Swanky categories, the difference in each case being size – Swanky are the largest, with enormous bathrooms, while Comfy (situated at the back) are the smallest. All rooms have pocket-sprung beds, cafetières with freshly ground coffee, and flat-screen TVs. The look is boutique-hotel sharp and prices are affordable.

Morgan

24 Bloomsbury Street, WC1B 3QJ (7636 3735/www.morganhotel.co.uk). Tottenham Court Road tube. **£**.
Round the corner from the British Museum, this cheap and cheerful hotel has no aspirations to boutique status, but the 21 rooms and suites have extras beyond basic B&B standard: modern headboards with inbuilt reading lamps, smart brocade drapes, bathrooms with granite sinks. The hotel's annexe of spacious flats is great value.

No.5 Maddox Street

5 Maddox Street, W1S 2QD (7647 0200/www.living-rooms.co.uk). Oxford Circus tube. **££££**.
Blink and you'll miss the entrance to this discreet bolthole just off Regent Street. Accommodation is in chic apartments, done up in the East-meets-West style that was all the rage when it opened in the late 1990s: bamboo floors and dark furniture mixed with sable throws and crisp white sheets. There's no bar, but the kitchen and fridge are full of treats, there's a decent Thai restaurant on the ground floor – and room service will do your shopping.

One Aldwych

1 Aldwych, WC2B 4RH (7300 1000/ www.onealdwych.com). Covent Garden or Temple tube/Charing Cross tube/rail. **££££**.
Despite weighty history – the 1907 building was designed by the architects behind the Ritz – One Aldwych is thoroughly modern. Upstairs, everything, from Frette linen through bathroom mini-TVs to the environmentally friendly loo-flushing system, has been

Haymarket Hotel p205

chosen with care. The hotel's cosy screening room has movie packages; other R&R options include spa treatments and a pool where classical music accompanies your laps. A real treat.

Piccadilly Backpackers

12 Sherwood Street, W1F 7BR (7434 9009/www.piccadillybackpackers.com). Piccadilly Circus tube. **£**.

International hostellers swarm into London's most central venue, attracted by the rates and location. The accommodation is basic, although graphic art students have painted the rooms on the third floor in an attempt to perk things up. Ten rooms feature 'pods' – six beds arranged three up, three down. There's a travel shop and a backpackers' bar nearby at 4 Golden Square (7287 9241).

Ritz

150 Piccadilly, W1J 9BR (7493 8181/ www.theritzlondon.com). Green Park tube. **££££**.

Founded by hotelier extraordinaire César Ritz in 1906, this hotel remains the epitome of luxury – recently embellished by the addition of the adjoining 18th-century Grade-II listed William Kent House. The real show-stopper, though, is the Long Gallery, an orgy of chandeliers, rococo mirrors and marble columns. The high-ceilinged, Louis XVI-style bedrooms have been painstakingly renovated, with 24-carat gold leaf features and magnificently heavy curtains. Mod cons include wireless internet, large TVs and a gym.

St Martins Lane Hotel

45 St Martin's Lane, WC2N 4HX (7300 5500/www.stmartinslane.com). Leicester Square tube/Charing Cross tube/rail. **££££**.

When it opened as a Schrager property nearly a decade ago, the St Martins was constantly buzzing, with guests giggling at the playful Philippe Starck decor. Although the novelty has worn off, it's still an exclusive place to stay. The all-white bedrooms have comfortable minimalism down pat, with floor-to-ceiling windows, gadgetry secreted in sculptural cabinets and limestone

bathrooms. The Asia de Cuba fusion restaurant is as good-looking as ever, and the Light Bar remains dramatic.

Sanderson

50 Berners Street, W1T 3NG (7300 1400/www.morganshotelgroup.com). Oxford Circus tube. **££££**.
This noughties Schrager/Starck creation is still one of the city's most stylish hotels. Generously sized guest rooms come with silver-leaf sleigh beds, piled high with cushions, and super-modern glassed-in bathroom areas with powerful steam showers and beautiful stand-alone baths. When it's time to mingle, slip downstairs to the Long Bar and Suka restaurant.

Savoy

NEW *Strand, WC2R 0EU (7836 4343/ www.fairmont.com/Savoy). Covent Garden or Embankment tube/ Charing Cross tube/rail.* **££££**.
See box p208.

Sherlock Holmes Hotel

108 Baker Street, W1U 6LJ (7486 6161/www.sherlockholmeshotel.com). Baker Street tube. **££**.
How do you transform a dreary, chintz-filled Hilton into a hip boutique hotel? It's elementary: hype up the Baker Street address, banish the bland decor and create a sleek lobby bar. That's what the Park Plaza chain did when it snapped up the Sherlock Holmes a few years ago. The rooms resemble hip bachelor pads, there's a gym with sauna, steam rooms and beauty treatments, and the memorabilia ranges from paintings to magnifying glasses.

Soho Hotel

4 Richmond Mews (off Dean Street), W1D 3DH (7559 3000/www.firmdale. com). Tottenham Court Road tube. **£££**.
Kit Kemp's 2004 shot at urban hip is still her edgiest creation. The large bedrooms are contemporary, with modern furniture, industrial-style windows and all mod cons, although they're also classically Kemp with bold stripes, trad florals, plump sofas, oversized bedheads

and upholstered tailor's dummies. The drawing room and other public spaces feature groovy colours, while Refuel, the loungey bar and restaurant, has an open kitchen. It's all very cool, but also wonderfully quiet and comfy.

22 York Street

22 York Street, W1U 6PX (7224 2990/ www.22yorkstreet.co.uk). Baker Street tube. **££**.
There's no sign on the door; people usually discover this immaculately kept B&B by word of mouth. Unpretentious and comfortable, it's perfect for those who loathe hotels and hate designer interiors. Rooms are subtly tasteful, with wooden floors, antique pieces and French quilts, and breakfast is a real occasion, served at a huge, curving wooden table in the traditional kitchen.

Weardowney Guesthouse

9 Ashbridge Street, NW8 8DH (7725 9694/www.weardowney.com). Marylebone tube/rail. **£**.
Amy Wear and Gail Downey – models turned knitwear designers – lived above their boutique for a decade. When they moved out, they opened it as a quiet corner establishment for paying guests. The seven rooms are adorned with hand-knitted throws and curtains, as well as art and photos from the pair's creative associates. A housekeeper does breakfasts and laundry, and there's a pretty roof terrace.

The City

Andaz Liverpool Street

NEW *40 Liverpool Street, EC2M 7QN (7961 1234/www.london.liverpoolstreet. andaz.com). Liverpool Street tube/rail.* **£££**.
In 2007 this former Conran hotel became the first property in Hyatt's new Andaz portfolio. Andaz means 'personal style' in Hindi, and the name reflects the vibe: out with gimmicky menus and closet-sized minibars, in with down-to-earth service, eco-friendliness and uncomplicated luxury. The bedrooms wear regulation style-mag

Swanking up the Savoy

If you're planning to do big-money luxury in London, 2009 will be a great year to get traditional: the superluxed **Savoy** (p207) is due to reopen in spring. Built in 1889 to put up theatre-goers from Richard D'Oyly Carte's Gilbert & Sullivan shows, the Savoy is the hotel from which Monet painted the Thames, where Vivien Leigh met Laurence Olivier, where Londoners learned to love the martini. Long known for its discreet mix of Edwardian neo-classical and art deco, the Savoy is currently undergoing £100m of renovations.

An impressive £2.5m is being dropped on the fifth-floor Royal Suite, with its two bedrooms (plus an optional third, if you've extra guests), kitchen (for your personal chef) and eight bay windows over the river. The famous cul-de-sac at the front entrance gets a garden of new topiary and centrepiece crystal fountain (Lalique, of course), but the welcome begins before you even arrive with a phone call to check out your particular needs – 'Anything that needs doing for a guest will be done in advance', as General Manager Kiaran MacDonald puts it.

There will be a new tea room, with glass-roofed conservatory, while the leather counter of the new champagne bar is set on a stage that once hosted big bands for dinner dances. Be reassured, though: the Savoy Grill, American Bar and rooftop swimming pool remain in place.
■ www.savoy2009.com

uniform – Eames chairs, chocolate shagpile rugs and white Frette linen – but management is keen to maintain the hotel's East End character, notably by its connections with local artists.

Apex City of London
1 Seething Lane, EC3N 4AX (7702 2020/www.apexhotels.co.uk). Tower Hill tube. **££**.
Part of a small chain, this sleek, modern business hotel has built a sturdy reputation. Service is warm and accommodating, room details are obliging (free Wi-Fi, pillow menu, rubber duck in the bathroom), rates are impressive (especially at weekends) and the location – right by the Tower – is terrific.

Boundary
NEW *2-4 Boundary Street, E2 7JE (www.theboundary.co.uk). Old Street tube/rail.*
See box p203.

Fox & Anchor
NEW *115 Charterhouse Square, EC1M 6AA (7012 3700/www.foxandanchor. com). Barbican tube/Farringdon tube/rail.* **££**.
See box p203.

Hoxton Hotel
81 Great Eastern Street, EC2A 3HU (7550 1000/www.hoxtonhotels.com). Old Street tube/rail. **££**.
A kind of postmodern country lodge, the Hoxton Hotel proves that budget needn't be boring. A well-designed bar and restaurant lends an air of excitement to the place. The rooms aren't big, but they are well thought out – the flatscreen TV can be turned to a cheekily tiny chaise longue or the Frette linen bed, there's free internet, a free Pret Lite breakfast, fresh milk in the fridge. Grab a room at the back on the fifth or sixth floor and you'll be blessed with great urban views. Weekend rooms are often less than £100 – and a few £1-a-night rooms periodically released.

Malmaison
Charterhouse Square, EC1M 6AH (7012 3700/www.malmaison.com). Barbican tube/Farringdon tube/rail. **££**.

Andaz Liverpool Street p207

Although it's part of a chain, Malmaison has real charm. Location is key: it's set in a lovely, leafy, cobblestone square by Smithfield Market, while rooms are equipped to high standards, with extra touches including free broadband. Reduced weekend prices keep most of the business crowd away at weekends.

Rookery
12 Peter's Lane, Cowcross Street,
EC1M 6DS (7336 0931/www.rookery
hotel.com). Farringdon tube/rail. **£££**.
Hidden away down a tiny alley, the Rookery is a kind of Dickensian Tardis. Like its sibling Hazlitt's (p204), it's decorated in period style, with Gothic oak beds, plaster busts and clawfoot bathtubs, but there are modern comforts too. All the rooms, generous in size, are individually furnished.

St Paul's Youth Hostel
36 Carter Lane, EC4V 5AB (7236
4965/www.yha.org.uk). St Paul's tube/
Blackfriars tube/rail. **£**.
You're one block from St Paul's in a former choir school, and only about the same distance from the Millennium Bridge across the Thames to Tate Modern. Share a dorm for about £20.

Threadneedles
5 Threadneedle Street, EC2R 8AY
(7657 8080/www.theetoncollection.
com). Bank tube/DLR. **£££**.
Occupying the former HQ of the Midland Bank, its lobby and bar area centrepieced by a magnificent atrium, Threadneedles successfully integrates modern design with monumental space. The decor is soothingly neutral, with Korres natural toiletries in the serene limestone bathrooms. Little stress-busting comforts reflect its business-friendly location: fleecy throws, a scented candle lit at turndown and a 'movie treats' menu.

Zetter
86-88 Clerkenwell Road, EC1M 5RJ
(7324 4444/www.thezetter.com).
Farringdon tube/rail. **££**.
Billing itself as a restaurant with rooms, the Zetter is in fact more than that: it's a fun, laid-back, modern hotel with some interesting design notes. The rooms are sleek and functional, but cosied up with choice home comforts such as hot-water bottles and old Penguin paperbacks, while the walk-in Raindance showers are stocked with gorgeous Elemis products.

ESSENTIALS

The best guides to enjoying London life

(but don't just take our word for it)

'Armed with a tube map and this guide there is no excuse to find yourself in a duff bar again'

Evening Standard

'I'm always asked how I keep up to date with shopping and services in a city as big as London. This guide is the answer'

Red Magazine

'You will never again be stuck for interesting things to do and places to visit in the capital'

Independent on Sunday

Rated 'Best Restaurant Guide'

Sunday Times

TIME OUT GUIDES WRITTEN BY LOCAL EXPERTS
timeout.com/shop

Getting Around

Airports

Gatwick Airport
0870 000 2468/www.baa.co.uk/ gatwick. About 30 miles south of central London, off the M23.

Of the three rail services that link Gatwick to London, the quickest is the **Gatwick Express** (0845 850 1530, www.gatwickexpress.co.uk) to Victoria Station, which takes about 30 minutes and runs from 3.30am to 12.30am daily. Tickets cost £15.90 single, £15.20 day return (after 9.30am) and £26.80 for an open return (valid for 30 days). Under-15s are £6.50 single, half-price open and cheap day returns; under-5s go free.

Southern (0845 748 4950, www.southernrailway.com) also runs a rail service between Gatwick and Victoria, with trains every 5-10 minutes (or every 25 minutes between 1am and 4am). It takes about 35 minutes, at £8.90 for a single, £9.20 for a day return (after 9.30am) and £17.80 for an open period return (valid for one month). Under-16s get half-price tickets; under-5s go free.

If you're staying in the King's Cross or Bloomsbury area, it's worth considering the **Thameslink** service (0845 748 4950, www.firstcapitalconnect.co.uk) via London Bridge, Blackfriars, Farringdon and King's Cross; journey times vary. Tickets cost £8.90 single, £9.50 day return (after 9.32am) and £17 for a 30-day open return.

Hotelink offers a shuttle service (01293 532244, www.hotelink.co.uk) at £20 each way (£24 online). A taxi costs about £100 and takes ages.

Heathrow Airport
0870 000 0123/www.baa.co.uk/ heathrow. About 15 miles west of central London, off the M4.

The **Heathrow Express** (0845 600 1515, www.heathrowexpress.co.uk) runs to Paddington every 15 minutes 5.10am-11.25pm daily, and takes 15-20 minutes. The train can be boarded at either of the airport's two tube stations. Tickets cost £15.50 single or £29 return (it's £1 cheaper online and £2 more if you buy on board); under-16s go half-price. Many airlines have check-in desks at Paddington.

A longer but cheaper journey is by tube. Tickets for the 50- to 60-minute **Piccadilly Line** ride into central London cost £4 one way (£2 under-16s). Trains run every few minutes from 5am to 11.57pm daily except Sunday, when they run from 6am to 11pm.

The **Heathrow Connect** (0845 678 6975, www.heathrowconnect.com) gives direct access to Heathrow Airport from various stations, including Ealing Broadway and Paddington. Trains run every half-hour. It serves Terminals 1, 2, 3 and 4, with a direct service from Paddington to the new Terminal 5. Ticket prices vary depending on which station you board at; a single from Paddington costs £6.90.

National Express (0870 580 8080, www.nationalexpress.com) runs daily coach services to London Victoria between 5am and 9.35pm daily, leaving Heathrow Central bus terminal around every 20-30 minutes. For a 90-minute journey to London, you can expect to pay £4 for a single (£2 under-16s) or £8 (£4 under-16s) for a return.

As at Gatwick, **Hotelink** (see above) offers an airport-to-hotel shuttle service for £19 per person each way. A taxi into town will cost roughly £100 and will take an hour or more.

London City Airport
7646 0000/www.londoncityairport.com. About 9 miles east of central London.

The **Docklands Light Railway** (DLR) includes a dedicated stop for London City Airport. The journey to Bank in the City takes around 20 minutes, and trains run 5.30am-12.30am Mon-Sat and 7am-11.30pm Sun. A taxi costs around £20 to central London, less to the City or to Canary Wharf.

Luton Airport

01582 405100/www.london-luton.com. About 30 miles north of central London, J10 off the M1.

Luton Airport Parkway Station is linked to the airport by a short shuttle-bus ride. The **Thameslink** service (p211) calls at many stations (King's Cross and City among them); it has a journey time of 35-45 minutes. Trains leave every 15 minutes or so and cost £11.90 one-way and £21.50 return. Trains from Luton to King's Cross run at least hourly through the night.

The Luton to Victoria journey takes 60-90 minutes by coach. **Green Line** (0870 608 7261, www.greenline.co.uk) runs a 24-hour service every 30 minutes or so at peak times. A single is £11, while returns cost £16; under-16s go half-price. A **taxi** costs £50 or more.

Stansted Airport

0870 000 0303/www.stanstedairport.com/www.baa.co.uk/stansted. About 35 miles north-east of central London, J8 off the M11.

The quickest way to get to London from here is on the **Stansted Express** train (0845 748 4950) to Liverpool Street Station; the journey time is 40-45 minutes. Trains leave every 15-45 minutes, and tickets cost £15 single, £25 return; under-16s go half-price, under-5s free.

The **Airbus** (0870 580 8080, www.nationalexpress.com) coach service from Stansted to Victoria takes at least an hour and 20 minutes and runs 24 hours. Coaches run roughly every 30 minutes, more frequently at peak times. A single is £10 (£5 for under-16s), return is £17 (£8.50 for under-16s). A **taxi** is about £80.

Arriving by rail

St Pancras International

Pancras Road, King's Cross, NW1 2QP (7843 4250/www.stpancras.com). King's Cross tube/rail.

In November 2007, Eurostar relocated to the newly refurbished St Pancras International Station. The new station is served by a high-speed rail line, cut-

ting journey times to Paris by at least 20 minutes. From 2009, the Eurostar will serve Stratford in east London too.

Mainline stations

For information on train times and ticket prices, call 0845 748 4950 or go to www.nationalrail.co.uk. You can get timetable and price information, and buy tickets, for any train operator in the UK via www.thetrainline.com.

All London's major rail stations are served by the tube.

Arriving by coach

Victoria Coach Station

164 Buckingham Palace Road, Victoria, SW1W 9TQ (7730 3466/www.tfl.gov.uk). Victoria tube/rail.

National Express (0870 580 8080, www.nationalexpress.com), Britain's most comprehensive coach company, is based here, while companies like Eurolines (01582 404511, www.eurolines.com) run services to Europe.

Public transport

The Transport for London **Travel Information Centres** provide maps and information about the tube, buses and Docklands Light Railway (DLR; p214). You can find them in the stations listed below. You can also go online to www.tfl.gov.uk/journeyplanner or call 7222 1234 for more information.

Heathrow Airport Terminals 1, 2 & 3 *Underground station* Open *6.30am-10pm daily.*
Liverpool Street Open *7.15am-9pm Mon-Sat; 8.15am-8pm Sun.*
Victoria Open *7.15am-9pm Mon-Sat; 8.15am-8pm Sun.*

London Underground

Delays are common. Escalators are often out of action. Some lines close at weekends for engineering. It's hot, smelly and crowded at rush hour (8am to 9.30am and 4.30pm to 7pm Mon-Fri). Nevertheless, 'the tube' is still the quickest way to get around London.

Using the Underground

A flat cash **fare** of £4 per journey applies across zones 1-6 on the tube; customers save up to £2.50 per journey with a pre-pay Oyster card (see below). Anyone caught without a valid ticket or Oyster card is subject to a £20 on-the-spot fine.

To enter and exit the tube using an Oyster card, simply touch it to the yellow reader, which will open the gates. Make sure you also touch the card to the reader when you exit the tube, otherwise you will be charged a higher fare when you next use the card to enter a station.

To enter using a **paper ticket**, place it in the slot with the black magnetic strip facing down, then pull it out of the top to open the gates. Exiting at your destination is done in much the same way, though if you have a single journey ticket, it will be retained by the gate as you leave.

There are 12 tube lines, colour-coded on the tube map on the back flap.

Oyster cards

Oyster, a pre-paid travel smart-card, is the cheapest way of getting around on buses, tubes and the DLR. There is a £3 refundable deposit payable for the card. Any tube journey within zone 1 using Oyster pay-as-you-go costs £1.50 (50p for under-16s). A single tube journey within zone 2, 3, 4, 5 or 6 costs £1 (50p for under-16s). Single tube journeys from zones 1-6 using Oyster pay-as-you-go are £3.50 (7am-7pm Mon-Fri); £2 at other times and £1 for children. You can charge up at tube stations, London Travel Information Centres (see above), some national rail stations and at newsagents. For more details visit www.tfl.gov.uk/oyster or call 0870 849 9999.

Travelcards

Using Oyster pay-as-you-go will always be 50p cheaper than the equivalent Day Travelcard. If you are also using National Rail services, Oyster may not be accepted: opt for a Day Travelcard. Peak Day Travelcards can be used all day, Monday to Friday (except public holidays). They cost from £6.60 for zones 1-2 (£3.30 child), up to £13.20 for zones 1-6 (£6.20 child). All tickets remain valid for journeys started before 4.30am the next day. The Off-Peak Day Travelcard meets most visitors' needs, allowing you to travel from 9.30am Monday to Friday and all day Saturday, Sunday and public holidays. It costs from £5.10 for zones 1-2, rising to £6.70 for zones 1-6.

Up to four under-11s can travel free on the tube (from 9.30am Monday to Friday, all day Saturday, Sunday and public holidays) as long as they are accompanied by a fare-paying adult. Another four can travel with an adult for £1 each (a Day Travelcard is issued) at the same times.

If you plan to spend a few days charging around town, you can buy a 3-Day Travelcard. The peak version can be used all day Monday to Friday on the start date and for any journey that starts before 4.30am on the day following the expiry date; it's available for £16.40 (zones 1-2) or £39.60 (zones 1-6). The off-peak version costs £20.10 for zones 1-6.

Travelling with children

Under-14s travel free on buses and trams without the need to provide any proof of identity. 14- and 15-year-olds can also travel free, but need to obtain an Under-16 Oyster photocard. For details, visit www.tfl.gov.uk/fares or call 0845 330 9876. An 11-15 Oyster photocard is needed by 11- to 15-year-olds to pay-as-they-go on the tube or DLR or to buy 7-Day, monthly or longer period Travelcards and by 11- to 15-year-olds if using the tram to/from Wimbledon. Photocards are not required for adult rate 7-Day Travelcards, Bus Passes or for any adult rate Travelcard or Bus Pass charged on an Oyster card. For details of how to obtain under-14, 14-15 or 16-17 Oyster photocards visit www.tfl.gov.uk/fares or call 0845 330 9876.

Underground timetable

Tube trains run daily from around 5.30am (except Sunday, when they start an hour or two later, depending on the line). The only exception is Christmas Day, when there is no service. Generally, you shouldn't have to wait more than ten minutes for a train, and during peak times services run every two or three minutes. Times of last trains vary, though they're usually around 11.30pm-1am daily except Sunday, when they finish 30 minutes to an hour earlier. Other than New Year's Eve, when tubes run all night, the only all-night public transport is by night bus (see below).

Docklands Light Railway (DLR)

DLR trains (7363 9700, www.tfl.gov. uk/dlr) run from Bank or Tower Gateway, which is close to Tower Hill tube (Circle and District lines). At Westferry DLR the line splits east and south via Island Gardens to Greenwich and Lewisham; a change at Poplar can take you north to Stratford. The easterly branch forks after Canning Town to either Beckton or London City Airport (from spring 2009, it should be going as far as Woolwich Arsenal on the south bank). Trains run 5.30am to 12.30am Monday to Saturday and 7am to 11.30pm Sunday.

The adult single **fares** on DLR are the same as for the tube (p213), except for a DLR-only zones 2-3 journey, which costs £1.50 (£1 using Oyster pay-as-you-go) or, for children 11-15, 70p (Oyster pay-as-you-go 50p).

Buses

All buses are now low-floor and accessible to wheelchair-users and passengers with buggies. The only exceptions are Heritage routes 9 and 15, which are served by the world-famous open-platform Routemaster buses. You *must* have a ticket or valid pass before getting on a bus in central London: inspectors patrol and board buses at random; they can fine you £20. You can buy a ticket (or 1-Day Bus Pass) from pavement machines, but, frustratingly, they're often out of order. Better to travel armed with an Oyster card or some other pass (p213).

Using pay-as-you-go on Oyster, the **single fare** is £1 a trip and the most you will pay a day will be £3. Paying with cash at the time of travel costs £2 for a single trip. Under-16s travel for free (using an Under-14 or 14-15 Oyster photocard; p213). A 1-Day Bus Pass gives unlimited bus and tram travel for £3.50. A book of six Saver tickets costs £6; they are sold at some newsagents and tube station ticket offices.

Many buses run 24 hours a day, seven days a week. There are also some special **night buses** with an 'N' prefix to the route number, which operate from about 11pm to 6am. Most night services run every 15 to 30 minutes, but many busier routes have a bus around every ten minutes.

Water transport

Most river services operate every 20 minutes to one hour between 10.30am and 5pm; visit www.tfl.gov.uk for details. **Thames Clippers** (www.thamesclippers.com) runs a reliable commuter-boat service, boarded at Embankment, Blackfriars, Bankside, London Bridge and Tower Pier.

Taxis

If a **black taxi**'s orange 'For Hire' sign is switched on, it can be hailed. If a taxi stops, the cabbie must take you to your destination, if it's within seven miles. It can be hard to find a free cab, especially just after the pubs close or when it rains. Rates are higher after 8pm on weekdays and all weekend. You can book black cabs in advance; both **Radio Taxis** (7272 0272) and **Dial-a-Cab** (7253 5000; credit cards only) run 24-hour services (booking fee £2).

Minicabs (saloon cars) are generally cheaper than black cabs, but only use licensed firms (look for the yellow disc in the front and rear windows) and avoid those who tout for business. They will be unlicensed, uninsured and possibly dangerous.

There are, happily, lots of trustworthy and licensed local minicab firms, including **Lady Cabs** (7272 3300), which employs only women drivers, and **Addison Lee** (7387 8888). To locate a licensed minicab firm, text HOME to 60835 – Transport for London will send you the phone numbers of the two nearest. Always ask the price when you book and confirm it with the driver.

Driving

Congestion charge

Drivers coming into central London between 7am and 6pm Monday to Friday have to pay an £8 fee. The area is defined as within King's Cross (N), Old Street roundabout (NE), Aldgate (E), Old Kent Road (SE), Elephant & Castle (S), Vauxhall, Chelsea, South Kensington (SW), Kensington, Holland Park, North Kensington, Bayswater, Paddington (W), Marylebone and Euston (N). Expect a fine of £50 if you fail to do so (rising to £100 if you delay payment). Passes can be bought from newsagents, garages and NCP car parks; the scheme is enforced by CCTV cameras. You can pay any time during the day of entry. Payments are also accepted until midnight on the next charging day, although it's £2 more. For more information, phone 0845 900 1234 or go to www.cclondon.com.

Parking

Parking on a single or double yellow line, a red line or in residents' parking areas during the day is illegal, and you may end up being fined, clamped or towed. However, in the evening (from 6pm or 7pm in much of central London) and at various times at weekends, parking on single yellow lines is legal and free; if you find a clear spot, look for a sign giving the regulations for that area. Meters are also free at certain

times during evenings and weekends. Parking on double yellow lines and red routes is illegal at all times.

NCP 24-hour **car parks** (0870 606 7050, www.ncp.co.uk) are numerous but pricey (£3-£12 for two hours). Central ones include Arlington House, Arlington Street, St James's, W1; Snowsfields, Southwark, SE1; and 4-5 Denman Street, Soho, W1.

Vehicle removal

If your car has gone, the chances are (assuming it was legally parked) it's been stolen; if not, it's probably been taken to a car pound. A release fee of £200 is levied for removal, plus £40 per day from the first midnight after removal. You'll probably also get a parking ticket of £60-£100 when you collect the car (it's reduced by half if paid within 14 days). To find out how to retrieve your car, call 7747 4747.

Vehicle hire

Easycar (www.easycar.com) offers competitive rates, as long as you don't mind driving a branded car around town. Otherwise, try **Alamo** (0870 400 4508, www.alamo.com), **Budget** (0844 581 9999, www.budget.co.uk) or **Hertz** (0870 599 6699, www.hertz.co.uk).

Cycling

London isn't the friendliest of towns for cyclists, but the **London Cycle Network** (see www.londoncyclenetwork.org.uk) and **London Cycling Campaign** (7234 9310, www.lcc.org.uk) help make it better. Call Transport for London (7222 1234) for maps.

Cycle hire

Both the **London Bicycle Tour Company** (1A Gabriel's Wharf, 56 Upper Ground, South Bank, SE1 9PP, 7928 6838, www.londonbicycle.com) and **Go Pedal!** (07850 796320, www.gopedal.co.uk) rent out bikes; the latter will also deliver and collect them.

Rainforest Cafe

A WILD PLACE TO SHOP AND EAT®

Rainforest Cafe is a unique venue bringing to life the sights and sounds of the rainforest.

Come and try our fantastic menu!
Includes gluten free,
dairy free and organic options for kids.

15% DISCOUNT

off your final food bill*

Offer valid seven days a week. Maximum party size of 6.

020 7434 3111

20 Shaftesbury Avenue, Piccadilly Circus, London W1D 7EU
www.therainforestcafe.co.uk

*Please present to your safari guide when seated.
Cannot be used in conjunction with any other offer.

Resources A-Z

Accident & emergency

In the event of a serious accident, fire or other incident, call **999** – free from any phone, including payphones – and ask for an ambulance, the fire service or police. The following have 24-hour Accident & Emergency departments.

Chelsea & Westminster Hospital *369 Fulham Road, Chelsea, SW10 9NH (8746 8000). South Kensington tube.*
Guy's Hospital *St Thomas Street (entrance Snowsfields), Borough, SE1 9RT (7188 7188). London Bridge tube/rail.*
Royal London Hospital *Whitechapel Road, Whitechapel, E1 1BB (7377 7000). Whitechapel tube.*
St Mary's Hospital *Praed Street, Paddington, W2 1NY (7886 6666). Paddington tube/rail.*
St Thomas's Hospital *Lambeth Palace Road, Lambeth, SE1 7EH (7188 7188). Westminster tube/ Waterloo tube/rail.*
University College Hospital *235 Grafton Road, NW1 2BU (0845 155 5000). Euston Square/Warren Street tube.*

Credit card loss

American Express *01273 696933.*
Diners Club *01252 513500.*
MasterCard/Eurocard *0800 964767.*
Switch *0870 600 0459.*
Visa/Connect *0800 895082.*

Customs

For allowances, see www.hmrc.gov.uk.

Dental emergency

Dental care is free for resident students, under-18s and people on benefits. All other patients must pay. NHS-eligible patients pay on a subsidised scale.

Dental Emergency Care Service
Guy's Hospital, St Thomas Street, Borough, SE1 9RT (7188 0511). London Bridge tube/rail. **Open** 9am-5pm Mon-Fri.
Queues start forming at 8am; arrive by 10am if you're to be seen at all.

Disabled

London is a difficult place for disabled visitors, though legislation is slowly improving access and general facilities. The capital's bus fleet is now more wheelchair accessible. The tube, however, remains escalator-dependent. The *Tube Access Guide* booklet is free; call the Travel Information line (7222 1234) for more details.

Most major attractions and hotels offer good accessibility, although sadly provision for the hearing- and sight-disabled is patchier. Enquire about facilities in advance. *Access in London* is an invaluable reference book for disabled travellers, available from Access Project (www.accessproject-phsp.org).

Artsline
54 Chalton Street, Somers Town, NW1 1HS (tel/textphone 7388 2227/www. artslineonline.com). Euston tube/rail. **Open** 9.30am-5.30pm Mon-Fri.
Information on disabled access to arts and entertainment events.

Electricity

The UK uses the standard European 220-240V, 50-cycle AC voltage, along with three-pin plugs.

Embassies & consulates

American Embassy *24 Grosvenor Square, Mayfair, W1A 1AE (7499 9000/www.london.usembassy.gov). Bond Street or Marble Arch tube.* **Open** 8.30am-5.30pm Mon-Fri.

ESSENTIALS

Australian High Commission
*Australia House, Strand, Holborn,
WC2B 4LA (7379 4334/www.uk.
embassy.gov.au). Holborn or Temple
tube.* **Open** 9.30am-3.30pm Mon-Fri.
Canadian High Commission
*38 Grosvenor Street, Mayfair, W1K
4AA (7258 6600/www.canada.org uk).
Bond Street or Oxford Circus tube.*
Open 8-11am Mon-Fri.
Embassy of Ireland *17 Grosvenor
Place, Belgravia, SW1X 7HR (7235
2171/passports & visas 7225 7700).
Hyde Park Corner tube.* **Open**
9.30am-1pm, 2.30-5pm Mon-Fri.
New Zealand High Commission
*New Zealand House, 80 Haymarket,
St James's, SW1Y 4TQ (7930 8422/
www.nzembassy.com). Piccadilly Circus
tube.* **Open** 9am-5pm Mon-Fri.
South African High Commission
*South Africa House, Trafalgar Square,
St James's, WC2N 5DP (7451 7299/
www.southafricahouse.com). Charing
Cross tube/rail.* **Open** 9.45am-12.45pm
(by appointment only), 3-4pm
(collections) Mon-Fri.

Internet

Most hotels have broadband or wifi.
Otherwise, there are cybercafés around
town, including the **easyInternetCafé**
chain. You'll also find terminals in
public libraries. For more options, go
to www.cybercafes.com. For wireless
access, check with your provider or visit
www.wi-fihotspotlist.com.

easyInternetCafé

*456-459 Strand, Trafalgar Square,
WC2R ORG (www.easyinternetcafe.
com). Charing Cross tube/rail.* **Open**
8am-11pm daily. **Terminals** 393.
Locations throughout the city.

Left luggage

The threat of terrorism has meant that
London stations tend to have left-lug-
gage desks rather than lockers; to find
out if a train station offers this facility,
call 0845 748 4950.
Gatwick Airport *South Terminal
01293 502014/North Terminal
01293 502013.*

Heathrow Airport *Terminal 1
8745 5301/Terminals 2 8759 3344/
Terminal 3 8745 4599/Terminal 4
8897 6874/Terminal 5 8283 5073.*
London City Airport *7646 0162.*
Stansted Airport *01279 663213.*

Opening hours

Banks 9am-4.30pm (some close
at 3.30pm, some 5.30pm) Mon-Fri;
sometimes also Saturday mornings.
Businesses 9am-5pm Mon-Fri.
Pubs & bars 11am-11pm Mon-Sat;
noon-10.30pm Sun. A small number
are now open much later.
Shops 10am-6pm Mon-Sat; some to
8pm. Many are also open on Sunday,
usually 11am-5pm or noon-6pm.

Pharmacies

Also called 'chemists' in the UK. Larger
supermarkets and all branches of
Boots (www.boots.com) have a phar-
macy, and there are independents on
most high streets. Staff can advise on
over-the-counter medicines. Most phar-
macies are open 9am-6pm Mon-Sat.

Police

Look under 'Police' in the phone book
or call 118 118/500/888 if none of the
following are convenient.
Charing Cross Police Station *Agar
Street, Covent Garden, WC2N 4JP
(7240 1212). Charing Cross tube/rail.*
Marylebone Police Station *1-9
Seymour Street, Marylebone, W1H
7BA (7486 1212). Marble Arch tube.*
West End Central Police Station
*27 Savile Row, Mayfair, W1X 2DU
(7437 1212). Piccadilly Circus tube.*

Post

Post offices are usually open 9am-6pm
Mon-Fri and 9am-noon Sat, although
the **Trafalgar Square Post Office**
(24-28 William IV Street, WC2N 4DL,
0845 722 3344) opens 8.30am-6.30pm
Mon-Fri and 9am-5.30pm Sat. For general enquiries, call 0845 722 3344 or
consult www.postoffice.co.uk.

Smoking

Smoking is now banned in all enclosed public spaces, including pubs, bars, clubs, restaurants, hotel foyers, shops and public transport. Many bars and clubs have smoking gardens or terraces.

Telephones

London's dialling code is 020; standard landlines have eight digits after that. If you're calling from outside the UK, dial your international access code, then the UK code, 44, then the full London number, omitting the first 0 from the code (Australia 61; Canada 1; New Zealand 64; Republic of Ireland 353; South Africa 27; USA 1).

US cellphone users will need a tri- or quad-band handset.

Public payphones take coins and/ or credit cards. International calling cards, offering bargain minutes via a freephone number, are widely available.

Tickets

Many smaller venues subcontract their ticketing to agencies; reliable ones include **Ticketmaster** (0870 534 4444, www.ticketmaster.co.uk), **Ticketweb** (0870 060 0100, www.ticketweb.co.uk) and **Keith Prowse** (0870 840 1111, www.keithprowse.com). For on-the-day theatre reductions, try **tkts** (p127).

Time

The UK operates on Greenwich Mean Time (GMT), which is five hours ahead of US Eastern Standard time. In autumn (26 October 2008, 25 October 2009) the clocks go back to GMT, having gone forward by one hour to British Summer Time in spring (29 March 2009).

Tipping

Tip in taxis, minicabs, restaurants (some waiting staff rely heavily on tips), hotels, hairdressers and some bars (not pubs). Ten per cent is normal, with some restaurants adding as much as 15%. Always check whether service has been included in your bill: some restaurants include a service charge, but also leave space for a tip on your credit card slip.

Tourist information

Visit London (7234 5800, www.visit london.com) is the city's official tourist information company. There are tourist offices in several major sightseeing areas. In addition to the following, there is a new facility by St Paul's (p158).

Britain & London Visitor Centre
1 Lower Regent Street, Piccadilly Circus, SW1Y 4XT (7808 3800/www.visit britain.com). Piccadilly Circus tube. **Open** 9.30am-6.30pm Mon; 9am-6.30pm Tue-Fri; 10am-4pm Sat, Sun.

London Information Centre
Leicester Square, WC2H 7BP (7292 2333/www.londontown.com). Leicester Square tube. **Open** 8am-6pm Mon-Fri; 10am-6pm Sat, Sun.

Greenwich Tourist Information Centre *Pepys House, 2 Cutty Sark Gardens, SE10 9LW (0870 608 2000). Cutty Sark DLR.* **Open** 10am-5pm daily.

Southwark Tourist Information Centre *Tate Modern: Level 2, Bankside, SE1 9TG (7401 5266/ www.visitsouthwark.com). Southwark tube or Blackfriars tube/rail.* **Open** 10am-6pm daily.

Visas

EU citizens don't require a visa to visit the UK; citizens of the USA, Canada, Australia, South Africa and New Zealand can also enter with only a passport for tourist visits. *Always* check the current situation at www.uk visas.gov.uk well before you travel.

What's on

Time Out remains London's only quality listings magazine. Widely available in central London every Tuesday, it gives listings for the coming week from Wednesday. For gay listings, also look out for freesheets *Boyz* and *QX*.

ESSENTIALS

Index

Sights & areas

ESSENTIALS

ESSENTIALS

z

Eating & drinking

a

b

c

d

e

f

g

h

i

j

k

l

ESSENTIALS

ESSENTIALS

London's most famous day out

What will you be doing on your trip to London?

Attending an A-List party? Going to a star-studded film premiere? Challenging your sporting heroes or taking to the stage with music's megastars? Will you be knighted by the Queen or address the world's leaders?

Do all these things and much, much more as you mingle and interact with the world's most famous figures at Madame Tussauds.

Visit www.madame-tussauds.co.uk to check out our best offers and book your fast track tickets

Madame Tussauds LONDON

Who do you want to meet?

⊖ **Next to Baker Street Tube Station**